THE NEW MIDDLE AGES

BONNIE WHEELER, Series Editor

The New Middle Ages presents transdisciplinary studies of medieval cultures. It includes both scholarly monographs and essay collections.

PUBLISHED BY PALGRAVE:

Women in the Medieval Islamic World: Power, Patronage, and Piety
edited by Gavin R. G. Hambly

The Ethics of Nature in the Middle Ages: On Boccaccio's Poetaphysics
by Gregory B. Stone

Presence and Presentation: Women in the Chinese Literati Tradition
by Sherry J. Mou

The Lost Love Letters of Heloise and Abelard: Perceptions of Dialogue in Twelfth-Century France
by Constant J. Mews

Understanding Scholastic Thought with Foucault
by Philipp W. Rosemann

For Her Good Estate: The Life of Elizabeth de Burgh
by Frances A. Underhill

Constructions of Widowhood and Virginity in the Middle Ages
edited by Cindy L. Carlson and Angela Jane Weisl

Motherhood and Mothering in Anglo-Saxon England
by Mary Dockray-Miller

Listening to Heloise: The Voice of a Twelfth-Century Woman
edited by Bonnie Wheeler

The Postcolonial Middle Ages
edited by Jeffrey Jerome Cohen

Chaucer's Pardoner and Gender Theory
by Robert S. Sturges

Crossing the Bridge: Comparative Essays on Medieval European and Heian Japanese Women Writers
edited by Barbara Stevenson and Cynthia Ho

Engaging Words: The Culture of Reading in the Later Middle Ages
by Laurel Amtower

Robes and Honor: The Medieval World of Investiture
edited by Stewart Gordon

Representing Rape in Medieval and Early Modern Literature
edited by Elizabeth Robertson and Christine M. Rose

Same Sex Love and Desire Among Women in the Middle Ages
edited by Francesca Canadé Sautman and Pamela Sheingorn

Listen Daughter: The Speculum virginum and the Formation of Religious Women in the Middle Ages
edited by Constant J. Mews

Science, the Singular, and the Question of Theology
by Richard A. Lee, Jr.

Gender in Debate from the Early Middle Ages to the Renaissance
edited by Thelma S. Fenster and Clare A. Lees

Malory's Morte Darthur: Remaking Arthurian Tradition
by Catherine Batt

The Vernacular Spirit: Essays on Medieval Religious Literature
  edited by Renate Blumenfeld-Kosinski, Duncan Robertson, and Nancy Warren

Popular Piety and Art in the Late Middle Ages: Image Worship and Idolatry in England 1350–1500
  by Kathleen Kamerick

Absent Narratives, Manuscript Textuality, and Literary Structure in Late Medieval England
  by Elizabeth Scala

Creating Community with Food and Drink in Merovingian Gaul
  by Bonnie Effros

Encountering Medieval Textiles and Dress
  edited by Désirée G. Koslin and Janet Snyder

Eleanor of Aquitaine: Lord and Lady
  edited by Bonnie Wheeler and John Carmi Parsons

Isabel La Católica, Queen of Castile
  edited by David A. Boruchoff

Homoeroticism and Chivalry: Discourses of Male Same-Sex Desire in the Fourteenth Century
  by Richard Zeikowitz

Portraits of Medieval Women: Family, Marriage, and Politics in England 1225–1350
  by Linda E. Mitchell

PORTRAITS OF MEDIEVAL WOMEN
FAMILY, MARRIAGE, AND POLITICS IN ENGLAND 1225–1350

Linda E. Mitchell

PORTRAITS OF MEDIEVAL WOMEN
© Linda E. Mitchell, 2003

All rights reserved. No part of this book may be used or reproduced in any manner whatsoever without written permission except in the case of brief quotations embodied in critical articles or reviews.

First published 2003 by
PALGRAVE MACMILLAN™
175 Fifth Avenue, New York, N.Y. 10010 and
Houndmills, Basingstoke, Hampshire, England RG21 6XS.
Companies and representatives throughout the world.

PALGRAVE MACMILLAN is the global academic imprint of the Palgrave Macmillan division of St. Martin's Press, LLC and of Palgrave Macmillan Ltd. Macmillan® is a registered trademark in the United States, United Kingdom and other countries. Palgrave is a registered trademark in the European Union and other countries.

ISBN 0–312–29297–X hardback

Cataloging-in-Publication data can be found at the Library of Congress.

A catalogue record for this book is available from the British Library.

Design by Newgen Imaging Systems (P) Ltd., Chennai, India.

First edition: July, 2003
10 9 8 7 6 5 4 3 2 1

Printed in the United States of America.

CONTENTS

Acknowledgments vii

1. Introduction 1
2. Agnes and Her Sisters: Squabbling and Cooperation in the Extended Medieval Family 11
3. Like Mother, Like Daughter: The Parallel Careers of Margaret de Quency and Maud de Lacy 29
4. Heroism and Duty: Maud Mortimer of Wigmore's Contributions to the Royalist Cause 43
5. Welshness, Englishness, and the Problem of Dowagers and Heiresses in Wales: The Lestrange Family's Marital Adventures in Powys 57
6. Murderous Maud? The Case Against Maud Mortimer of Richard's Castle 79
7. Isabella de Vescy and the Lords Ordainer: Marital Politics and the Crown, 1272–1327 93
8. Martyr to the Cause: The Tragic Career of Alice de Lacy 105
9. The Rise and Decline of the Medieval English Noble Widow? 125

Abbreviations 139
Notes 141
Bibliography 173
Index 181

ACKNOWLEDGMENTS

I am grateful to quite a number of funding sources and institutions for their assistance in this project. The Fulbright–Hays Commission provided me with a dissertation research grant for research in London—the foundational research for many of the case studies in this volume. Alfred University has supported me with two Alfred Faculty Summer Research grants and the NEH endowment fund has supported me consistently throughout the process of researching and writing this and other works. The National Endowment for the Humanities provided me with a summer stipend. The Public Record Office in London, the British Library, the Lambeth Archives, and the county record offices of Lincolnshire, Shropshire, Worcester, and North Yorkshire all graciously allowed me access to their manuscript collections. The invaluable assistance of the librarians and staff who oversee the Interlibrary Loan department at Herrick Library at Alfred University made completion of this project possible. My splendid colleagues at AU, especially Fiona Tolhurst and the members of the Division of Human Studies, have read portions of this text, provided support and sustenance, and have made the writing of this book bearable. I cannot begin to express the depth of my gratitude to them. I also owe a debt of gratitude to Bonnie Wheeler and Michael Flamini, of Palgrave Press, for their support, encouragement, and assistance. Finally, this volume would not have been completed without the hard work of Christopher Michael Romanchock, my student research assistant. As always, all errors are my own.

CHAPTER 1

INTRODUCTION

The fascination for learning about individual people's lives through the ages has never diminished. No doubt Greek men and women in the fifth century B.C.E. enjoyed the stories of Odysseus and Achilles in part because they opened a window on the past. In the same vein, the eighteenth- and nineteenth-century delight in historical biography can be traced to the compulsion the living have to find out about the dead. Even our modern-day interest in tabloid-style sensationalist biographies of movie stars and dead presidents contains the same prurient enjoyment of peering into worlds into which we cannot usually go.

The medieval world is one that is particularly difficult to penetrate. If the lives of medieval men seem shrouded by a veil of darkness, then the lives of medieval women must seem shrouded by an opaque curtain. Historians can find out a great deal about the ways in which certain groups of people interacted, but aside from the royal family and some highly notable members of the nobility, it is usually impossible to identify them on individual bases, or to differentiate one from another. In the later Middle Ages, when family letter collections appear (such as that by the members of the Paston family), it is possible to know more about specific individuals. Nevertheless, even these avenues of exploration are limited, since most of the letters deal more with public business than with the emotional upheavals of the writers.

The sources most usually available to medieval historians contain evidence of public activity and of the transfer of property: official documents, charters, deeds, agreements, contracts, royal writs, records of litigation, chronicles. These records can tell us much about what people did, but not very much about who they were. Public documents can be quite fascinating, but they do not tell the researcher anything about the context for, say, a transfer of property. The historian must identify a context and explore the possibilities of the relationship between the document and the context.

This is particularly the case with chronicles, which have been used for decades as reliable illustrators of personality and character. We are only now beginning to question the validity of the chronicler's perspective and to question the authenticity of his (and they are all male) view in comparison to the requirements of the narrative itself.

What medievalists usually do in order to flesh out the bare bones of documentary evidence is extrapolate, recommend, suggest, and speculate. This collection of case studies is devoted to the outcome created by the combination of certain kinds of sources and such an individualistic methodology, within a population of medieval people—women—whose life experiences are very imperfectly delineated by the available records. Such a task necessitates a clear vision of what can be accomplished by using sources that outline activity rather than personality and a willingness to develop interpretations knowing that such sources do not provide a transparent context. The task is not easy: the danger of anachronism and self-referentiality is always present when focusing on a population that is imperfectly revealed in available sources. Nevertheless, I have devised some guidelines that I feel enhance the legitimacy of my approach and inform my conclusions.

First, I believe that one can infer some of the personality traits of an individual by looking at the activities of that person. The process of amassing very large quantities of data can be instructive in suggesting motivations for action. In addition, patterns of activity are sometimes revealed by the records and these are useful guideposts to behavioral individualities. Does a woman hide behind the cloak of her widowhood or does she step into the center of the conflict? Are relations with certain members of her family cordial or hostile? Is there evidence of interaction between her and adult children or grandchildren; if so, what kinds of interaction? Although identifying motivation is virtually impossible, given the dearth of personal information in such sources, it is possible to speculate, at the very least, answers to these questions. The sources do identify action, although mediated through the lens—and pen—of the court clerk, the estate official, and the notary. These actions, especially when evaluated in context with other actions, reveal interactive behavior, which then can be used to extrapolate, speculate, and interpret.

Second, I have learned not to take at face value anything written down by a medieval clerk. This is particularly true for chronicle and other narrative sources, but it has validity in the realm of public documents as well. Just as Natalie Zemon Davis has uncovered "fiction" in the archives of Early Modern France, it is possible to misread English chancery and legal sources by believing them to be transparent. Although it is impossible to know the context for every document available, the speculative tools developed by every historian and a willingness to question seemingly canonical sources can serve to help clarify the circumstances of an individual's actions.

Historians have been turning a critical eye to chronicles and "histories" for a number of years, aided in part by New Critical methodologies of close reading that developed an apparatus of motifs by which to evaluate texts. This can be seen particularly with respect to famous chroniclers' treatments of specific male historical figures, such as Matthew Paris's depiction of Richard, earl of Cornwall. Historians, for some reason, are far less critical of depictions of women in the same chronicles, perhaps because, if they were to subject depictions of women to the same critical lens, no depiction of a medieval female could be considered accurate or legitimate.

The development of sensitivity toward social constructions of gender has aided the historian immeasurably in this evaluative process. By admitting that not only named authors but unnamed mediators—such as chancery clerks—abide by social norms when identifying, locating, and evaluating the activities of both men and women, it is possible to view such information as useful in a variety of contexts, but never entirely neutral. In this process, I believe that the sociological theory and method known as ethnomethodology can be quite useful.

Ethnomethodology posits that human interactions within a social and cultural context are mediated by internally accepted norms that define the way social interchanges are ordered. The "reality" of a given culture is constructed: it is not organic. For example, the "reality" of a culture in which cannibalism is an acceptable, even necessary, mode of behavior considers cannibalism to be both acceptable and necessary—thus normal. Nevertheless, cultural change can occur when a new "reality" is inserted that fractures the conventions of the old "reality."[1] Such a fracturing occurred in the 1970s when the Women's Movement successfully advocated for the position that women have a legitimate place and role in the male-dominated cultures of the marketplace, the marble halls of government and law, and the academies of higher learning. This fracture is an ongoing process, one to which both deliberate and automatic actions contribute.

The cultural norms understood and accepted by the typical medieval clerk—that women could not be independent actors in the legal procedures surrounding the conveyance of land from one generation to the next; that women could not sustain a military action on their own; that women's roles confined them to a domestic sphere in which they had no political voice—were periodically "fractured" as a result of changes in the law or in the social underpinnings of the culture. At these times, "new" realities of female participation and action occurred and provided a means by which women could insert themselves into public discourse. It is also possible that such changes reflect cultural norms within a different context—that of the secular world of family and land rather than the clerical world of Church and Scripture—and thus did not "fracture" reality at all, but instead attempted to integrate two competing cultural systems. A mechanism of archaic enplotment might have occurred in the mind of the medieval clerk who wrote the chronicles and transcribed the plea rolls: he might not identify the presence of women in the midst of battles or in other areas where a male presence dominated because he assumes they are not there. The veracity of clerical accounts of the absence of women in the Crusades, except as camp followers and washerwomen, has been challenged quite recently for this very reason.[2] Interestingly, a fracturing of reality seems also to occur frequently for the traditional historian trained literally not to "see" women in the sources. Claims that women are "invisible" in the sources of medieval public history, made by both traditionalists and revisionists, are nothing more than a blindness to the presence of women—both named and unnamed—because of an equally blinkered acceptance of the cultural norms of traditional, post-Enlightenment history, which posits that women simply did not appear in such activities evidenced by these sources. In other words, women are invisible because historians have assumed they are not there. The historical studies of the last thirty years have fractured that particular reality with a vengeance, yet it is still possible to read very recent works of history that persist in lending credence to that old "reality." Nevertheless, their presence ultimately cannot be ignored: reality is fractured; a new reality must take its place.

Although I have avoided theoretically based conclusions in the individual case-studies, where such a device could become tedious with repetition, I have included a discussion of the ways in which the experiences of women in thirteenth- and fourteenth-century Britain could be considered as exemplary of this ethnomethodological position in the concluding chapter. The weight of evidence that I hope to demonstrate through the case studies underpins this conclusion in significant ways, but the studies themselves are not dependent on the theoretical position developed in the last chapter.

Finally, I remain convinced that the complexities of human nature have not changed all that much in the last seven hundred years. We live in a technologically advanced culture that would mystify and alarm the typical woman or man of the thirteenth—or even the eighteenth—century. Nevertheless, the emotions that motivate human action, whether they be desire for money, fame, stability, or human companionship, have not been transformed by the coming of the computer age. Moreover, I believe that, with extreme care, this view does not lead inherently to anachronism: this is one of the reasons why historical biography continues to fascinate. It is wrong to imbue people from the past with the value systems of the present; it is ridiculous, for example, to suggest that the feminist philosophy of the late twentieth and early twenty-first centuries was echoed by Heloise or Hildegard von Bingen in the twelfth century. Emotions, however, are another story entirely. All people are motivated by emotional responses and those responses are limited by our own chemistry: attraction, fear, hate, delight, love, lust, anxiety are all consistent with the human animal no matter the time or the place. The differences lie in how these emotions are expressed and repressed by culture. Medieval people lived in a culture that we would find alien, but they experienced emotions that we would recognize and with which we could empathize. For that reason, I believe that the historian's tendency to speculate and suggest has validity. I can say, with conviction, that Heloise and Hildegard both remained convinced of their talents, despite the fact that the culture in which they lived tended to denigrate the abilities of women, and that they chafed at the restrictions that came from the legal, political, and social perspectives of their world. "Equal pay for equal work" might have meant nothing to them and they might have remained genuinely convinced of the inferiority of women compared to men, but that did not stop them from striking out against the frustrations they experienced.

The issue of emotional consistency is a delicate one. Three decades ago, Philippe Ariés claimed that the modern-day relationship between parent and child is the result of Enlightenment attitudes toward child rearing changing premodern notions. Since then, many historians have demonstrated convincingly that medieval people loved, valued, and enjoyed their children. They celebrated their successes and mourned their early deaths. Certainly modern-day statistics of child abuse and neglect suggest that not all parents today share those same values. Should we deny that medieval people's attitudes toward their children were any less complex? This is another "reality" that deserves to be "fractured."

Similarly, can we deny that medieval people's attitudes toward *themselves* were any less complex? Marriages were arranged for various reasons—yet popular literature extolled "romantic" love as an ideal (even though they defined it differently from us). Husbands mourned the death of wives, and wives the death of husbands. People divorced—or tried to divorce—on the basis of incompatibility. Is this all that different from the emotional issues with which we struggle today? Might this, too, be a "reality"—an accepted norm for historians—that ought to be "fractured"?

The difficulty of evaluating emotional responses in people from the past is, of course, a prickly issue, made thornier when the people in question do not identify their own motivations themselves. Nevertheless, emotional motives did drive behavior then as it does now; how can we not speculate as to what those motives were, even knowing that our evaluation might be wide off the mark?

In the long run, these issues are addressed best when the sources for them are plentiful and varied. One of the reasons why medieval England and its "colonial" possessions—Wales, Ireland, and (to some extent) Scotland—have become the center for much of the work on the medieval family and medieval women is because, by the early thirteenth century, England's royal government had become thoroughly dependent upon a chancery that spewed forth thousands of documents a year[3] ranging from writs, charters, and deeds, to account records and the lists compiled by commissions, escheators, and the like, to the massive documentation of the royal courts of law: King's Bench, Common Pleas, Exchequer of Pleas, county courts, courts in eyre, and so on. Such a mass of written evidence and the systematic administration that survived because of it was not matched anywhere else in Western Europe, with the possible exception of the Norman kingdom of Sicily and Southern Italy, and it might even have rivaled the two greatest administrative systems of the medieval world—the papal chancery and that of the emperors of Byzantium. This material is plentiful, but its survival is often uneven, especially in the twelfth and early thirteenth centuries. By the end of the thirteenth century, however, the reliance on documents was so great that they tend to survive in overwhelming quantities. For example, the size of plea rolls for the fourteenth century is so daunting as to discourage comprehensive viewing. It becomes necessary to sample and to rely on more manageable document collections. Nevertheless, the fourteenth-century administrative evidence has survived in such quantity that I feel I have been able to do justice to those women whose careers continued into that century.

The motivation behind much of the administrative effort to maintain archives came from the development of a centralizing legal system that owed much of its evolution to the interest of the three monarchs of the thirteenth century—John, Henry III, and Edward I. The original system devised largely by Henry I and Henry II in the twelfth century was expanded, improved, and made more complex (never really streamlined) in the thirteenth. Most important to these studies was the development of "private" law—that which oversaw land, inheritance, provisions for widows and younger children, relations between tenants and overlords, and those between families, peers, and colleagues. It is thus necessary to explain some of the developments that had the greatest impact on women's lives.

Legal systems throughout medieval Europe recognized three specific states in women's lives, based upon marital status. Unlike men, who were either minors (under the guardianship of parents or custodians) or men-of-full-age with legal autonomy, women were unmarried maidens, wives, or widows. In moving among these states, a woman's legal status changed. Maidens remained under their fathers' control—or that of a guardian—until they married. When married, husbands assumed legal control over their wives. During widowhood, women in post 1066 England— unlike many on the Continent—were released from guardianship and were able to govern themselves and their property without the intervention of a male tutor, although they did not automatically have control over their choice to remarry or to remain single.

Women most typically interacted with medieval legal systems, such as that of England, when issues arose concerning transfer of property, changes in marital status, and maintenance of property holdings. Since virtually all Englishwomen achieved independence only as widows, the issues of inheritance, dowry, dower, and the bequeathing of moveables were less significant, perhaps, during marriage. Once widowed, however, medieval Englishwomen found themselves in the midst of a legal and administrative system that neither privileged them in, nor particularly hindered them from, gaining the advantages of independence.

Widows did not have to appoint or receive a guardian of any kind, they had total control over their landed property, and they could bequeath their own moveables by testament, including the crops grown on their dower lands.[4] Widows also had unusual legal advantages with respect to some landed property, in particular, lands held in dower or as their *maritagium*.[5] Unlike some continental systems, remarriage did not damage an English widow's claim to land she had received from her late husband's estate.[6] Indeed, widows could collect property from each successive marriage and were consequently valued marriage candidates in feudal England. They could also purchase their own remarriage, the guardianship of their children, and wardship of the family's lands, but they were not automatically assured of receiving any of these.

Women were significantly disadvantaged when it came to inheriting lands held in feudal tenure, in which primogeniture (eldest son inherits) was the norm. In fact, feudal forms of tenure disinherited not only daughters but younger sons as well. On the other hand, customary law usually dictated that if no male issue survived, daughters could inherit. Anglo-Norman law (the basis of English Common Law) attempted to unify these two disparate requirements by developing a practice of primogeniture for male issue but retaining partible inheritance if only females survived. Consequently, if more than one sister survived, each acquired equal shares of the family's estate, with the eldest receiving the oldest title.[7]

Englishwomen who were not heiresses were restricted in their ability to control real property to two forms of tenure: *maritagium* and dower. The Common Law marriage-portion—frank-marriage or *liberum maritagium*—differed from the typical continental dowry. It was a specific type of voluntary but customary grant, consisting of land, cash, moveables, or any combination thereof, which the grantor (not necessarily the bride's father) could choose to give either to the wife and heirs of her body, to the husband alone, or to both spouses and their issue. If the grant contained land or rents, no feudal services were due on the gift for three continuous generations. If the woman died without issue, her *maritagium* returned to her natal family.[8] Widows assumed control over their *maritagia*, whether they had issue or not. Indeed, the 1258 Petitions of the Barons, c. 7, complained that widows alienated their marriage-portions to the detriment of the grantor; as a result, the reforming Statute of Westminster of 1275 stipulated (or was interpreted to state) that *maritagia* were inalienable to the fourth degree, when they would presumably become fully the property of the grantee's heir.[9] A later English development was the joint enfeoffing of married couples with inherited land. Widows had complete control over this jointure, even to the detriment of the heirs.

English Common Law dower—the widow's portion of her late husband's real property—existed in two forms. The most typical dower was the so-called reasonable dower, which amounted to life use of one-third of the husband's landed estates (including "appurtenances" such as advowsons of churches, lands, rents, issues, rights of common pasture, pannage, and other non-regalian rights).[10] "Nominated" dower, which existed more frequently in the twelfth century, was less typical in the thirteenth and fourteenth centuries, but was often used to establish a widow's portion for the wives of kings and princes and for the wives of young heirs who had no lands of their own, but who stood to inherit them upon the death of the current holder. In this form, a specific group of properties was delineated as the wife's dower; it rarely comprised the full one-third of the estates. If it was lower than the "reasonable" third, the widow could sue in court for dower in other properties to make up the shortfall; if it comprised more than the "reasonable" third, she had to give some back to the heir. Both forms of dower were incorporated into the medieval English marriage ceremony: wives were dowered "at the church door" with the worldly goods of their new husbands. Although a widow could not alienate her dower properties away from the heir (she had only usufruct, not ownership, of them) and she was restricted from "wasting" the property, she did not have to relinquish it upon remarriage. Consequently, widows who remarried several times could amass large estates in dower from several husbands; they were also sought after as marriage partners.

A widow's dower in her husband's estates might look like a significant benefit—and it was—but it pales in comparison to the property a husband could attain should his wife predecease him. By "curtesy of England," a widower had usufruct of *all* his late wife's holdings (such as her inheritance or her *maritagium*) until his own death, when the property would devolve upon the actual heir. The grant's only requirement was that the marriage had produced children. This form of male dower had a significant impact both on the individuals inheriting the land in question and on the status of the husband, who could even retain a title "by right of his wife."

When it came to property of any kind, medieval Englishwomen were disadvantaged to the greatest extent as wives. Bracton's formula—a married couple is one person, and that person is the husband—meant that women could not prevent their husbands from selling or giving away their inherited property or alienating lands that had been designated as nominated dower. They had recourse to the courts as widows, but if the alienation had been recorded in a chyrograph, it was impossible to get the land back. Wives were also severely disadvantaged with respect to moveable property. The husband had complete and unfettered control over chattels, even those brought by his wife to the marriage and those considered to be her "paraphernalia," that is, her clothing and jewels. Thus, medieval wives could not make wills without their husbands' permission. There was some pressure brought to bear on husbands, however, when it came to granting such permission. Bracton states that it is "only proper" that a husband should grant his wife permission to make a will, since she would receive chattels if he predeceased her.[11] A widow usually inherited one-third of her husband's chattels after his death if they had produced children, one-half of his goods if the marriage was barren. The remaining property then went to designated heirs or recipients by testament, usually including the Church.[12] Widows themselves (as mentioned above) could make wills with impunity.

Thus, it is clear that the stage of a woman's life in which she was most independent, had greatest access to material wealth, and the greatest potential influence on her family was as a widow. Unfortunately, this was also a life stage that carried significant dangers and anxieties. Widows were vulnerable because of the privileges they had gained and because of their independence. This juxtaposition of power and powerlessness had an impact on the lives of women and seemed to be an important factor in the ways in which widows determined the life choices they made.

The case studies that follow are the product of extensive researches in the public archives in the United Kingdom and in the printed sources available more widely. The plea rolls, chancery records, deeds, charters, final concords, letters, and exchequer documents that can be found at county archives as well as at the Public Record Office and the British Library number in the hundreds of thousands. The sheer quantity of material available to the researcher is daunting, but it is even more daunting when searching for specific people through these masses of un-indexed sources. As much as one can find from these documents, even more remains tantalizingly opaque. As a result, these case studies are not complete biographies; rather, they focus on specific activities of the people under review in ways that can place them in somewhat larger contexts. Some of the studies are more fully delineated than others—the fault lies in the imperfections of the archives and the researcher—but all contain at their core a solid quantity of information derived from a broad array of sources. Some of the case studies are also interconnected; the activities of certain noble families are easier to identify because of royal connections or the serendipitous preservation of documents.

English medieval history has had a long tradition of family studies and the methodology known as medieval prosopography was more or less invented for use with English historical documents. Both of these historical genres—as well as biography—have helped to inform this work.[13] I have also used some of the techniques of micro-history[14] to develop a reliable method of historical speculation, one that provides a note of authenticity without resorting to anachronism. This hybrid methodology is dependent on a labor-intensive form of research that has sent me to national and county archives, to national libraries, to ecclesiastical collections, and to the collections of printed sources at the Institute of Historical Research at the University of London, and the libraries of Indiana University, the University of Rochester, and Cornell University among others. For this kind of work, both quantity and quality are essential in historical sources. Carlo Ginzburg's inquisition transcripts, from which he wrote *The Cheese and the Worms*, do not have a parallel in the body of my research. Moreover, the need to explore and reinforce speculative conclusions or to clarify answers to questions often necessitated surveying a huge number of documents in order to amass a relatively small amount of data. As a result, I have undoubtedly missed quantities of potentially useful information, but I plead indulgence on the basis that the hardest taskmaster—time—prevented me from exploring more avenues for research. It is to the products of that research that I now turn.

CHAPTER 2

AGNES AND HER SISTERS: SQUABBLING AND
COOPERATION IN THE EXTENDED
MEDIEVAL FAMILY

Students of history often experience the medieval period as a series of relatively disconnected actions performed or influenced by a group of relatively disconnected people—usually male—whose lives seem defined by relationships to which we, as moderns, do not really relate. The relationships between lord and vassal, lord and villein, guild master and apprentice: all are foreign to us. We tend to perceive professional relationships as economically grounded and do not usually feel obligated by loyalty or devotion to our employers or employees. We instead tend to extend our devotion and loyalty to friends and, more particularly, to family. Most histories, however, do not explain or analyze the ways in which families operate until the subject under study is the nineteenth century; their topic is, almost invariably, the development of the so-called nuclear family in the Industrial Age. Historians who do focus on particular noble families in the Middle Ages tend to concentrate on the men of each generation whose political careers provided the family with its defining fame and influence, rather than viewing the family as a particular unit of both public and private action, one which included both males and females.[1]

It is a mistake to ignore or dismiss the importance of the family in any historical age, and especially in the Middle Ages. For one thing, the very influential analysis of premodern family structures by Philippe Ariés, who believed that both the nuclear family and the concept of parental devotion to children developed *after* the Enlightenment, has been largely debunked by other historians who have shown that medieval and early modern families also reflected a "nuclear" model.[2] In addition, historical biographies show many instances of parents who devoted themselves to bettering their children's lives and furthering their careers. Although the traditional view of the feudal relationship sees only ties between a lord and an individual retainer, in fact the feudalism of the thirteenth century was completely immersed in family relationships, ones that had far-reaching effects on the political developments of the period. Families inherited land; each generation's heirs usually had no more than stewardship in property held in feudal tenure. Families also distributed land among their members and retained ties to their feudal overlords both collectively and as individuals. Women inherited fees in the absence of male heirs, which meant that a family's feudal associations could be influenced by women's actions as well as by those of the men in the family. Since the basis of inclusion in the medieval English political community was control of baronial property, land tenure was not simply a private or domestic issue.

Thirteenth-century English inheritance law was based on primogeniture: the eldest son was the sole heir of his parents. However, when parents produced no surviving male offspring, Common Law stated that all their female children should inherit equal portions of the estate. Theoretically, the inheritance of property by women should not have disrupted the feudal structure, since unmarried heiresses were governed by male guardians and married heiresses relinquished virtually all control over their property to their husbands. Common Law, however, protected free widows, including widowed heiresses, from forced remarriage, thus providing noble heiresses in the thirteenth century with the opportunity to exercise direct and total control over their inherited property. This inclusion of women into the structure of land governance altered the reality of feudal tenure. An heiress could be a baron, even a countess, in her own right. Moreover, when more than one daughter survived and the property was divided among a number of coheiresses, natal family relationships, which might have been less important in other circumstances, tended to become magnified in their significance to the maintenance of the family and to the development of political and social alliances. This case study is about one such family in the thirteenth and fourteenth centuries.

William de Ferrers, the eldest son and heir of William, earl of Derby, and his first wife, Sibyl, daughter of William le Marshal and Isabella de Clare, had seven daughters: Agnes, Isabel, Maud, Sibyl, Eleanor, Joan, and Agatha. They had no surviving male children, which put the integrity of the earldom at risk as long as Sibyl lived. If William had no male progeny, then the earldom of Derby would be divided among his seven daughters, thus effectively obliterating the earldom itself, as no one heiress would have enough land to sustain the title.

Sibyl la Marshal was also from a large family. Her parents, the earl and countess of Pembroke, had had ten children—five boys and five girls. At the time William de Ferrers married Sibyl, sometime in 1218 or early 1219,[3] she stood no chance to inherit any of her father's and mother's huge estates. There were five apparently healthy brothers standing in line ahead of her.[4] Nevertheless, despite the probably small marriage portion that Sibyl had brought to the marriage, the linkage between Derby and Pembroke would have been one desired by the less prestigious earl of Derby as a way of fortifying his connection to the most powerful nobleman of the early thirteenth century.[5] Other marriages arranged between Marshal daughters and prominent titled noblemen and the heirs of titles served similar functions in the political community surrounding the young King Henry III.

Sibyl's seven daughters were born between 1220 and 1237, when she died. William's father did not die until ten years later, by which time several significant events had changed the relationship between the Ferrers and Marshal families that would have effects well beyond the familial. William very quickly remarried, wedding Margaret, daughter and coheir of Roger de Quency and Helen of Galway, earl and countess of Winchester (and another connection between both the Pembroke and the Chester earldoms) who obliged him by producing a son, Robert, who inherited the earldom of Derby upon his father's death, thus mitigating against the dissection of the estate that William de Ferrers must have feared was inevitable. He also arranged reasonably advantageous marriages for his four eldest daughters sometime before 1245—before his own father died—all to shore up political connections to the families with which he had become allied (more on this later). Interestingly, he apparently never considered dedicating any of his daughters to the monastic life. Perhaps the most significant event for the seven Ferrers sisters, however, was the death in 1245 of the last two of their Marshal uncles, all five of whom died without legitimate progeny. As a result, the vast estates of the earldom of Pembroke and Striguil in England and Wales and the lordship of Leinster in Ireland were divided among the Marshal's five daughters, of whom Sybil de Ferrers was the fourth. This meant that Sibyl's seven daughters became heirs to one-fifth of the largest, wealthiest, and most prestigious inheritance in the British Isles. Their share included the town and manor of Sturminster Marshal in Dorset, various manors in Kent, Wiltshire, Bedford, and Norfolk, and the castle, town, and county of Kildare in Ireland, with all the rents, issues, income, advowsons, knights' fees, and services that belonged to those properties.

It is most unlikely that any of the daughters and grandchildren of William and Isabella Marshal had anticipated such a windfall; the Ferrers sisters were thrust from relative obscurity into the bright glare of a long and complicated series of negotiations for the division of the immense Marshal estates, even before their father could enjoy the benefits of inheriting his own title. Their future careers were changed irrevocably by the inheritance of their grandparents' estates; how they managed the transformation is a fascinating story.

The seven daughters of Sybil la Marshal de Ferrers provide a dynamic demonstration of the strategies employed when a family of women jointly inherit a large estate. Six sisters survived their first husbands. Of the sisters who lived beyond their first marriages, two never remarried, two married twice, and two married three times. Moreover, only one of the six died while she was married; the remaining five died as widows and three of them lived as widows for long periods of time. Survival of children also played a role in the family dynamics experienced by the Ferrers sisters. Of the seven sisters, six had children who survived them; one of the sisters, Maud (probably the next to eldest), had four daughters who jointly inherited her share of the "maternity." The interactions of the first cousins, necessitated by the unusually complex division of property among the coheirs, followed patterns established by their parents in the previous generation. Finally, since the Ferrers sisters collectively inherited only one-fifth of their maternal grandfather's and grandmother's estates, they were not just coheirs of each other, but also coheirs of their Marshal family cousins who inherited the remaining four-fifths of the property.

By using the records of the central courts and the rolls of the royal chancery it is possible to discover what benefits the Ferrers sisters received from their inheritance, how they managed and maintained their property, and how they interacted with each other and with others outside their immediate family. Their actions reveal the sisters to have been intelligent and effective landholders who protected their interests and their property even when they bickered among themselves for greater shares of their inheritance. Both the spirit of cooperation among them and the antagonisms directed against some of the family members continued to be played out in subsequent generations, especially among the first cousins.

At the time the sisters inherited, three were married, one was widowed and about to be married again, and the three youngest were still minors. Their inheritance made the unmarried sisters wards of the king, who also controlled their marriages. Making advantageous marriages was one of the most important things a medieval parent did for his or her children and William Ferrers—and likely Sibyl as well, while she lived—seem to have planned carefully for the futures of their eldest daughters. Well before there was an inkling of the eventual dispersal of the Marshal inheritance, Agnes, Isabel, Maud, and Sibyl had been married to significant barons of middling to high rank: Agnes married William de Vescy, an important lord in Yorkshire and a member of the inner circle of the Lacy family of Pontefract who became the earls of Lincoln in the 1230s; Isabel married

Gilbert Basset, a follower and friend of Earl Richard le Marshal, Isabel's uncle;[6] Maud married Simon de Kyme, an important landholder in Lincolnshire and another member of the Lacy family's "inner circle"; and Sibyl married Franco de Bohun, lord of Midhurst, Sussex, and a cousin of the earl of Hereford and Essex, Humphrey de Bohun. These marriage arrangements reveal several things about the relative status of William de Ferrers and his wife, Sibyl la Marshal. For William, marriage to a daughter of the prestigious house of Pembroke raised his status. This seems to have been reflected in the marriage choices made for their daughters: all of the connections either directly or tangentially moved toward or into the Marshal orbit of political and marital alliances, or into the Marshal–Chester circle that was cemented by William's and Sibyl's own marriage.[7] An indication that this was a deliberate strategy of association with the more powerful earldoms of Pembroke and Chester can be seen in the gift that Isabel de Ferrers received when she married Gilbert Basset: her uncle, Earl Richard le Marshal, gave her a manor in Hampshire, including the town of Greywell, as part of her *maritagium*.[8] This strategy of alliance through marriage, which began well before the Ferrers sisters had any idea that they would eventually inherit part of the Marshal estate, became far more overt after the sisters became heirs and also gained control of their own remarriages when they were widowed.

Between 1245 and about 1270 the Ferrers sisters added nine more husbands to their list, marrying a total of thirteen times. Agnes, the eldest, and Agatha, the youngest, each married once; Isabel, second sister, and Joan, next-to-youngest, each married twice; and Maud, third eldest, and Eleanor, third youngest, each married three times. The middle sister, Sybil, who had married Franco de Bohun, predeceased her husband and, indeed, died before a share of the Marshal estate could fall into her hands; her son, John de Bohun, inherited her portion.[9]

With few exceptions, the sisters who married (or remarried) after they had become heiresses again turned almost exclusively to men within the Marshal family orbit. Their husbands included other barons of the Welsh March and the palatine county of Cheshire, which the earls of Pembroke dominated after the death of Earl Ranulph of Chester; families with local ties to counties in which the Marshals had centralized their authority, such as Somerset and Dorset; and brothers and cousins of other men who had married into the Marshal family. These marriage patterns within the family that controlled the earldom of Derby suggest that the overriding agenda was to deliberately and specifically strengthen its ties to the *maternal* line, not to the paternal.[10] This suggests that, even at the most rarified level of the nobility, the wife's status could have enormous significance on the political and social viability of the family. Traditional historians and anthropologists tend to state that the wife shares the status of her husband. In this case, just the opposite seems to have occurred: the husband shared his *wife's* status.

Agnes and her sisters thus achieved a significant status by virtue of their inheritance through their mother. A question one might ask is how did this rise in status affect their lives? The short answer is that, aside from Sibyl—the middle sister who died before she could make an impact—Agnes and her remaining five sisters did indeed embark on careers in which their connections to the Marshal family gave them opportunities to advance socially and to gain influence. One advantage they had was health: only one of the surviving sisters—Joan—died before her last husband; the five remaining sisters (Agnes, Isabel, Maud, Eleanor, and Agatha) all lived for many years as widows (Agnes was a widow for thirty-seven years, Agatha for over thirty, and Maud outlived her third husband by ten years). Widowhood placed noblewomen, in particular, in an advantageous situation. Widows received life use of one-third of their late husbands' property and did not have to relinquish it if they remarried (so someone like Maud, who married three times and survived all three husbands, controlled a great deal of property as dower). They were not subject to guardianship. Widows could make wills and act as executors for other peoples' wills; own, buy, sell, and rent property; act as guardians for their children and arrange their marriages; act as patrons for priests and monasteries; hire estate managers and attorneys; pursue litigation in the royal law courts. Moreover, they were subject to taxation and to supplying soldiers to the king's armies. In short, noble widows could do almost everything noblemen did, except assume magisterial positions (judge, baron of the exchequer, royal administrator), lead armies into battle (although they often assumed leadership in the defense of castles), attend the king's annual court as a member of the informal house of lords or the formal house of commons, or other specifically male professions (although they had to be formally acquitted of the common summons to attend such councils). The combination of family connections and dowager status could make a woman a powerful and influential member of the nobility. Indeed, it made the careers of many women possible, and the Ferrers sisters are excellent examples of this phenomenon.

Agnes and her sisters, in particular Maud, Eleanor, and Agatha—who happened to live longer than the other three—all made the best of a very good situation. Eleanor parlayed her position into a series of prestigious marriages and died a countess.[11] Maud used her status to solidify her economic and political position in the West Country through a profitable second marriage with a fellow baron in Somerset and Dorset and also gained entry into the royal court through a third marriage to a landless but socially prominent Poitevin noble.[12] Agatha became a powerful figure in the Welsh Marches, having married a collateral relation, Hugh de Mortimer of Chelmarsh, who happened to be the younger brother of Roger de Mortimer, one of the most important barons of the March (Roger's wife, Maud de Braose, was also the Ferrers sisters' first cousin).[13] Agnes had the most successful career of all the sisters, becoming lady of Kildare, gaining political and economic control over a large part of Yorkshire and Northumberland through her dower settlement, and seeing her eldest son marry into the royal family itself, not once, but twice.[14]

Throughout their lives, Agnes and her sisters had to work both within and through the family to achieve many of their political and economic aims. What detailed searching through the records reveals was a situation not unlike those that occur even today among members of a family: the sisters cooperated with each other, but also bickered among themselves. They helped each other when it was advantageous to do so, but individual sisters were not unwilling to antagonize their siblings when their own profit was at stake.

The Ferrers sisters did, indeed, work together to their mutual benefit. As discussed in greater detail later, they acted as co-plaintiffs with other Marshal family heirs to secure property or to sue tenants for trespass, debt, or other proprietary actions. They also acted together as sisters and coheirs when the property they had inherited directly was threatened or when they felt they were not receiving the privileges due to them. The Ferrers sisters at times also contributed to the well-being of each other's children. However, the very real problems of six, or even five, individuals, sharing ownership of property—not to mention the additional problems of succeeding generations, unexpected deaths, and the turmoil created by remarriage—seemed to have soured relations between some of the sisters.

The division of the Ferrers's share among the seven sisters must have been a laborious process.[15] Although each of the sisters had to have at least some land in all of the property they held jointly, there was no way to distribute it equally, so each sister received jurisdiction over specific local courts, advowsons, and profits and rents from specific manors to make their shares more equal. Although an attempt was made to make the seven shares mutually exclusive, this was not possible in all cases, so the sisters had to cooperate with each other in the lands they controlled together. The situation was complicated further by the need to grant dower properties or cash settlements to the four surviving widows of the Marshal men. Two in particular, Eleanor Plantagenet, widow of William le Marshal the younger and wife of Simon de Montfort, earl of Leicester (and also sister of King Henry III) and Margaret de Quency, *suo jure* countess of Lincoln and dowager countess of Pembroke, posed unusual problems.[16] Indeed, the circumstances were so bedeviling for all involved that it is worth discussing here before going any further.

Eleanor de Montfort was still a child when her first husband, William le Marshal the younger, died: it is not even clear whether the marriage had been consummated. She seems to have had a "nominated" dower, including precisely those English lands that fell to the Ferrers portion, among them Luton, Bedfordshire, the family *caput* in that county.[17] The Irish lands that formed the lordship of Leinster were not divided at this time. Instead, Eleanor received an annuity of £400 taken from the profits of the lordship. When both Walter and Anselm le Marshal died in 1245, the problems of dividing the estates among the thirteen coheirs looked so overwhelming that King Henry III made the fateful decision to pay Eleanor—his sister— her annuity from his own coffers. In proposing this, Henry made a serious miscalculation of the heirs' willingness to assume this responsibility. Not only did the Marshal heirs almost never pay the yearly amount allotted to them, but they amassed hundreds, even thousands, of pounds of debts to the Crown as the years progressed, while Henry's exchequer faithfully paid £400 a year to his sister. The Liberate Rolls attest to the payments made to Eleanor and Simon de Montfort.[18] The rolls of the King's Remembrancer attest to the extensive debts amassed by the heirs. For example, in 1255–56 five of the seven Ferrers heiresses each owed £217 2s 10 1/2d.[19]

Margaret de Quency's Marshal dower was even more burdensome to the heirs, however, because her husband, Walter, had been the last male heir invested with the earldom and she was entitled to a full one-third of the property. Again, the burden fell on the Ferrers sisters, who were compelled to relinquish the most prestigious portion of their inheritance, the Irish county of Kildare, for the duration of Margaret's life. The king mandated that the other heirs remunerate the Ferrers sisters from their own portions, but these cash payments did not begin to match the actual estates and were, moreover, subject to controversy.[20]

It is clear that, in these instances, the family members were willing to cooperate with each other to avoid paying debts, which would have diminished all their incomes. However, these same family members were not unwilling to drop such cooperative attitudes in order to thwart one of their own in similar suits. For example, Agnes de Vescy pursued a case of partitioning of debt in the court of Exchequer of Pleas against all her coheirs, more than thirty years after the division of the Marshal estates. The case was still appearing in the court records ten years later, indicating that quite a few delaying tactics had been employed by the litigants. Not only did Agnes sue her sisters, cousins, nephews, and nieces; several of the defendants sued each other for apparent nonpayment of the debt, which amounted to a mere 125 marks among all thirteen coheirs.[21]

The Ferrers sisters were not unusually litigious, but they were not afraid of conflict, either. All of them sued for dower when their husbands died and all litigated against tenants, bailiffs, and the like over debts, detinues, and trespasses committed by them. They were also occasionally sued for such things themselves. The activity of each sister individually, however, is not as significant in this context as their activity collectively—in joining together against a common antagonist, in fighting among themselves, and in more peaceful interactions among them. It is to these issues that I now turn.

Tenants occasionally sued one of the heirs for novel disseisin or for entry into property she held. In these situations, having multiple coheirs was an advantage for the defendant. By law, all of the heirs had to be listed in the writ and all had to appear before the case could be heard in court. It must have been virtually impossible for a plaintiff to win a case in which over thirteen powerful codefendants were involved.[22]

Occasionally the sisters joined together to pursue a mutual interest through the courts—or to attempt to garner more than their rightful share of profit. In 1293, the abbot of St. Thomas near Dublin complained that the Ferrers heirs had impinged upon the privileges of his priory—given, he claimed, to the abbots of St. Thomas by William le Marshal, himself—and were demanding that he appear before their liberty court of Kildare to answer a case of darrein presentment. The heirs—in this case Maud, Agatha, and William de Vescy, Agnes's son—insisted that the abbot was required to attend their court, while the abbot insisted equally strongly that he did not need to do so. The case appeared in the court of the King's Bench at every session for two years, but no final judgment is stated in the record. However, an inquisition did discover that the heirs were not entitled to summon the abbot to their court, and it was the abbot's own default that delayed the rendering of justice.[23]

Agnes and her sisters also had a number of disputes with other Marshal coheirs. In 1273, Humphrey de Bohun (coheir by right of his late wife, Eleanor de Braose, and the father-in-law of Robert de Ferrers, their brother) sued the Ferrers sisters for trespass. He also engaged in a lengthy contest with them over the wardship of a tenant's lands.[24]

Joan and William de Valence were among the coheirs tapped to reimburse the Ferrers sisters for the lands Margaret de Quency held in dower (Joan had inherited a full one-fifth portion of the estate)[25] and this necessitated a number of complicated agreements and propelled a significant conflict between the Valences and Agatha de Ferrers, who was able to compel her far more powerful cousins to release property they owed her after a four-year battle.[26]

Despite these antagonisms, there tended to be more cooperation than opposition among the large group of Marshal heirs. The Ferrers sisters sometimes exchanged property with the heirs outside their immediate family: a maneuver that helped to consolidate more scattered holdings. For example, a three-way exchange apparently occurred between Gilbert de Clare, earl of Gloucester and Hertford, Maud de Ferrers, and Agatha de Ferrers because they were involved in suits of warranty of charter with each other in the 1270s and 1280s.[27]

The sisters were also engaged in transfers of property within their smaller family circle. These arrangements were often not nearly as cordial, however. When Sibyl de Ferrers's son, John de Bohun of Midhurst, decided to sell part of his inheritance to Maud de Ferrers and other heirs, Agnes tried to impinge on the sale by suing John for entry as of her right.[28] Isabel (de Ferrers) Basset de Mohun was forced to sue her own sister, Joan, and her brother-in-law, Robert Aguillon, for dower after Reginald de Mohun's death in 1258.[29]

The most significant conflicts among Agnes and her sisters, however, occurred because of the complicated arrangements in their Irish inheritance. In 1257, Agnes made an agreement with her sister Joan and Joan's husband, Robert Aguillon, concerning the profits from a mill in Kildare, which was supposed to be part of Joan's inheritance, but was still controlled by Margaret de Quency in dower. Both Margaret and Joan died in 1266, which caused a chaotic situation in the Irish lands—and an excellent opportunity for the ever-acquisitive Agnes to wrestle away a bit of her sister's portion: Agnes never surrendered the mill to Robert Aguillon, who was entitled to it by right of curtesy. Robert sued Agnes and forced her into making a concord.[30]

Another conflict, in 1277, involved the newly widowed Agatha, who sued her sisters for withholding lands worth £12 6s 4d, which were part of her share in the vill of Newton-near-Jerpoint. None of her sisters answered the summons, so Agatha recovered the land by default.[31]

By far the most spectacular—and protracted—conflict among the sisters occurred when Margaret de Quency/de Lacy/la Marshal died in 1266 and the county of Kildare was finally released to the heirs. Agnes received the castle and capital manor, which then became the lordship of Kildare, while the other sisters received scattered manors and vills in the county. More importantly, the four surviving sisters—Agnes, Maud, Eleanor, and Agatha—were to receive approximately equal shares of the issues from the pleas and perquisites of the county and its court and to appoint jointly a seneschal, chancellor, and treasurer who would administer the county and divide the proceeds among the coheirs. As soon as Margaret died, however, Agnes appointed her own administrators and appropriated all the profits of the county. Maud (along with her third husband Emery), Eleanor, and Agatha sued Agnes for their respective shares. The Irish common pleas court found in their favor and demanded that Agnes give up the county profits to her sisters. She refused, claiming that she had been ejected from her seisin without having been summoned to defend herself. The case was adjourned to the court of the King's Bench in 1272 and continued to be delayed until Hilary term, 1275, when judgment was supposed to be made. Agnes attempted to forestall judgment by pleading that Eleanor's death the previous year nullified the writ. The court decided that since Eleanor left no surviving issue and her share was simply redistributed among her sisters and their heirs, the case would continue. They found in favor of Maud and Agatha and outlined precisely what they expected Agnes to do, how and when new officials of the county were to be appointed by all three sisters, and directed Agnes to pay any profits in arrears to Maud and Agatha.

This circumstance, in which one heir attempts to wrest more than her due from her coheirs, could have serious consequences. In the case of the Ferrers sisters, the result was an endless series of expensive petitions to the king and writs in the royal courts made not only by the sisters whose income had been appropriated by their sister, but by their heirs as well, after their deaths. The situation worsened when King Edward I removed Agnes's heir, William de Vescy (her second son), from his position as justiciar of Ireland and forced him to concede all his lands to the Crown as payment of his outstanding debts.[32] Just when Agatha and Maud had recovered their shares of the pleas and perquisites of the county, their property was again taken from them because the escheator never determined which parts of the Irish property belonged to William de Vescy and which belonged to his aunts. Eventually, the sisters and their heirs received yearly cash settlements for their shares in the county of Kildare.[33] Litigation of this kind was costly and frustrating, but the result must have been worth the cost, since the profits of a county as large as Kildare were extensive and provided all the sisters with badly needed cash.

Another effect of this kind of strife within the community of the Ferrers sisters must have been, in certain ways, its emotional impact on the family. Since all these women established households all over England and even in Ireland, they probably did not meet very often. Since they shared ownership in significant properties, particularly in Ireland and in the west of England, they nonetheless had to develop a useful working relationship. It seems that the younger sisters almost always allied themselves with each other, especially in opposition to their eldest sister. Since Agnes, in other contexts, appears to have been an unusually combative person—at least according to legal records that indicate that she had a consistently adversarial relationship with her tenants, her children, and the religious communities for which she stood as patron—it is not beyond the realm of possibility to imagine her acquisitiveness taking precedence over a less-profitable spirit of cooperation with her younger sisters.

Obviously, the economic relationship that Agnes and her sisters shared out of necessity must have had an effect on their personal relationships with each other. Although all of these activities and responsibilities might be defined as "domestic" in character, domesticity does not preclude political effects as well as personal. As mentioned before, land ownership (to the extent that people other than the king "owned" land) carried political responsibilities. One of the reasons why the Ferrers sisters seem to have taken their conflicts into the public arena of the king's court, instead of thrashing them out among themselves, is because the question of what belonged to whom carried consequences beyond their familial, domestic, private interests. Having an official record of the resolution of a conflict had become an important issue by the thirteenth century in England and the Ferrers sisters were clearly aware of the need to maintain their archives. If the county court of Kildare was administered *en famille*, then it behooved the sisters to establish clear boundaries regarding who was responsible, should they be called to account for poor administration of justice, for example. If all the sisters were subject to supplying the feudal levy, then it was vital for each one to know exactly how many soldiers she needed to supply. If a rebellion occurred—and several did occur during the lifetimes of the Ferrers sisters—then it was necessary, even imperative, that the family close ranks whenever possible, in order to protect their property from undue confiscation. This, in fact, occurred among the Marshal heirs during the Barons' War and the rebellion of Simon de Montfort: those who inherited land (including Agnes and her sisters) remained, for the most part, loyal to the Crown while many of those who had not yet inherited or whose family associations lay more outside the Marshal family circle turned against the Crown and supported the earl of Leicester—for example, Agnes's sons John and William, and the sisters' half-brother, Robert de Ferrers, earl of Derby. Indeed, Agnes was rewarded for her support of the Crown,[34] while her son, John, was fined a substantial amount before being forgiven his disloyalty.

The combination of cooperation and hostility that the Ferrers sisters exhibited during their lives appears in subsequent generations as well. The six sisters who had surviving children seem to have been protective of them and of their rights in the family property. Interestingly, they were also protective of each other, especially the children whose more favorable economic circumstances gave them opportunities to act as patrons for their less well-endowed cousins and nephews.

As the genealogical table indicates (see table 2.1), the sisters' ability to sustain their lineage beyond one generation was uneven. Eleanor had no surviving children; Agnes's sons all died without legitimate progeny;[35] Isabel's children all apparently died without producing heirs. Maud, Sibyl,

THE EXTENDED MEDIEVAL FAMILY

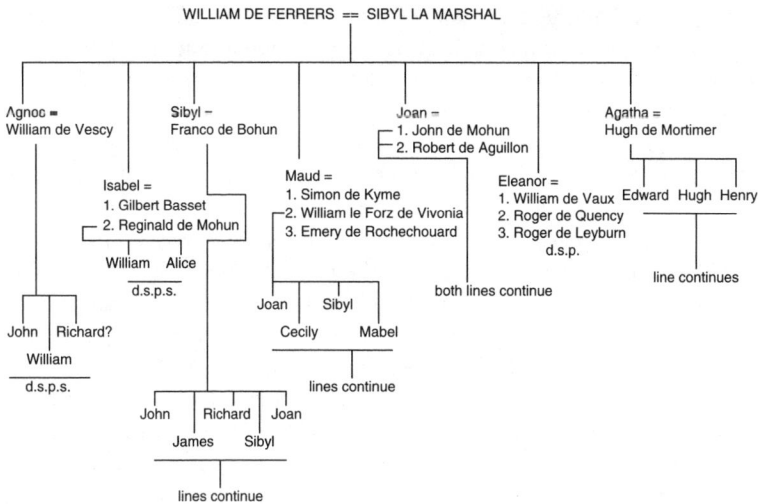

Table 2.1 The Ferrers Sisters

Joan, and Agatha all had successful lineages that continued into the fourteenth century; this was complicated further by Maud's heirs being four daughters (their father was William "le Fort" de Vivonia), who together shared Maud's one thirty-fifth of the Marshal estates and who each gained one-fourth of the Vivonia patrimony.

Since Maud's heirs were all female, their experiences mimicked those of their mother to a large extent. Maud's involvement with her daughters was, however, far more concentrated than that of her sisters and their own progeny, and is worth discussing in greater detail.

Maud's second husband, William "le Fort," was the son of Hugh de Vivonia, a Poitevan nobleman, and Mabel Malet, an heiress in the West Country. The Vivonia family appears in English records in the twelfth century, when an earlier Hugh gained a position in the household of Henry II and his son, young Henry.[36] As was typical in that period, Hugh's family was eventually rewarded for their service to the crown with marriage to an heiress; in this case to one whose property was confined to the counties of Somerset and Dorset, but whose lands lay alongside those of William le Marshal, earl of Pembroke. Maud's marriage to William was thus a politically and economically advantageous move for both adults, as it connected the Vivonia family more thoroughly to the Marshals and consolidated power over a larger portion of both counties. Their daughters—Joan, Cecily, Sibyl, and Mabel—were connected, in much the same way as Maud's marriages connected her, to continuing Marshal family alliances along the Welsh March and to the Poitevan alliances established within the Vivonia family. What makes these marriages so interesting is that they were probably arranged and organized by Maud, herself, in a series of manipulations that prevented the king from gaining control of the young women and also prevented him from using them as profitable marriage "properties." Amazingly, Maud managed to retain this control in the teeth of royal threats to her security and position: she refused to turn her daughters over to the king to be married to his choices and seems never to have been punished for her behavior, although the Close Rolls reveal a great deal of irritation on the part of Henry III when he was unable to gain control of the four girls.

The king, in 1259, had granted the girls' wardships and marriages to four members of his household—Ingram de Percy, Peter de Chauvent,[37] Imbert de Munferant, and Laurence de Sancto Mauro—with the stipulation that if none of the knights to whom he granted the marriages actually married the girls, then Maud could purchase their marriages. In fact, Maud resisted giving up her daughters to their guardians for two years and then sent her two younger daughters, Mabel and Sybil, to live overseas with their Vivonia relatives. The king finally granted Maud custody of her two elder daughters, Joan and Cecily, but retained their marriages. In the end, none of Maud's daughters married the men originally chosen by the king.[38] Joan married Reginald fitzPeter;[39] Cecily married John de Beauchamp; Mabel married Fulk de Archiaco; and Sybil married Guy de Rochechouard. Since none of these names ever appeared in the chancery records as possible marriage partners for the four girls and, moreover, because of Maud's marriage to Emery de Rochechouard—who must have been related to Sybil's husband, Guy—it is likely that Maud organized these marriages, probably by purchase, and subsequently negotiated for her daughters' best interests. That her protection of them met with their approval can be evidenced by the fact that Maud's daughters almost never interfered with the peaceful seisin of either her inheritance or her dower throughout her long life.[40] Moreover, after Maud's death in 1299, her three surviving daughters seem to have remained largely cordial and cooperative with each other—perhaps a testament to their upbringing, and quite a contrast to the volatile relationship between their mother and their aunts.

Maud's daughters also seem to have been relatively successful in preserving their lineage, as their progeny and grandchildren continue to appear regularly in chancery records into the mid-fourteenth century.[41] They also tinkered with the distribution of lands in their joint inheritance in an attempt to consolidate holdings and establish more discrete divisions in the property and to simplify tenurial relationships that, by the second decade of the fourteenth century, had become positively Byzantine.

Cecily de Beauchamp and Joan de Vivonia, wife of Reginald fitzPeter (she always called herself by her patronymic), survived far longer than their two sisters; they were also widows for a very long time. Consequently, they are seen more frequently in interactions regarding land distributions, both within their immediate kin group and among the other Ferrers heirs. Cecily purchased her sister, Sibyl's, portion of their inheritance for £1000 in 1300, a sale endorsed by her sister, Joan, and their nephew, Aymer de Archiaco. Cecily continued to receive hers and Sibyl's shares of the issues of Kildare's county court as late as 1315.[42] In 1318, Cecily and her cousin, Hugh de Mortimer of Chelmarsh (Agatha's son) exchanged property: her share of Luton, Bedfordshire (Agatha's designated *caput*) for his share of Sturminster Marshal, Dorset (Maud's designated *caput*).[43] A generation later, Cecily's son, John de Beauchamp "of Somerset" assisted Hugh de Mortimer's son, Hugh, with converting part of the Luton land into a jointure for Hugh and his wife, Margaret.[44] Joan de Vivonia sued her nephew, Aymer de Archiaco, for debt in 1307.[45] A few years later, Aymer sold a part of his inheritance to Joan and her younger son, Reginald fitzReginald, to whom Joan had earlier granted remainder of much of her inheritance in England.[46]

That the progeny of the Ferrers sisters remained closely allied is also demonstrated amply by the unusual level of patronage offered to one of the less wealthy and influential branches of the family. The Mohun family (lords of Dunster, Somerset) had married two of the sisters: Reginald had married Isabel, the second sister, after her first husband, Gilbert Basset, died; and Reginald's eldest son, John, married Joan, one of Isabel's much younger sisters, around the time of the sisters' inheritance of their mother's Marshal claim. Neither benefited significantly from these marriages. Reginald had a number of children from his first marriage and Isabel's dower was not all that significant; John had three or four children with Joan and died soon after the birth of the last child. Although Isabel did not remarry, Joan did—Robert Aguillon, who held her inheritance in curtesy for the rest of his life. It was perhaps for this reason that Joan's younger son, James, received such a significant level of patronage from his aunts and cousins. Agnes de Vescy presented James to the ecclesiastical living of Bubwyth in 1283 while he was still a subdeacon.[47] James advanced to the deaconate later that year.[48] In 1286, Agnes removed him from his first living and presented him to the church of Brompton.[49] James must have attained the priesthood shortly thereafter because he was listed as such when Isabella Beaumont de Vescy (Agnes's daughter-in-law, who held Brompton in dower) confirmed his presentation.[50] James's career continued to advance; he was called Master when he acted as one of Agnes de Vescy's executors.[51]

James seems to have been particularly close to another cousin, Joan Vivonia fitzPeter (daughter of Maud de Ferrers and her second husband, William le Fort, and widow of Reginald fitzPeter). Both owed money to Robert fitzPayn, which they agreed to repay through an enrolled agreement with the court of the Exchequer of Pleas.[52] A few years later, Joan's son, Peter, agreed to his mother's enfeoffing of James with part of her inheritance in Somerset, a transaction that was actually part of an arrangement to regrant some of her land in fee tail to her younger son, Reginald.[53] Finally, James acted as Joan's executor at her death.[54] Although this focus on the career of one particular family member is not that unusual—Maud de Clare, countess of Gloucester and Hertford, strenuously advanced the ecclesiastical career of her son, Bogo, and Joan de Vivonia fitzPeter herself supported her own son, William, in his clerical ambitions.[55] The fact that this family member was a nephew and cousin rather than a son, grandson, or brother suggests that James was something of a "project" for the Ferrers sisters.[56] Joan de Ferrers's relatively early death and the subsequent control of her property by her second husband (whose absence in the records of family interaction suggests that he was not engaged in the family's cooperative endeavors) might have necessitated their adoption of James as a needy member of the kin group, but his continued ties with more remote relations (such as his cousin's widow, Isabella Beaumont) suggests a more important relationship. The fact that James acted as executor for two generations of Ferrers relations demonstrates those close connections.

The tenacity with which the connections among the Ferrers heirs were maintained obscures the very real difficulties inherent in such maintenance. It seems as though once the most annoying obstructions had been removed—Agnes and her son, William—the remainder of the Ferrers kinship coalesced into an efficiently organized collective. Other large families who had, of necessity, to share power in a relatively confined district occupied themselves more with battling over their possession than with protecting their holdings from outside interference.[57] This was not the case here. No commissions of oyer and terminer appear in the Patent Rolls to demonstrate strife among the coheirs. In fact, the records are so bare that one could assume that the families had merely died out, or had lost track of their connections to each other, were it not for two moments in the mid-fourteenth century when the Ferrers heirs as a collective had to be identified because of generational events that necessitated their presence. The circumstances suggest that, even as late as 1339, the family derived from the Ferrers sisters was still viable and interactive. In 1339, the death of one of the coheirs, Mary [Archiaco?] wife of John Meyer, without heirs of her body, resulted in her inheritance being distributed among the extant heirs: John de Beauchamp of Somerset, Henry fitzRoger fitzPeter

THE EXTENDED MEDIEVAL FAMILY 27

fitzReginald [fitzPeter], John de Bohun of Midhurst, John de Mohun of Dunster, and Hugh de Mortimer of Chelmarsh.[58] In 1344, when the last widow connected to the Vescy family died (Clemencia, widow of John; son of William—Agnes's grandson) the same group of heirs requested that her dower in the Marshal–Ferrers estates be distributed among them.[59] The cohesion established by the younger sisters in response to the aggressive actions of their eldest sibling thus survived multiple generations and withstood multiple tests of its stability. In particular, Maud, Joan, and Agatha had built a coalition within their sisterhood of which they could be proud.

The experiences of the Ferrers sisters in managing and retaining their inherited property present a paradigm for analyzing the activity of female heirs in medieval England. Unlike the more familiar heiresses of great baronies, these women were only middling important: their lands only as extensive as those of the middle baronage. They had the influence and the political significance of neither their male coheirs nor even of their female cousins who inherited larger portions of the estate, such as Joan de Valence. The Ferrers sisters were unusual because so many of them survived to inherit and all but one produced heirs of their bodies, but their lives and activities were not unusual for their station in life. They made businesslike arrangements with each other concerning their joint inheritance rather than ones influenced by affection and family. Although they often acted in tandem, they also acted against each other, especially when one sister exhibited an unfamilial greed toward her siblings' portions. The sisters also distributed their lands in varied ways. Some retained their whole inheritance during widowhood; others gave portions of their shares to their children; still others alienated it from their family by enfeoffing tenants with their property. In other words, they did exactly as they liked with their inheritances, making sure that those who were important to them benefited.

The following generations often took their cues from the actions of their mothers. This continued reliance on family associations might not have been possible had the seven Ferrers sisters not been forced to maintain their own association with each other. Nevertheless, the actions of the daughters and sons of the Ferrers sisters suggest that the cognate ties that bound them together were as significant as those that bound them to their fathers' families. This family might have become close-knit out of necessity, but the support for less-empowered members of the family, such as James de Mohun, demonstrate that it was also close-knit by choice. Barbara Hanawalt, when talking about medieval criminal behavior, has noted that the family that slays together, stays together, but it can also be said that the family that is sued together becomes glued together. The property arrangements among the Ferrers sisters and their heirs and other children were so tortuous that the family's continued success depended on their ability to get along. Moreover, such alliances led to much closer personal ties among specific family members, ones that they maintained through succeeding generations and trying times. I contend that the picture of this family might be unusual, but it is not unique. Family, both direct and extended, had to have been among the most accessible and sensible potential partners for all medieval people. It is merely the complexities of this particular relationship among the Ferrers sisters and their progeny that guaranteed the visibility of their experiences.

CHAPTER 3

LIKE MOTHER, LIKE DAUGHTER: THE PARALLEL CAREERS OF MARGARET DE QUENCY AND MAUD DE LACY

When historians discuss intergenerational influences within medieval noble families, they usually focus on the relationships between fathers and sons. Such relationships are relatively easy to uncover: chronicles, for example, often characterize rebellions such as the Barons' War and the rebellion of Simon de Montfort as conflicts in which the younger generation pits itself against the "Establishment" identified with their parents. Nevertheless, by neglecting to identify and analyze similar relationships between mothers and daughters in noble families,[1] the story of the dynamics of medieval noble families will never be complete.

It might be argued that the records available to medieval historians do not reveal the ways in which mothers and daughters interacted. It might also be argued that there was comparatively little contact between them, especially because daughters tended to marry when very young—aged thirteen or fourteen being the norm—and might have had little contact with either parent while still in the nursery (if, indeed, they lived with their parents at all beyond the age of six or seven). Nevertheless, while it is admittedly more difficult to discuss relationships between mothers and daughters, it is hardly impossible. Moreover, the system of fosterage in medieval noble society more or less guaranteed that parents had relatively little day-to-day contact with *any* of their children—male or female—once they had left the nursery, and this was especially the case with the oldest children. Thus, sons could have been as much strangers to their fathers as daughters were to their mothers. Such lack of contact did not, however, dictate the absence of genuine feelings and the desire for familial associations.

The relationships between mothers and daughters might be more difficult to tease out of the documentary sources, but they are there, albeit usually in indirect, perhaps even ambiguous, ways. Widows appear more often in medieval records, so often the mother–daughter interactions revealed in them occurred between generations in which either one or both parties were dowagers. While such evidence usually describes an adversarial moment in the relationship—such as litigation over dower, inheritance, or *maritagium*[2]—this does not mean that the relationships were always adversarial.

Developments in Common Law after Magna Carta tended to disperse property into women's hands—both dower and inheritance—with fewer barriers than in the previous century.[3] Noble daughters after 1217 often witnessed their widowed mothers bearing the burdens of feudal landholding. There are a number of such mother–daughter combinations in the thirteenth century: Hawise de Forz, countess of Aumale, and her daughter, Isabella, and Ela Longespee, countess of Salisbury, and her daughter, Ela, come to mind. Another pair is Margaret de Quency de Lacy la Marshal, countess of Lincoln and Pembroke, and her daughter, Maud de Lacy de Clare, countess of Gloucester and Hertford. These two women benefited significantly from legal innovations that transferred both more property and greater autonomy into their hands. Although Maud's life, in particular, has generated some considerable attention by historians,[4] no one has discussed the lives and actions of this mother–daughter pair in the context of each other's careers. I believe that Margaret served as one of several models for her daughter—despite the absence of any overt filial relationship between them. This absence might, indeed, be the result of certain issues raised early in Maud's marriage, which pitted Margaret against her new son-in-law (which will be discussed later). Nevertheless, Maud's actions as a widow seem to reflect a level of influence from her mother—even when that influence can be viewed as negative.

Margaret was not born to the position she eventually assumed in the baronial hierarchy. Her father was Robert de Quency, younger brother of Roger de Quency, earl of Winchester. Her mother was Hawise, sister of Ranulph de Blundeville earl of Chester and Lincoln. Although derived from two of the most significant lineages of the twelfth century, being the product of the cadet branches of both houses could have been a social disability for Margaret. This, however, was not to be. About ten years after her marriage to John de Lacy, which occurred sometime around 1221, Margaret's maternal uncle, Ranulph, received dispensation to grant her widowed mother the earldom of Lincoln as an *inter vivos* gift.[5] This arrangement was highly irregular, especially in the early thirteenth century. First, there was a serious question as to whether women could inherit noble titles at all, since they were seen to be disconnected to the land that defined them, and the convention of "courtesy" titles that typified the noble lineages of future centuries had not yet developed. Second, even though Ranulph had acquired the earldom of Lincoln as a secondary title, it comprised a significant portion of his estate, which was destined to go not to a son, but to the progeny of all four of his sisters, including Hawise. Ranulph, by transferring the earldom to her (and thereby to his niece and nephew-in-law), effectively disinherited his other heirs of a substantial portion of their rightful inheritance. Even more surprising is the lack of evidence of any litigation arising from this arrangement, which suggests that the rest of the family either had granted tacit approval of the transfer or did not care.[6] In fact, this highly irregular grant occurred only a few years after Henry III's minority had ended (Earl Ranulph had been one of the guardians of the kingdom, along with Earl William le Marshal) and Ranulph still retained a significant amount of influence with the young king. He very likely manipulated his position in order to effect the transfer of such an important property.

Ranulph and Hawise probably had had something like the transfer of property in mind for awhile, and this agenda is reflected in their choice of marriage partner for Hawise's daughter and sole heir, Margaret: that is, John de Lacy. The family most thoroughly associated with the earls of Chester was the Lacys of Pontefract, Yorkshire. They controlled the office of Constable of Chester, but had never attained a noble title independent of the palatine county. Ranulph and Hawise must have sought to change this situation by arranging a marriage in 1221 between John (whose first wife, Alice de l'Aigle, had conveniently died) and Margaret. In 1232, in a move reminiscent of Ranulph's, Hawise received permission from the king to grant the earldom of Lincoln jointly to Margaret and John.[7] Thus, with a few swift strokes of the pen, Margaret went from being the daughter of a fairly minor baron to being a countess in her own right. John enjoyed the benefits of the earldom for only eight years: he died in 1240, leaving his wife and two young children behind (one of whom was already married).[8] His son, Edmund, would also die at a relatively young age;[9] his daughter, Maud, and grandson, Henry, would be the significant beneficiaries of this change in status.

Before John's death, he and Margaret had been able to negotiate a brilliant marriage for their daughter. In 1238, after paying King Henry III the enormous sum of £5000, they married Maud to Richard de Clare, the teenaged earl of Gloucester and Hertford, whose first clandestine marriage to the daughter of Hugh de Burgh, earl of Kent, had just been annulled.[10] This marriage was a guarantor that the Lacys of Pontefract would retain their political connections to the Welsh March forged in John and

Margaret's marriage. Richard de Clare's elite status was not confined to his paternity: his mother was Isabel la Marshal, the fourth daughter of William le Marshal and Isabella de Clare, the earl and countess of Pembroke.[11] A series of events subsequent both to this marriage and to John de Lacy's death would result in Margaret becoming thoroughly intertwined with the life of her daughter and son-in-law, but in ways that were not guaranteed to produce harmony between them.

The marriage effected for John and Margaret's son, Edmund, in 1247 was equally brilliant, but not one over which they had any significant influence, since John was already dead and the boy was in wardship to the king, who also controlled his marriage. Even so, this marriage made significant collateral connections to the families with whom the Quencys and Lacys were traditionally allied. Edmund married Alice, the eldest daughter of Manfred, viscount of Saluzzo (a cousin of Henry III's wife, Eleanor of Provence), while his primary vassal, John de Vescy, was married to Agnes, Alice's younger sister.[12] This marriage clearly reflects both the change in the Lacy family's status and the king's understanding of the family's need to retain the important connections in Yorkshire that had benefited them in the years before attaining an earldom. Although this marriage into the royal family guaranteed that Edmund's children would have careers close to the throne, it did not significantly benefit Edmund himself, who was unable to gain control of the lion's share of the family estates—those controlled by Margaret, his mother, as countess of Lincoln.[13]

Margaret's control of the earldom of Lincoln during her widowhood associated her with some of the most important and interesting people of the mid-thirteenth century. One such relationship deserves scrutiny. At the time of John de Lacy's death, the bishopric of Lincoln was held by Robert Grosseteste, one of the most important intellectuals in the English church, one of the first chancellors of Oxford University, and teacher of notables such as Roger Bacon. As bishop of Lincoln, Robert Grosseteste must have had a fairly intimate acquaintance with Margaret de Lacy, countess of Lincoln, particularly in the year or so between the death of John de Lacy and Margaret's remarriage. Unfortunately, no details concerning this relationship exist. Nevertheless, sometime between 1240 and 1242 Bishop Grosseteste wrote the *Rules Seynt Roberd*, a treatise on estate and household management, and dedicated it to countess Margaret.[14] The *Rules* were popular among estate administrators throughout the century, declining in interest only when methods of estate management changed in the late fourteenth century.[15] What is important in this context is that Grosseteste, certainly the most significant intellectual of his day and one of the most influential thinkers in medieval England, recognized Margaret's position as countess of Lincoln to be both legitimate and important. He viewed her as both patron and peer and took pains in the dedication of the work to acknowledge her position. Even if the friendship between Bishop Grosseteste and countess Margaret was purely "professional," the bishop's desire for recognition from the countess demonstrates how the local power system between diocese and earldom probably operated. Without Countess Margaret's patronage, the bishop of Lincoln might have found himself dangerously lacking in powerful allies.

Margaret remained a widow for a relatively short time. She was young, wealthy, and a brilliant potential marriage partner—which she could arrange herself, as she had gained control over her own remarriage. Armed with both her inheritance and with dower from the lordship of Pontefract and the Constablecy of Chester, she parlayed a stunning marital coup around 1242: she married Walter le Marshal, the fourth son of Earl William and Countess Isabella and the holder of the titles earl of Pembroke, lord of Striguil, and lord of Leinster, since his three older brothers had already died without legitimate progeny. Walter began using the title earl of Lincoln almost immediately[16] and Margaret appended the Pembroke title to her list of honorifics as well. If they had succeeded in having surviving children, the story of the thirteenth century would have been very different. However, Walter did not succeed in begetting an heir, and when he and his youngest brother, Anselm, both died unexpectedly in 1245,[17] the entire, massive, Marshal inheritance was divided among thirteen different coheirs connected to the five daughters of William and Isabella. Margaret, as the dowager countess in possession at the time of Walter's death[18] received the greatest benefit of all: dower that outweighed any of the heirs' individual holdings. Not surprisingly, Margaret eschewed another marriage and enjoyed her twenty-one year widowhood to the fullest.[19] She died in 1266, survived by her daughter, Maud, Maud's children, her other grandchildren—Henry de Lacy and Margaret de Lacy—and her daughter-in-law, Alice of Saluzzo.[20]

One of the more convoluted results of the division of the Marshal estates was that Margaret's son-in-law, Richard de Clare, became heir to one-fifth of the earldom of Pembroke and the lordships of Striguil and Leinster, and thereby also became the guarantor of the dower of his own mother-in-law, Margaret. The complexities of this relationship were extraordinary; they might also have influenced adversely the relationship between mother and daughter.

Armed with her immense inheritance, dower from John de Lacy, and the architecture of the law behind her, Margaret set about the process of gaining hold of her "reasonable third" of the vast Marshal estates. The heirs were unenthusiastic about granting her a share, which amounted to more than any of them had attained individually, but the law was clear: Margaret was entitled to the full third, and she would not be satisfied—as other Marshal widows had been—with cash payments and compromises. Ultimately, the least powerful of the heirs—the seven Ferrers sisters and their progeny—gave up the most: they had to turn over the profits of the county and lordship of Kildare to Margaret, receiving repayment from the other heirs for the term of her life. Richard de Clare and his cousin Joan de Munchensey (who was married to King Henry III's half-brother, William de Valence) were assigned the task of compensating the Ferrers sisters for the dower payments made out of their share.[21] Thus, not only did Richard have to accommodate his mother-in-law as to her dower in his own share, but he also had to help reimburse his cousins, also in favor of his mother-in-law. The addition of this wealth to Margaret's already overflowing coffers must have rankled the young couple to some degree. Indeed, Margaret was forced to sue the coheirs over arrears in her dower payments, which suggests that there was opposition to her control of the Marshal estates.[22]

Although the assignment of Margaret's dower from the earldom of Pembroke must have created tension between the countess and her daughter and son-in-law, they were also allies in the coheirs' attempt to keep Eleanor de Montfort and her husband, Simon, earl of Leicester from enjoying Eleanor's dower from her first husband, William le Marshal the younger. As was mentioned in chapter 2, at the time of William's death, Henry III dowered William's widow, Eleanor (who was also the king's sister) with £400 a year from the Marshal's Irish lordship of Leinster. William's brothers must have paid the cash settlement fairly regularly, because Eleanor did not issue any protests. When the last Marshal son died, however, Henry III agreed to pay his sister her dower from his own treasury until the estate could be divided between the coheirs and each one's share of her dower had been determined. Henry's intervention, rather than making the arrangement easier to manage, succeeded in making the system break down completely: the heirs and the other surviving widows of the Marshal brothers neglected to repay the exchequer for the annuity that Henry was releasing to his sister and brother-in-law. Ironically, the greatest debtor was Walter le Marshal's widow, Countess Margaret, because she controlled more of the earldom of Pembroke and the lordship of Leinster than any single coheir. In 1260–61, Margaret owed 2800 marks for the Montfort dower.[23] In 1272–73, her estate was still 800 marks in debt.[24]

If the relationship between Margaret and her daughter had been strained by the division of the Marshal inheritance, such tensions might have been exacerbated after Edmund de Lacy's death in 1258 because of Margaret's obvious preference for her grandson, Henry, and his mother, Alice, over her own child.[25] Alice de Lacy paid substantial sums to the exchequer to retain the guardianship of her son, Henry's, vast estates. Guardianship of Henry's lands meant control over not only the Lacy holdings and their title of constable of Chester, but also over the earldom of Lincoln once Countess Margaret had died. Alice originally shared some aspects of the wardship with her mother-in-law—principally the actual maintenance of the heir— but assumed full responsibility after Margaret died.[26] Thus, the earldom of Lincoln—the most powerful titled position in northeastern England[27]— was largely in female hands from 1245, when Margaret was widowed a second time, to 1272, when Henry reached his majority. Alice de Lacy and her mother-in-law, Margaret, seem to have maintained a remarkably cordial relationship while sharing wardship of Alice's son. For example, the payment Alice was required to make to the Crown to hold the guardianship of Henry's lands made a significant impact on her treasury; as a result, Margaret granted Henry an annuity for his maintenance that specifically mentions Alice's fiscal pressures as one of the motivating forces behind the grant. The fact that Henry was Margaret's heir as well probably contributed to the sense of partnership between the two women: they were both concerned about the boy's welfare.

There are no similar records of cordial interactions between Margaret and her daughter, although Maud and Richard named their own second daughter after her.[28] It is notable that Maud never referred to either of her parents in any ecclesiastical donations, which she made during her long widowhood. Thus, virtually the only interactions between Maud and her mother during her marriage were financial ones involving the distribution of Richard's Marshal inheritance and Margaret's Marshal dower. Their necessary alliance in the quarrel with Simon and Eleanor de Montfort over Eleanor's Marshal dower seems to have been unable to neutralize either their wrangling over Kildare or whatever slights Maud might have felt occurred during her childhood. This lack of connection is rather unusual in the extended family of the earldom of Pembroke: parents and children among all the Marshal heirs tended to retain fairly close ties to one another (as exhibited, e.g., by the relations between the Ferrers sisters and their progeny, as discussed in chapter 2) and also tended to marry and remarry within the family orbit. Maud de Lacy married into that cohort (as did her mother), but she seems to have been somewhat hostile to it: her children were to find marriage partners elsewhere, largely as a result of her machinations.

Maud's husband, Earl Richard, died in 1262, about four years before Maud's mother would reach the end of her life. Thus, for virtually all of her married life, Maud's status as the wife of one of the most powerful noblemen in the thirteenth-century political community was limited by her mother's control of a third of the Marshal inheritance and her status as countess of Lincoln and dowager countess of Pembroke. Maud's career as a widow both paralleled and diverged from that of her parent and the patterns of these conjunctions and divergences cannot be explained entirely by personality or circumstance.

Richard de Clare died during the lull between the Provisions of Oxford in 1258 and the revival of the baronial party under the auspices of Earl Simon de Montfort. Similar to the experience of her mother, Maud's son, Gilbert, was a minor in royal wardship. Unlike her mother, however, Maud was not the heiress of a massive estate, so she was dependant upon the generosity of the king in her dower assignment—and Henry III was very generous, indeed. In fact, he was *too* generous, including in her assignment the Welsh castle of Usk and the family honor of Clare, Suffolk. Gilbert was forced to sue her for admeasurement of her dower as soon as he reached his majority.[29] There could have been compelling reasons for King Henry to have made the excessive dower assignment. The political situation, particularly in Wales and the March, was highly volatile and Gilbert, like many of the "younger generation,"[30] were clamoring for the maintenance and expansion of the Provisions of Oxford, which limited the powers of the Crown in essential ways. Moreover, Gilbert's father, Richard, had been active in the development of the Provisions. Henry seems to have made use of widows of Maud's generation—such as Agnes de Vescy, whose sons actually joined the rebellion of Simon de Montfort—to establish royalist strongholds in areas where the followers of Earl Simon were also strong.[31] Henry III's maneuver in this instance, however, backfired: had he felt that the king had dealt fairly with him during his minority, Gilbert might have begun his career in the royalist camp, rather than with the rebels.

Why would Maud agree to the deliberate defrauding of her son while he was a minor in wardship to the king and, thus, powerless to protest? It is possible that she had been feeling a sense of ill-usage for some time with respect to the financial arrangements made during her marriage; this attitude could have contributed to her willingness to go along with the king's scheme. Maud's fiscal dissatisfaction might have had a legitimate origin: in 1249 or 1250, Maud agreed to the transfer of the manor of Navesby, Northamptonshire—which had formed the bulk of her *maritagium*—to Richard's niece, Isabella (the daughter of Amicia de Clare and Baldwin de Redvers, earl of Devon), and her husband, William de Fortibus, count of Aumâle, as part of Isabella's *maritagium*.[32] Whether Maud really approved of this grant is unknowable; according to the Common Law, her participation in the writing of the chyrograph outlining the grant signified her consent.[33] Maud waited until Isabella's husband died and, in 1275, sued her for Navesby on the basis that it had been demised to her against Maud's will. Although she almost succeeded—Isabella defaulted and Maud claimed the manor on that basis—in the end Isabella was able to produce the chyrograph and Maud was amerced for litigating a false claim.[34]

Maud clearly did not have the resources to amass the kind of extensive landed wealth enjoyed by her mother. Although she was by no means poor (she was, in fact, probably the wealthiest thirteenth-century widow who was not also an heiress), Maud could never command the kind of authority that landholders who held by independent tenures—as tenants-in-chief or in fee—achieved. Her activities in widowhood, however, suggest a pattern of behavior and a personality that was both highly competitive and somewhat embittered. For example, Countess Margaret engaged in surprisingly little litigation during her widowhood, much of it involving the consolidation of her dower soon after Walter le Marshal's death.[35] Once that had been accomplished, Margaret apparently did not see the need for extensive litigation, bringing only the occasional suit into the central courts.[36] Margaret was apparently a careful overseer of her property and tenants, as well, because there were remarkably few suits introduced against her during her long widowhood.[37] In contrast, Margaret's daughter, Maud, was one of the most litigious women of the century. She brought thirty-three suits (fourteen dower-related) into the central courts and was sued forty-four times during the twenty-seven years of her widowhood.[38] This latter figure suggests that Maud was not only more acquisitive than her mother—the difference in their wealth perhaps a motivating factor—but that she was also far more adversarial in her associations with tenants, estate officials, and her peers.

Maud was equally competitive—and seems to have been equally idiosyncratic—in her participation in the "marriage market." While Margaret worked assiduously to promote the marriage of her grandson, Henry, to Margaret Longespee, granddaughter and heir of Ela, countess of Salisbury,[39] Maud was equally assiduous in promoting the careers of her own children. Maud's sons' marriages were in the king's gift after Richard de Clare's death, but her daughters' marriages were her responsibility, one that she fulfilled with the help of her son, Bogo.[40] She seems to have followed an agenda that furthered the family's relations with the royal family rather than following the agenda of her natal relations to consolidate territory in the west and north along the Welsh and Scottish Marches. The eldest daughter, Isabel, married the marquis of Montferrat; Margaret, the second daughter, was married for a time to Edmund, earl of Cornwall (they divorced); and Rose, the third daughter, married Roger de Mowbray who served a number of terms in the royal chancery and was an important member of the royal administration.[41] None of these marriages furthered relations with the earldoms of Lincoln, Chester, Pembroke, or Winchester—the lineages most associated with Maud's mother—unlike many of the Pembroke coheirs' marriages. Instead, they focused on the royal court as being the most important connection. This association with the Crown was furthered even more significantly by Gilbert's two marriages, to Alice de Lusignan,

Henry III's niece, and to Joan of Acre, daughter of King Edward I and Queen Eleanor of Castile. Maud thus apparently rejected the marriage strategies of both her husband and her parents. It is not clear why she was so hostile to what had developed as a highly successful series of marriage strategies, and her daughters suffered materially to some extent by these arrangements. Isabel de Montferrat, for example, was unconnected to any significant barony in England. Margaret's and Edmund of Cornwall's marriage was a disaster that ended in divorce in 1293. While Roger de Mowbray was evidently a competent administrator and an honorable courtier, he was not at the social level of his wife's family. In contrast, the marriage of Edmund de Lacy to Alice of Saluzzo created a relationship with the Crown that benefited the family to a significant degree, and the marriages of their son Henry were advantageous to the furthering of the family fortunes. Moreover, Henry's sister's marriage to George de Cantelou, while he was a relatively minor recipient of Marshal estates, nevertheless re-associated the Lacy family with that important lineage as well as with other prominent families of the Welsh March, among them the Braoses and the Mortimers.[42] The marriages arranged by Margaret were thus politically astute, financially remunerative, and far-sighted. Maud's strategies were not nearly as clearheaded and were less successful.

Maud herself, after her husband's death, was a wealthy woman and, as she was a settled matron with plenty of children, she made no attempt to negotiate another marriage. She concentrated her energies, instead, on promoting the clerical career of her son, Bogo, to such a degree that their interactions seem to overshadow all other relationships. In fact, Bogo was notoriously acquisitive during his career in the Church and Maud seems to have encouraged his ambitions with a zeal that does not reflect well on her reputation. Bogo has been described by Michael Althschul as "the greatest pluralist in the English Church." Despite the fact that he was never ordained to the priesthood, remaining in minor orders, he amassed an enormous collection of rectorships, canonries, and important offices, making him not only the "greatest pluralist," but also probably the wealthiest churchman of the century.[43] Maud was responsible for quite a few of the benefices enjoyed by her son. One such grant created difficulties within her own family: her attempt to present Bogo to Aldingfleet church (in Yorkshire) in 1268–69. Maud sued her son, Gilbert, and John de Eyville, the holder of the advowson, for impeding her right to make the presentation to the living. She claimed that Gilbert and John had colluded with the archbishop of York, Walter Giffard, in order to present Walter's brother, Godfrey, to Aldingfleet. Maud wanted the church to go to Bogo. The court pronounced in Maud's favor and awarded her £100 in damages, which she then promised to Bogo. Ten years later, he sued his mother for the hundred pounds. Maud proved that John de Eyville had never paid the damages; the two original litigants finally made a concord in 1279 in which Maud quitclaimed the advowson to John in exchange for one hundred marks, plus the original damages, which she then granted to Bogo.[44]

Although in other contexts she was a notable patron of the Church (which will be discussed later), Maud's acquisitiveness, evidenced by her relationships with lay tenants, apparently tended to sour her relations with ecclesiastical neighbors and sub-feofees. Although mostly small suits of debt and detinue, Maud was nevertheless sued by parsons, priors, and abbots associated with the family throughout her widowhood.[45]

One such case, which was more spectacular than the norm, can serve to illustrate Maud's adversarial approach to her ecclesiastical neighbors. The prior of Derhurst, Oxfordshire, sued Maud in 1277 over the enrollment of a writ in her hundred court concerning his own independent court.[46] The next year he returned to the court, claiming that Maud's estate officials had invaded his property and had unjustly carried off the prior's oxen and sheep.[47] The case dragged on for four years in the Court of Common Pleas before being adjourned to the King's Bench in 1283.[48] There, the entire story was revealed: the prior's attempt to enroll the writ in 1277 was designed to protect him from such distraints, and he argued that position before the justices of the Bench. Maud, who had delayed the proceedings in Common Pleas by defaulting and demanding adjournments, finally answered the prior's charges by arguing that she had acted simply as the king's representative: the sheriff of Oxford had instructed her to make the distraint. Although Maud was proved to be in the right, her bailiffs were nevertheless chastised for being overzealous, since they had carried off more animals than the writ of distraint had specified.[49] Thus, even though Maud was in the *right* and, moreover, had the power of the royal administration behind her, she still chose to antagonize her neighbor and to use the opportunity to gain an undeserved profit from her actions, even if her actions could be construed merely as turning a blind eye to the corruption of her estate officials.

Maud's career as it paralleled that of her mother, Margaret, seems to suggest a radically different agenda as well as a radically different style. Where Margaret seems to have been gracious—in dealings with her son's children and her tenants and neighbors—Maud seems to have been grasping. Perhaps she felt the need to compete with heiress-dowagers whose wealth was not entirely dependent on the life-interest they gained in their late husbands' estates, such as Margaret herself and her contemporary, Countess Ela of Salisbury.

In one activity, Maud's career diverged significantly from that of her mother: she was far more vigorous in her support for Clare family

Augustinian foundations than Margaret was in the Lacy foundation of Pontefract priory or the Marshal-supported Tintern Abbey, where her second husband was buried. Maud, although she had no inherited land of her own save her *maritagium*, oversaw the continued endowment of Stoke-by-Clare Priory (which her husband, Richard, had founded in 1248) after his death. Most of the donations actually came from tenants who granted their land to Maud. She then warranted the tenants and donated the property to the priory.[50]

Maud's most impressive grant, however, was the foundation of Canonsleigh Priory for forty Austin nuns in 1284. Maud had originally proposed founding a house in Sandelford, in the diocese of Salisbury. Pope Gregory X even ordered the archbishop of Canterbury to carry out her plans.[51] Nothing came of this foundation, apparently, because ten years later Pope Martin IV mandated the bishop of Exeter to establish Maud's house at Leigh, Devon.[52] Maud's initial grant was probably the £200 per year she had originally intended for Sandelford. In 1285 and 1286, however, Maud donated an additional two manors and convinced the bishop of Exeter to donate a third.[53] As with her donations to Clare Priory, Maud also solicited grants from her tenants, who then donated lands to the priory in her name or gave her the land to donate herself.[54] Maud's desire to found Canonsleigh evidently came from her dissatisfaction with the tiny foundation of six male Austin friars in the same location; this was dissolved to make room for her much larger community of nuns. Maud's desire for a more efficient utilization of her religious grants did not extend to a personal desire to dedicate her life to religious devotions: unlike Ela Longspee, countess of Salisbury, who founded Lacock Abbey, Maud did not enter her religious house as a vowess (Ela eventually became the abbess of Lacock). Thus, Maud's foundation can be seen as a supreme example of what might be called "conspicuous piety": she created Canonsleigh as a monument to her generosity and to her position in the local noble community. Given her overwhelming support of her son, Bogo's, clerical career—which was a model for everything that was wrong in the medieval Church—it is difficult to look at the program of Maud's donations without a slightly cynical eye. Her piety failed to reveal itself in other contexts, as well. For example, although her mother, Margaret, received two papal dispensations in 1251, the first to erect a portable altar so that "she and her household can celebrate the divine offices" and the other so that she, "accompanied by three or five honest matrons" could hear mass in the Cistercian monasteries in England,[55] no such dispensations appear for Maud, suggesting that she had never sought those kinds of privileges.

The charters outlining clerical donations by the laity always include memorials to loved ones both living and dead, which can be used to speculate on emotional relationships within families. Maud's charters specify that the donations are made to benefit the souls of herself and her husband. Maud's parents are conspicuously absent in this list of memorials. Although it is impossible to make any definitive conclusions based on such evidence, given the lack of positive contact between mother and daughter during their lives, it is possible to consider this silence as indicative of their relationship.

Given the apparent coldness between Countess Margaret and her daughter, Countess Maud, as well as the ways in which their lives intersected, especially following the death of Walter le Marshal, Margaret's second husband, it is reasonable to view Maud's personal agenda as designed to compete with, even to overshadow, her mother. Maud could never compete with her mother with respect to personal wealth, but she could compete successfully in placing favored children in positions of power and in self-promotion through the use of demonstrably generous clerical donations. This view could be reinforced by looking at Maud's relationships with her own daughters and sons. Although vigorous in promoting the careers of her sons (parallel to Margaret's support of her grandson, Henry), Maud seems to have been less enthusiastic about retaining contact with her daughters after their marriages: there is no evidence of any interaction between them after they reached adulthood.

Characterizing Maud's career as a widow as being motivated by competitiveness with her mother is reinforced by the possibility that Maud was, simply, competitive with everyone within her aristocratic circle. Another figure against whom Maud might have invited adverse comparison is the remarkable countess of Salisbury, Ela Longespee, whose granddaughter and heir, Margaret, married Maud's nephew, Henry de Lacy. If trying to compete against the image of her mother might seem a futile attempt to modern eyes, how much more difficult it must have been for Maud to measure herself against such a figure. Nevertheless, measure herself she seems to have done. After William Longespee's death on Crusade, Ela fashioned a magnificent tomb for him in the newly constructed Salisbury Cathedral. Maud, after Richard de Clare's death in 1262, designed and commissioned a tomb for him at the Clare family-patronized abbey of Tewkesbury, which the Chronicle of Tewkesbury describes as being decorated "with gold and silver and precious stones."[56] Ela transformed the disorganized and deteriorated male foundation at Lacock into a bustling, successful foundation for Austin nuns. Maud transformed the virtually defunct priory of Leigh into the wealthy and successful foundation of Canonsleigh for forty Austin nuns—but she herself never assumed an abbatial post there, as Ela did at Lacock. While the tomb for Richard was certainly motivated in part by Maud's desire to honor the memory of her late husband, the combination of the two comparisons also could suggest other, less altruistic, motives.

Even though this seeming competition does not appear at first glance to be directed at her mother (or at her memory), the two towering female figures of the mid-thirteenth century—Countess Ela and Countess Margaret—had connections to each other through marriage as well as proximity that might have made them silent allies and unseen partners. Ela and Margaret were of the same generation, with close family ties and with similar political agendas. It might be possible that Maud considered both of them to be models of behavior as well as objects of competition. By competing against *both* women, Maud might have felt she could outshine them both.

If the devotion of family members can be considered a mark of the status of a person within that family, then Maud invites invidious comparisons with both her own mother, Margaret, and her sister-in-law, Alice of Saluzzo. She alienated her eldest son, Gilbert, because of the fracas over her dower assignment. She apparently ignored both her daughters and her son, Thomas, who were compelled to make their own way in the world.[57] The one object of her maternal devotion, Bogo, was scarcely worthy of such attention. It could be argued that the blame for Maud's problematic life choices could be laid at Margaret's feet. After all, Margaret seems to have been just as careless with her daughter as Maud was with her own. While it is likely that nurture—or lack of it—might have played a part in the development of Maud's personality, it is impossible to state definitively what combination of environment and personality molded either Margaret or Maud into the figures they became.

Indeed, one could almost describe Maud as a somewhat distorted reflection of her mother. Both women were powerful, active, obviously intelligent, wealthy, and blessed with long lives. Maud's idiosyncratic life choices mirrored those of her mother—and, perhaps, of Ela Longespee, as well—but if so, "through a glass, darkly." Where Margaret and Ela had a golden touch, Maud's was slightly tarnished silver. Such a characterization, however, dismisses the very real struggle Maud must have experienced to make a place for herself in the competitive world of the thirteenth century. If she was ambitious and competitive, she was also very successful in achieving her goals. In the end, she might well have used her resemblance to her mother as a tool to help her realize her ambitions and, with that recognition, she might have come to value her legacy. With respect to Margaret, her possible neglect of her daughter and her obvious conflicts with her son-in-law might have soured her relationship with Maud. Nevertheless, it is not inappropriate to speculate that had Margaret survived beyond the chaotic years of the mid-1260s, she might have come to value and regard her daughter more highly, perhaps for the strength of will and the determination that so resembled her own.

CHAPTER 4

HEROISM AND DUTY: MAUD MORTIMER OF WIGMORE'S CONTRIBUTIONS TO THE ROYALIST CAUSE

The thirteenth century was witness to considerable political tumult in the British Isles. Beginning with the rebellions of the barons against the reign of King John, culminating in the creation of Magna Carta, the kingdom experienced a number of significant political and military actions by and against the Crown, as well as countless small conflicts. These actions affected the entire kingdom, but they also tended to be localized in regions controlled by particular families who became embroiled again and again in both baronial attempts to limit interference by the king and royal attempts to limit the growing power and autonomy of the baronage. The principle center for most of these activities was the Welsh March, which stretch from the mouth of the River Wye in the south, along the western portion of the Severn, and to the upper reaches of the River Dee.[1] On the English side, the counties of Cheshire, Shropshire, Hereford, and Gloucester "marched" from north to south. On the Welsh side lay a collection of small-to-large baronies held by Anglo-Norman conquerors and Welsh allies, running roughly from Glamorgan in the south, past the large native principality of Powys, and up to Denbigh and Flint in the north.[2]

Until the Edwardian conquests of the 1280s, Wales was divided between native Welsh princes whose power had coalesced under the Gwynedd-centered Principality of North Wales, and the cluster of marcher baronies that formed an encircling crescent around them, from St. Davids in Pembrokeshire and up through the river valleys nearly to Liverpool. The Principality of North Wales (under the control of Llewelyn ab Iorwerth for the first half of the thirteenth century) might have been hemmed in by Anglo-Norman marcher baronages—who also conveniently controlled the southeast coast of Ireland, especially the old kingdom of Leinster—but he was hardly powerless. Moreover, Llewelyn was able to manipulate the baronages surrounding the principality to some extent through intermarriage, treaty, negotiation, and, occasionally, war. In fact, the Welsh principality survived largely through Llewelyn's effective leadership, until the force of Edward I's combination of crusading zeal and desire for conquest was unleashed upon the Welsh in the 1280s.

The life and career of one woman and her family can serve to exemplify the ways in which both the complex relationships among the marcher barons and the Welsh princes and the growing power of the marcher barons against the English king could change the political architecture of a region. Maud de Mortimer of Wigmore, the granddaughter, daughter, wife, and mother of marcher barons and the coheir to two great marcher lordships, had the sort of career that most historians envisage as the exclusive province of the medieval noble*man*. Through both her proximity to the centers of power in the Welsh March and the accidents of life and death, Maud could easily be seen (as R. R. Davies has described her husband) as "one of the great architects of the late medieval March."[3]

In order to discuss Maud's career, it is necessary to identify the reasons why Maud was able to be so active in the thirteenth-century political arena. Her position within a large extended network of interrelated families had an impact on her effectiveness; the unusual nature of the Common Law regarding inheritance—and Maud's position as an important heiress—also had an impact. It could be said that Maud's career bridged the boundaries between public and private activity much as the bridges over the Wye and Severn rivers created the means for crossing the border between two radically different cultural and political milieus.

Historians usually divide medieval law into two discrete categories: feudal and customary, or public and private. The first category describes law relating to the system of military and political obligation between the king and his nobles and between a lord and his knights. The second contains laws regarding inheritance, secular considerations in marriage, and land tenure. English Common Law, developed after the Conquest, achieved a blending of feudal and customary law for the free Anglo-Norman people who lived in the English kingdom and its environs: Wales, Scotland, and Ireland. All landholders in England held more or less directly of the king, even when intermediaries existed, so Common Law dealt with the relation between the Crown and the people. The hegemony of the king over all lands held in his kingdom also placed virtually all interactions regarding land tenure into his hands and, ultimately, into his courts.[4]

The paradox that, in a society based upon military tenure, the Common Law protection of widows' and heiresses' rights to family property overrode the feudal requirements of the tenant's military service to his lord makes it difficult to construct realistic models of medieval political culture based on an androcentric notion of land ownership. The feudal ideal could be achieved only by the survival of sufficient male heirs to remove women from its sphere. Medieval English Common Law contradicted both feudal and social attitudes about the inappropriateness of women as landholders; this contradiction was accepted by the ruling class and even strengthened through Magna Carta, a document created by the same barons who relied upon feudal custom to thrive. The ideology of military service also stipulated that women could not bear arms or lead troops. Thus, the military nature of feudal holdings should in theory have prevented women from performing the duties of the fee. In reality the medieval noblewoman governed when her husband was away, defended the family property, and commanded the respect of kings and barons alike. She was, moreover, expected by her husband and her peers to perform all these duties efficiently and with skill.

Maud de Braose, wife and widow of Roger de Mortimer, lord of Wigmore (whose grandson, Roger, became the first earl of March) is a perfect example of a woman who obviated the restrictions her sex placed upon her and succeeded in placing herself squarely at the center of the political milieu in the areas under her domestic control. Maud's success was probably the result of a number of factors that together created a realm of activity for her: the endemic rebellions along the Welsh March in the second half of the thirteenth century; the wars between the Crown and the baronage that occurred at the same time; and the coincidence of both her own inheritance of significant property in Wales and the March and that of her husband. Maud was not unusual, however, in her ability to exploit these factors in order to create such a realm of activity.

The beginning of Maud's story lies in the early thirteenth century, in the generation of her grandparents (see table 4.1). Her paternal grandparents were Reginald de Braose, the lord of Abergavenny and Bramber,[5] and Grecia de Briwerre; her maternal grandparents were William le Marshal and Isabella de Clare, earl and countess of Pembroke. Reginald and Grecia had a number of children, among them their eldest son, William, who inherited the lordship. William was one of the most important marcher lords in the early thirteenth century, especially after the wars between King John and the Braose family had been resolved—largely as a result of the intervention of the thirteenth century's "Great Communicator," Earl William le Marshal. The position of the Braose lords of Abergavenny was demonstrated in the next generation by the marriage of Reginald and Grecia's son, William, to one of the daughters of the earl and countess of Pembroke, Eve la Marshal. William and Eve, in turn, had

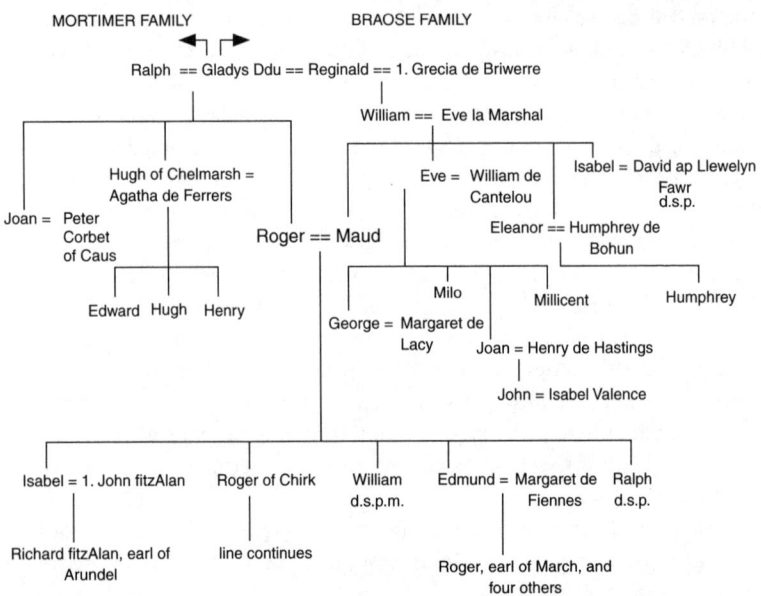

Table 4.1 The Mortimer of Wigmore and Braose Families

four daughters: Maud (the eldest), Eve, Eleanor, and Isabel.[6] At the time of the birth of their last daughter, neither William nor Eve could have anticipated that the four girls would inherit the substantial estates of the Braose family and share in the dispersal of the enormous earldom of Pembroke.

The Braose family tended to ally itself with other marcher barons in ways that put them in conflict with the Crown. Reginald, Maud's grandfather, had in fact inherited the family estates because of the outlawry of his brother William, who had fled to Ireland in order to escape the wrath of King John. Unfortunately, John vented his wrath on the wife and son of this earlier William de Braose, starving them to death, much to the fury of the magnates of the realm.

Maud's father, the younger William, does not seem to have fared much better, at least in areas in which diplomacy was the better method than use of force or impulsive action. In 1230, he was staying at the court of Llewelyn ab Iorwerth, where they were engaged in negotiating a marriage between William and Eve's youngest daughter, Isabel, and Llewelyn's son, David.[7] At court, William apparently encountered—and fell passionately in love with—Llewelyn's young wife, Joan Plantagenet, illegitimate daughter of King John. His feelings were evidently reciprocated, because the two were apparently found *inflagrante delicto* by Llewelyn's guards. William was summarily tried and executed, an act for which Llewelyn made no apology in a letter that he wrote to William le Marshal the younger, earl of Pembroke, right after the event.[8] Even more bizarre was the letter that Llewelyn sent to William de Braose's widow, Eve (who was the sister of Earl William le Marshal), whom he saluted as "his dear friend," sending her his "fondest greetings." In this letter, Llewelyn states that he is still interested in completing the negotiations for the marriage between Isabel and David, and that these negotiations should not be affected adversely by the late unpleasantness between the two families.[9] In fact, the marriage did take place.

Eve's unexpected widowhood at such a time meant that she was more or less responsible for her four very young daughters and herself. She managed, despite the shocking circumstances of her husband's death, to gain control of her dower and to retain guardianship of her daughters so that the family seems to have stayed together. She also seems to have deliberately delayed the marriage of her daughters for some years, perhaps to ensure that they would be connected to families who had gained her trust.[10] Indeed, Eve's actions must have influenced the ways in which Maud interacted with the men and women who were connected to the affinities of both herself and her husband. The horrible shock of her father's death, coupled with the rapidity of her mother's consolidation of her power and the rallying around them of the Marshal family seem to have served as models of behavior for Maud's later career.

Eve seems to have become involved with the rebellion of her brother, Richard le Marshal, in 1234, and indeed might have acted as one of the peacemakers between the king and the rebellious siblings after Richard's murder in Ireland, because she received a safe conduct in May 1234 in order to speak with the king. By the end of the month, she had a writ from King Henry granting her seisin of lands and castles, which he had seized because of the rebellion, and a formal statement that she was back in his good graces again.[11] Eve's foray into political activity along the Welsh Marches might have been short-lived, but it must have served as an object lesson for her daughters: that swift and decisive action would gain beneficial results. Such lessons must have been amplified by the events of 1245: Eve's two youngest brothers, Walter and Anselm, both died, leaving the Marshal earldom of Pembroke as the inheritance of the five daughters of William and Isabella, the first earl and countess.[12] Thus it was that Eve's daughters not only inherited their father's estates, but their mother's as well—one-fifth of the earldom of Pembroke and the lordships of Striguil and Leinster. Eve died in 1246, but not before managing yet another brilliant political coup, the marriage of her daughter, Maud, to Roger de Mortimer of Wigmore, which occurred in 1247.

In fact, Roger's family had been intimately connected to the same affinity as the Braoses since the beginning of the century and he and Maud were related by ties of marriage, if not of blood. In 1215, after the death of Grecia de Briwerre, Reginald de Braose, Maud's grandfather, remarried: Gladys Ddu (Dark-eyed Gladys), the daughter of Llewelyn ab Iorwerth and Joan Plantagenet.[13] This marriage produced no children; Reginald died in 1227. Three years later, Gladys married Ralph de Mortimer, lord of Wigmore. The marriage between Gladys and Ralph lasted sixteen years and produced at least three children, sons Roger (born ca. 1232) and Hugh and daughter Joan.[14] Gladys did not remarry after Ralph's death in 1246; she remained active until her own death in 1251. Roger, the heir of Wigmore, in an arrangement probably negotiated by his mother and his future mother-in-law, married Maud, eldest daughter of Gladys's stepson, William de Braose, in 1247 (she was probably several years older than he, since he was born about two years after her father had died). By means of this marriage Roger more than doubled the wealth and prestige of the Mortimer family, thus making it possible for historians of medieval Wales to identify him as one of the most important landholders of the March.[15]

Roger and Maud were thus connected in multiple and complex ways to each other and to the families with whom their own kin were allied. Roger, through Maud, became a part of the Marshal family affinity (which would have important consequences later on); both had connections to the family of Llewelyn ab Iorwerth; both enjoyed the benefits of holding a wide bloc of land in the Welsh Marches that stretched from the south coast to the border between Hereford and Shropshire. They had an eventful married life lasting thirty-five years and producing six children who survived infancy: sons Ralph (who died before inheriting), Edmund (originally destined for the Church but ultimately his parents' heir), William (who died without issue in 1297), and Roger (first lord of Chirk in Shropshire); and daughters Isabel (who married John fitzAlan lord of Oswestry and Clun in Shropshire and *de facto* earl of Arundel) and Margaret (who married Robert de Vere, heir apparent of the earl of Oxford). Roger died in 1282, before the Edwardian conquest of Wales, and Maud achieved control of her inheritance as well as dower from Roger's holdings. She never remarried, although she lived another nineteen years, and was very active in managing and administering her considerable inheritance. At the time of her death, in the winter of 1301, Maud must have been close to eighty years old.

The bare bones of this outline of Maud's life after marriage do not begin, however, to describe the extraordinary level of activity in which she engaged. Maud's connections to the most important lineages in the Welsh March contributed significantly to her effectiveness in the region during both her marriage and her widowhood. She was able to achieve the respect of her own and Roger's tenants and both Henry III and Edward I came to rely on her position in the March in their negotiations with—and wars against—the Welsh princes. What makes Maud's situation different from some of her female peers is the fact that some of her most significant contributions to the Crown apparently occurred *before* her widowhood. The political circumstances of the time effectively nullified the usual restrictions against female political and military activity that typified more peaceful times and less volatile regions.

By the middle of the century, most members of the baronage were disgusted with King Henry III's enthusiastic support of his half-siblings and the Poitevans who populated his wife's household. In fact, the Mortimers could have counted themselves among the aggrieved, considering Henry's appropriation of one of the Marshal heiresses, Joan, daughter of Warin de Munchensey and Joan la Marshal, as a marriage partner for his youngest brother, William de Valence. William had a reputation for acquisitiveness that soon caused conflict in those portions of the Marshal inheritance that required cooperation among the heirs. Matters came to a head in 1258, when a committee of barons formulated a list of grievances and forced Henry III to accept them at a meeting in Oxford. The Provisions of Oxford went well beyond Magna Carta in their expression of baronial independence and in the control of royal activity. Unfortunately, no one with a reputation for diplomacy—another William le Marshal—was available to soften the edges of the Provisions of Oxford. Most of the Council of Twenty-Four belonged to the younger generation of barons who were convinced that Henry III's support of his relatives and in-laws impinged on their rights and privileges and negated the principles of the Great Charter. Among the most vocal in their displeasure were the barons associated with the Marches of Wales and Scotland, in particular those who had not lived through the mayhem caused by the revolts at the end of King John's reign.

The Provisions of Oxford acted as a sort of constitution for the governance of England for two years, by which time Henry III had reasserted his control of the government, recalled his relatives to his service, and had begun to make inroads again into the baronial privileges he felt interfered with regalian rights. Unfortunately, Henry's tactics were hardly those of a diplomatic and wise ruler and he succeeded in alienating not only a significant portion of the baronage, but his own sons as well. The younger generation of barons and the heirs of important lordships were particularly aggrieved. They rallied around the closest thing the mid-thirteenth century had to a "grand old man": Simon de Montfort, earl of Leicester, son of the leader of the Albigensian Crusade, a veteran of the first Crusade of Louis IX, and husband of Henry III's full sister, Eleanor, dowager countess of Pembroke.[16] The rebellion of the baronage and the revolt of Simon de

Montfort took on the character of a civil war, with Simon playing something of the role of Oliver Cromwell in the government that resulted. Although he initially had the sympathy of Lord Edward, the king's son and heir, Edward soon realized that Simon's intentions were not benevolent with respect to the royal family: he and his father were imprisoned and the government was under the virtual rule of Earl Simon.[17]

This civil war took on the structure of an intergenerational conflict, as well. Although Simon was himself a mature man in his late forties, his adherents were almost entirely young men who either had recently inherited their estates or who were waiting in the wings to succeed their long-lived fathers. For example, most of the Marshal heirs, contemporaries of Earl Simon, supported the king and Lord Edward, while their children tended to adhere to Montfort's side. Some younger barons, such as Earl Gilbert de Clare, straddled the fence, siding at first with Earl Simon and then shifting their allegiances to the king when they felt that they had not been treated fairly by the baronial party.

The one true constant in this deadly situation of shifting alliances was the Mortimer family.[18] Roger and Maud appropriated the role Maud's grandfather, William le Marshal, used to play: that of unswerving devotion to the Crown. Roger's position as an unassailable royalist was extremely dangerous to the baronial party's ambitions: he was responsible for breaking Edward free from his imprisonment and assisted him in his escape. As barons of the Welsh March, with Earl Simon gaining the support of the Welsh princes especially Llewelyn ap Gruffud, prince of North Wales against them, the Mortimer lands were constantly beset by attacks from both Welsh adherents of Montfort and English troops led by the earl himself. Although he was related by blood or marriage to both Roger and Maud, Llewelyn nevertheless invaded their Welsh lands when Roger invaded those of Earl Simon. The Mortimers' holdings at Wigmore and Ludlow were particularly targeted by Llewelyn and Simon.[19] Nevertheless, Roger and Maud never wavered in their support of Henry III and Lord Edward—and they were virtually the only truly powerful barons to be that devoted.

What makes this situation so interesting is that their royalist support was apparently not only well known by all, but was also something of a goad for other fence-straddlers to abandon their support of the earl in favor of a renewed royalist party. Roger was the model for Gilbert de Clare's decision to return to the royalist position; other relatives of Maud, such as Humphrey de Bohun, earl of Hereford, and Roger Bigod, earl of Norfolk, also joined the cause to oust Earl Simon. The fact that Simon was trying to impinge on their Marshal estates must have contributed to this decision. In the Battle of Evesham, which ended the conflict, Roger's and Edward's troops decimated Simon de Montfort's army and the victorious forces dismembered Simon's corpse in their killing fury.[20]

Who did the troops consider to be responsible for the great victory of the royalist army over the numerically superior forces of the earl of Leicester? If the aftermath of the battle is reliable as evidence, the royal army considered Maud de Mortimer, who was staying at Worcester Castle at the time of the battle, to be one of the important associates of their cause: they awarded her Simon's head and genitals to commemorate the victory. Actually, the genitals might have been an afterthought, since, according to the Annals of London, the soldiers had shoved them into the mouth of the corpse before the head was presented to Maud.[21] This grisly acknowledgment of her role was supplemented later by Henry III's grant of lands and money from the forfeited estates of the rebels.[22] Unlike other grants, however, which would have been subsumed under her husband's control, Henry specified that his grant to Maud was to be independent of Roger, and that she would have total control over it—something that contradicted both Common Law and medieval custom.

What in the world did Maud do? Therein lies the mystery. No sources, either public or literary, identify the contributions Maud made to the royalist cause in the years between 1258 and 1265. Nevertheless, if one extrapolates from activities in which she engaged in the years following the Montfortian rebellion, it is possible to suggest some of the ways in which Maud's activity might have benefited the royalists. Later sources, especially those surrounding the Welsh rebellions in the early years of Edward I's reign and his subsequent conquest of the Principality of North Wales, suggest that Maud was an adept spy, a messenger and go-between in the conveyancing of information between the Welsh Marches and Westminster, a competent victualler (or "vittler") of the army, and a staunch defensive strategist in the lands of her family.[23] Roger was forced to spend almost the entire period of the rebellion trying to evade capture: not only was he an opponent of Earl Simon, he had also agreed to go into exile in Ireland after the battle of Lewes in 1264, but had failed to depart.[24] Although he was apparently strong enough to be the architect of Edward's escape from Hereford Castle (when the guard saw Mortimer's standard they refused to engage his army), Maud must have been significantly responsible for much of his success. She would have been able to remain for longer on the family estates—at least until Llewelyn destroyed both Wigmore and Ludlow in 1265—and, once she was evacuated to Worcester Castle, she could have continued to direct the royalist effort from that location. One tool that Maud seems to have had, which might have proved highly beneficial, was that her children seem never to have been demanded by Earl Simon as hostages for Roger's good behavior. Armed not only with a loyal collection of followers but with the assurance of knowing that her children were safe from direct harm, Maud might have felt emboldened to heroic levels of activity that the sources simply fail to identify. Certainly, the gifts of Simon's body parts (however revolting to modern sensibilities) and the grants of land awarded by the king were unlikely to have been made just because of the gratitude of the royalists for the activities of Maud's husband. To emphasize this point, if Maud had not been an active participant, it is unlikely that she would have been called upon to participate in other royal campaigns that followed the end of the Montfortian rebellion—but, in fact, she was called upon, and while she was still married to Roger.

In 1274, Maud de Mortimer received a letter from one Hywel ap Meurig. He wrote to inform her that Llewelyn was going to be arriving shortly at Cydewain to inspect the new castle he was building there. While there, Llewelyn, according to Hywel, was planning to enter the forest of Clun to inspect the site of yet another castle, "and it is rumoured that a party of the great men of England are coming thither to speak with Llewelyn. The writer does not know whether this will be for good or evil." Hywel then advises Maud to tell her husband and asks that she herself keep watch at Clun and elsewhere, to be prepared for trouble.[25]

In order for this letter to have any significance, Maud must have been both well known and well respected in the territory north of Wigmore. The author of the letter must also have expected that she would know what to do, should the meeting between Llewelyn and the "great men of England" devolve into violence. Maud was acting as a spy during a potentially explosive juncture in the decade before Edward's invasion of Wales.

Sometime around Roger's death in 1282, Maud was again called upon to serve. Roger Lestrange wrote to King Edward in late November to inform him of Llewelyn's whereabouts, and to request that the king tell the Mortimers (by this time Maud and Roger had established a separate lordship for their younger son, Roger, at Chirk, and Edmund had inherited Wigmore)—and specifically mentions Maud—to guard their territory so that Llewelyn's supplies could not get through to his army.[26] This request was only the beginning of a long association of Maud with the Edwardian conquest of North Wales and the pacifying of the region after the conquest had been effected.

Maud's duties began almost immediately after Roger's death. In March 1283, Edward I ordered her to send soldiers to Montgomery, where he was amassing an army.[27] In 1287, at the height of the Welsh war, Maud was required to victual the army from her market-sellers of Radnor; to send three hundred foot soldiers to the king's aid; to dispatch men, horses, arms, and aid to Gilbert de Clare in the campaign against Rhys ap Meredoc; and to spend the winter in Wales, along with the other barons of the March, in order to repulse Rhys's attacks.[28] The king again ordered Maud and the other marcher lords to remain in Wales in 1294 and he respited her from all pleas except dower, *novel disseisin*, and *darrein presentment* for the duration of her time there.[29] In 1297, when Edward was going overseas, he requested that Maud send some of her men to advise and consult with Prince Edward.[30] As an active baron of the Welsh March, Maud's responsibilities in both her own and her husband's properties were extensive. She was responsible for the completion of Roger's plans to build a castle at Dinbaud, Maelienydd, which became one of the most important strongholds in the region.[31]

Maud was not merely subjected to the hardships of being a tenant-in-chief, however. The grant of land forfeited by the Montfortians made by Henry III to her was not to be the last she would receive. As soon as she was widowed King Edward gave her a wardship worth £60 a year for at least six years and later granted her escheated manors in fee farm.[32] She received numerous quittances from the common summons (as a female she would not be summoned to attend the parliaments, but she nevertheless required a formal quittance or she would have been compelled to attend) and was respited from paying her debts during the decade of the Welsh conquest.[33] The king eased the path she trod as one of the executors of Roger's will in paying his debts and making his bequests; as she grew older, he sent her timber and other small gifts.[34] When her children (especially her son, Edmund), apparently disgruntled by her continued longevity, refused to surrender her dower to her and worked to delay her peaceful seisin indefinitely, Edward permitted her to grant some of her inheritance to her most demanding children, her sons Edmund and William.[35] It did not work. Edmund seems to have been hostile to his parents' generosity in granting lands to his other siblings and cousins. This is demonstrated by his refusal to accept the charters that had alienated the lands away from his seisin, on the grounds that he had been a minor at the time of the grants and thus had no way of preventing them.[36] The result of his refusal was a lengthy and tedious series of litigation between Edmund and his mother and siblings that plagued Maud's widowhood.

King Edward was not entirely openhearted in his treatment of Maud, however. She was clearly considered to be just like his other barons in that he had no compunction about summoning the widow to his court *quo warranto* to defend her marcher liberties. She was in court twice, arguing that her family had always held their land as marcher lords, free from the king's writ, but the decision of the court as to the legitimacy of her claim is lost.[37]

It is important to reiterate that, unlike most women—and many men— marked for royal favor, Maud was not related to the royal family by blood, and only tangentially by marriage after her son, Edmund, married Margaret de Fiennes. This circumstance makes her position even more significant, since Henry III and Edward I were not bound by family loyalties to advance her position. They could have used her for their own ends, especially during her widowhood, when Maud would have been vulnerable to royal influence, and then overlooked her when they distributed the rewards of service. Maud did not have the personal authority to do what Gilbert de Clare, earl of Gloucester, and Hertford did: he rebelled after the Montfortian rebellion had failed because he felt that he had not received a fair share of gifts for his support of the royal side. She would not have been able to protest Edward's demands on her during the conquest of Wales if he had failed to provide her with adequate protection. Maud's Braose and Marshal antecedents certainly contributed to her prestige, but personal wealth and social status cannot have been the only reasons for Maud's royal patronage. If interactions with her family (both natal relatives and children) and tenants are any indication of her character, Maud de Mortimer was a forthright and wholly competent landholder as well as a concerned and generous, but nevertheless firm, parent, who was more than qualified for the important roles she accepted during her widowhood. She managed to maintain a high degree of stability in her lands during her nineteen-year widowhood, as evidenced by the scarcity of litigation with her tenants. Her level of authority is exemplified by the success she achieved in those cases that were presented before the justices.[38]

Maud de Mortimer's life was shaped by the tragicomedy of her father's death, the boldness of her mother's determination to protect her daughters and herself, and the spider's web of family loyalties that included her marriage to Roger de Mortimer. It was, moreover, one devoted to service to the Crown and to her family in ways that make her an exemplary figure. It is impossible to say which of the experiences of her formative years were the most significant, but if her actions as an adult woman, wife, mother, and widow demonstrate anything they demonstrate that she learned from the events of her childhood some cardinal rules. There was no hint of scandalous behavior in her adult life, unlike that of her grandson, Roger, who became the lover of Queen Isabella, Edward II's wife. She and Roger were unusually generous to their children, both in giving up land and in being sensitive to their happiness—Roger, for example, purchased the right of remarriage of his daughter, Isabel, after the death of her husband, John fitzAlan, and then gave it to her.[39] However, Maud was also determined not to be exploited by her children: her generosity did not extend to beggaring herself or denying herself the rightful dower to which she was entitled after Roger's death. Most of all, Maud seems to have embodied the ideal of service that had made her grandfather, William le Marshal, such a towering figure in the late twelfth and early thirteenth centuries. Perhaps more than any of his grandchildren, she seems to have resembled him. Tellingly, her son Roger, lord of Chirk, and her grandson, Roger, earl of March, were both antiroyalists during the reign of Edward II[40]—in much the same way that Earl William's five sons (and Maud's mother) fought against the Crown when Maud was a small child, and resembling, as well, the generational breakdown of royalists and Montfortians in mid-century. The younger generation clearly had few expectations of preferment at the hands of Edward II and no profound sense of loyalty to the image of the king, perhaps the result of the same kind of intergenerational conflict that was seen in the period between 1258 and 1265.

Maud's marriage to Roger was one that could not have succeeded without their mutual partnership and a shared agenda. Without Maud, Roger would have been disastrously ill-prepared for his role as preserver of the royal dignity in the Barons' War and the rebellion of Simon de Montfort. Without Roger, Maud might well have found no appropriate outlet for her prodigious energies, or a husband who so clearly respected her abilities. Guided by their mutual dedication to defending royal power, their mutual antipathy for Simon de Montfort and his adherents—including Llewelyn—and their mutual devotion to all of their children, Maud and Roger had a profound impact on the development of the Welsh March in the second half of the thirteenth century.

CHAPTER 5

WELSHNESS, ENGLISHNESS, AND THE
PROBLEM OF DOWAGERS AND HEIRESSES
IN WALES: THE LESTRANGE FAMILY'S MARITAL
ADVENTURES IN POWYS

The March of Wales—that volatile border between the two distinct regions of England and Wales—produced some of the most significant political events and the most important political actors of the thirteenth and early fourteenth centuries. Barons who attained marcher status, such as the earls of Hereford, Pembroke, and Gloucester (who controlled specific lordships in Wales) and the barons of Oswestry, Ewyas, and Wigmore, enjoyed significant benefits because of that status, but they also experienced uniquely difficult and dangerous disadvantages. Marcher status granted a baron many of the regalian rights the king enjoyed in the more settled portions of England. As the medieval formula stated: "the king's writ does not run in marcher territory." This meant that the sheriffs of adjoining or conjoined counties had no jurisdiction in the marcher lordship; that the lord was solely responsible for justice in that region; and that the lord enjoyed all the privileges of sovereignty in that region—the rights of wreck and waste among them. In exchange, the marcher baron was solely responsible for the protection of the border between England and Wales, a situation that required the maintenance of a large and mobile military force at all times. The marcher baron also had to negotiate the delicate relationship between "Englishry" and "Welshry" who had to live, work, and fight together in these lordships.

Some marcher lordships, such as the earldom of Pembroke, operated in much the same way as an English county. This was also the case in the hybrid palatinate county of Chester, which was considered to be in England but whose earls attained the status of marcher lords because of the location of the county. Other marcher lordships were more "*ad hoc*" in their administration and in their legal systems. Nevertheless, all marcher lordships tended to conform to at least the basic principles of English Common Law and all English and Anglo-Norman residents lived under—and were supposed to abide by—the standards set by Common Law with respect to inheritance, dower, trespass, and disseisin. Welsh tenants, however, often lived under an entirely different system, that of Welsh customary law (recorded in the thirteenth century under the direction of Llewelyn ab Iorwerth, prince of Gwynedd, as the Laws of Hywel Dda).[1] These were two radically different legal systems, especially with respect to the transfer of property from one generation to the next. As can be imagined, this difference served to exacerbate the tensions between Welsh and English residents, often provoking the kind of violence the marcher regions were designed specifically to mitigate. The situations could worsen even further if a Welsh family intermarried with an English family and the status of their tenure changed.

The laws regarding inheritance and the protection of widows in English Common Law make significant provision for the women involved. Although male primogeniture (inheritance by the eldest son) was the ideal, daughters could inherit in the absence of sons; male collateral relatives were barred from inheriting if there were more direct female heirs (e.g., a sister would inherit rather than a more distant male cousin); all illegitimate children were barred from inheriting; daughters were entitled to receive a portion of family lands and moveable wealth at marriage as a marriage-portion (*maritagium*), which passed to their own children as their maternal inheritance; and widows were guaranteed life use of one-third of their late husbands' real property and total control over at least one-third of their moveable wealth, all of which had to be turned over to the widow within forty days of her husband's death. This could tie property up for years, should a widow prove long-lived.

Welsh law, in contrast, provided virtually no provision for daughters or widows. In the system known as "gavelkind," not only were daughters banned from inheriting, they could be superceded by male cousins and, sometimes, illegitimate half-brothers as well. Widows were entitled to half of their late husbands' moveable wealth, but this amount was not absolute and could be ignored by the heirs. All property was inherited jointly by all available male relatives—usually sons, but also brothers, nephews, even cousins—of the dead landowner, and daughters were barred from receiving real property even as a dowry, although they did receive a portion of moveable property at the occasion of marriage. Those Welsh families that had *no* collateral male relatives at all could use daughters as conduits of real property to a new Welsh lineage, by which means their sons would assume matrilineal connections.[2]

This radical form of partible inheritance has been viewed by historians of medieval Wales as one of the principle reasons for the volatility of the region. In order to gain independent control of a reasonable amount of land, Welsh heirs literally had to get rid of collateral coheirs. The result was endemic warfare within families, tensions among the Welsh princes, which militated against alliances that might have prevented the wholesale Norman takeover of southern Wales, and intergenerational strife. These laws of inheritance also might have served the Norman conquerors quite effectively, since their application kept their Welsh subjects and tenants divided among themselves and prevented the kinds of power blocs that the English law of primogeniture encouraged.

Even more mayhem could result if land changed from Welsh tenure to English tenure as the result of an intercultural marriage alliance. While land never seems to have changed from Common Law tenure to Welsh customary tenure, the opposite occurred fairly frequently, especially after the death of Llewelyn ab Iorwerth, when most of the native Welsh lords recognized the suzerainty of the English Crown and many of them married into Anglo-Norman noble families. One such family changed its status so significantly that its heads attained the status of lords of the March: the lords of Southern (or Upper) Powys.

Gwenwynwyn ab Owain Cyfeilog of Southern Powys had been one of Llewelyn ab Iorwerth of Gwynedd's most specific targets.[3] His estates occupied the space between central Wales and the English county of Shropshire and were the most prominent administrative center in the region after the dissolving of the Montgomery earldom of Shrewsbury in the mid-twelfth century.[4] A. J. Roderick describes Powys as being "between the Scylla of Gwynedd and the Charybdis of England,"[5] a situation that must have contributed to the political choices made by Gwenwynwyn himself and his progeny that moved the family away from their earlier Welsh alliances and toward a greater association with the baronages that marched on Powys's eastern border.

Gwenwynwyn was the last prince of Southern Powys to come from Welsh stock on both sides—his parents were Owain Cyfeilog and Gwenllian, daughter of Owain Gwynedd and sister of Iorwerth ab Owain, whose son, Llewelyn, parlayed his dominance of North Wales into a united principality. Gwenwynwyn's marriage strategy (or perhaps that of his father), while one also used by his own cousin, Llewelyn, associated him more fully with his English neighbors: he married Margaret, daughter of Robert Corbet, lord of Caus, and Emma Pantulf (yet another neighboring marcher baronage).[6] They had three children, Gruffud, Owain, and Madoc, but only Gruffud's line survived.[7] Gruffud, himself, used a similar strategy when he made connections to yet another local marcher family by marrying

Hawise, daughter of John Lestrange of Knockyn and Lucy daughter of Robert Tregoz[8] (see table 5.1).

Both Gwenwynwyn and his son, Gruffud, were notoriously slippery in their political alliances, shuttling between the camp of Llewelyn ab Iorwerth, prince of Gwynedd, and that of the English kings. Gwenwynwyn, in 1198, initiated an uprising in Wales against the English that was, by all accounts, a spectacular failure.[9] The rebellion led, in 1207, to his capture—along with his wife and eldest son, evidently—by King John, who gave Llewelyn ab Iorwerth *carte blanche* to invade Upper Powys. This move prompted Gwenwynwyn to change sides, joining John against Llewelyn in 1210.[10] When Pope Innocent III, in 1212, encouraged the Welsh princes to rebel against John (who was refusing to seat Stephen Langton as archbishop of Canterbury), Gwenwynwyn changed sides again, joining with Llewelyn and the other Welsh partisans.[11] The ink was barely dry on Magna Carta, however, when Gwenwynwyn returned to the royalist camp, much to the annoyance of Llewelyn.[12]

Gwenwynwyn died in 1218; Henry III's regency council granted Llewelyn ab Iorwerth custody of the lands of his heir, Gruffud ap Gwenwynwyn, who was still a minor living in England with the royal court. Gruffud would not be able to gain control of his patrimony and to marry until 1241, a year after Llewelyn ab Iorwerth's death. This situation did not endear him to the family of Gwynedd, but he had no love for Henry III, either, as will be seen later.

Morris Jones's criticism of the political machinations of Gwenwynwyn ab Owain Cyfeiliog and his family is typical of most Welsh historical perspectives:

> [I]t is difficult to fix upon the precise period in the history of the ancient Princes of Upper Powys when they can be said to have definitely acknowledged the supremacy of the English Crown. . . Their position was for a lengthened period of an equivocal anomalous character—they asserted their princely prerogatives whenever circumstances permitted, and they could act independently of the English sovereign—but whenever adversity overtook them, and they were threatened with destruction by their rival princes or by superior force, they forthwith claimed English protection, and submitted themselves to the foreign yoke.[13]

Such vacillation between "Scylla" and "Charybdis" as described in the quoted extract could be interpreted quite differently if one accepts the possibility that such maneuverings formed the foundation of an agenda devised by Gwenwynwyn to preserve his patrimony *by any means necessary*. In such a circumstance, the fluidity of the family's alliances, especially in the years before the Edwardian conquest, takes on the character of inspired and

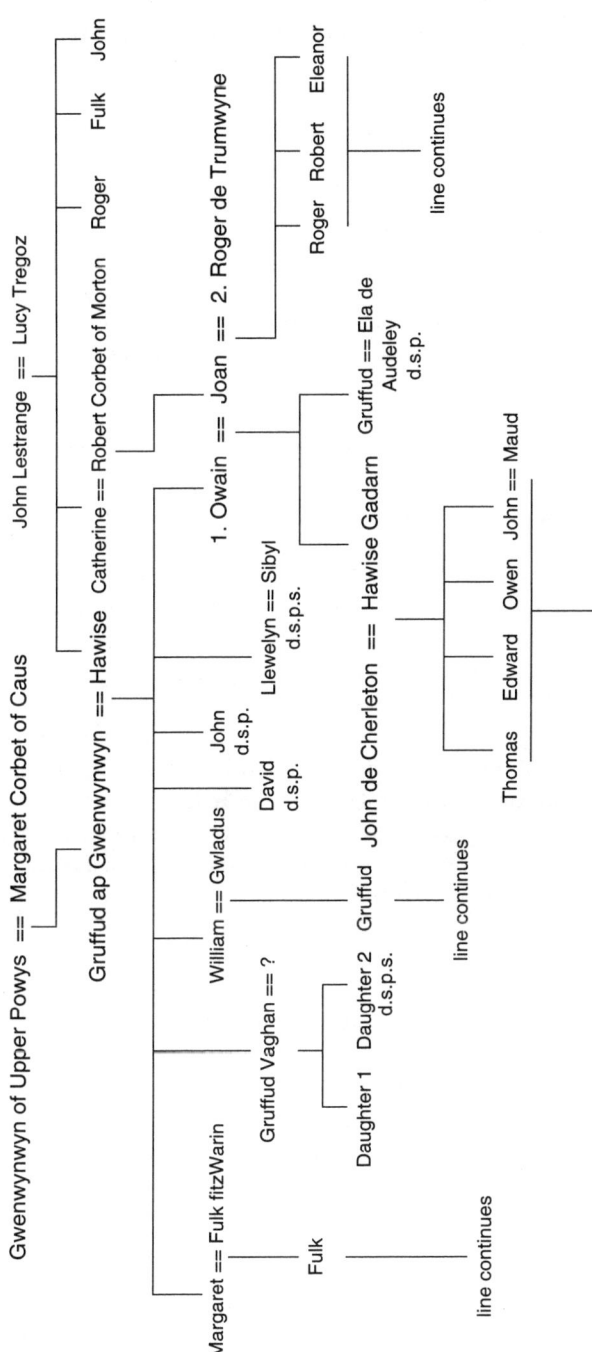

Table 5.1 The Families of Powys and Lestrange (names in large type are significant to the chapter)

pragmatic flexibility, rather than haphazard and cowardly vaccilation. Moreover, it worked.

Gruffud ap Gwenwynwyn seems to have been convinced by the experiences of his father that his only protection against the incursions of the House of Gwynedd lay in more alliances with the local marcher baronage and with further "Englishness." He married Hawise Lestrange, the daughter of an Anglo-Norman neighbor and a connection of his mother, Margaret Corbet. He received a royal charter in 1242, soon after his marriage, that secured for her a dower property in Derbyshire that could not be alienated from her "even if Griffin [sic] or his heirs abandon the service and fealty of the king."[14] He would eventually reconfigure the organization of the lordship after he had regained his Welsh lands in order to provide her with a more appropriate dower as well as to provide his eldest son with a clear tenurial title, but organized in such a way as to retain some of the principles of Welsh customary inheritance, an arrangement that "embodied both the principles of primogeniture and gavelkind, a compromise between English and Welsh hereditary practice."[15]

Gruffud also continued his father's policy of making strategic political alliances that were based on expedience rather than ethnic or cultural loyalty. Firmly in the royalist camp from 1241, he is mentioned in the *Annales Cambriae* as being one of the "English" barons who were allies of Lord Edward in 1257, when a convocation was called between the Welsh leaders in the south and the "English" barons (Gruffud and his brother-in-law, John Lestrange) to deal with the situation that resulted from Gruffud's son, Llewelyn, attacking Gruffud's own castle of Trallwng and his burning of the village there.[16] In 1264, he nonetheless sided with Gwynedd and Simon de Montfort against King Henry after the battle of Lewes. This turnabout, however, might have been motivated by his intense dislike of Roger de Mortimer, who had followed his own father's practice to ally with Llewelyn ab Iorwerth in his attacks on Upper Powys.[17] The alliance with Gwynedd lasted longer than the others, but Gruffud was back in the royalist camp by 1275, and there he would stay.[18]

As a result of their support of the English kings, the family of Owain Cyfeiliog were awarded marcher baronial status—something no other Welsh lordship had attained—and effectively assumed control over the region that the Norman Montgomerys had earlier ruled as part of the now-defunct earldom of Shrewsbury. By abandoning a Welsh cultural-political identity, Gruffud guaranteed that his family had the opportunity to survive and thrive.[19]

The transformation of the principality of Upper Powys into the marcher barony of Powys Wenwynwyn was apparently formalized in 1283—the year after Gruffud's death—when Owain ap Gruffud ap Gwenwynwyn appeared at the parliament at Shrewsbury and surrendered his lands—and his crown—to King Edward I and received his lands back as a baron of England.[20] The actual arrangements, however, must have been hammered out years before, by Owain's father.

Gruffud must have planned to convert the principality into a marcher barony, in part in order to guarantee that his wife, Hawise Lestrange, would receive a legal "reasonable" dower beyond the minimal endowment that had occurred at the time of their marriage. Gruffud's and Hawise's eldest son, Owain, received an English title to the land, as lord of Welshpool, or Upper Powys, or Cyfeiliog (depending on the situation), while his five younger brothers[21] held their inheritances as his sub-feofees, but for Welsh services. Thus, Gruffud guaranteed that all of his sons would receive their rightful shares, according to Welsh law, but his wife and eldest son would benefit from the transformation of the entire lordship from Welsh custom to English Common Law tenure. He then rhetorically reinforced the "Englishness" of his tenurial position by adopting the patronymic "de la Pole."[22]

The incredible complexities inherent in inventing a hybrid form of tenure within a baronial family are highlighted by the numerous charters, deeds, and royal confirmations that exist describing the arrangement. In brief, Owain received control over all of Upper Powys, both in demesne and as liege lord of his younger brothers, in order of birth: Llewelyn, John, David, William, and Gruffud. Llewelyn, William, and Gruffud were awarded lands that they held either in life tenure (in order to accommodate Hawise's dower) or in fee tail; John and David, who were both priests, were awarded lands in life tenure only. Eventually, Owain had to modify the grants to include his nephew, Llewelyn ap Gruffud, who received specific lands in fee tail. In exchange, all Owain's younger brothers and Gruffud's son, Llewelyn, released their rights to the lordship that remained to Owain.[23]

In making this radical move, Gruffud no doubt believed that such an arrangement would ultimately benefit future generations of his family. He might have recognized the inevitability of English dominance in Wales and therefore sought to take the steps necessary to ensure his family's survival. He might also have decided that, given the hostility of the princes of Gwynedd, his best chance for preserving his estates and the viability of his family lay in associating himself completely with the English culture of the marches, both politically and with respect to the familial alliances he negotiated for himself and that he and Hawise organized for their children. This prescience—an example of political astuteness and pragmatism not imitated by other Welsh lords (ultimately to their detriment)—guaranteed the family's survival through the Welsh conquests of King Edward I. Unlike the rest of the Welsh baronage, the "de la Poles" of Upper Powys survived as an independent entity, rather than being absorbed into the Crown Principality of Wales after the Edwardian conquest.

Owain ap Gruffud ap Gwenwynwyn took care to renew both the grants and the releases several times during his life. Nevertheless, they failed to prevent the entire countryside from erupting upon his death. His careful, methodical planning and the original intentions of his father availed him nothing.[24] Gruffud's younger sons and grandsons did not recognize the move toward Englishness as a wise and beneficial one. The transformation of the principality of Upper Powys into the marcher barony of Powys Wenwynwyn served to disinherit them from the bulk of the family's land, ensured their eternal subjection to the progeny and heirs of their eldest brother (since their lands were still subject to the Welsh law of gavelkind and were thus divisible among all their male relations), and inserted another population into the political mix: that of the women in the de la Pole family, who would henceforth be privileged with dower and *maritagium* rights and who could inherit the entire lordship, if Owain or his male progeny failed to produce a male heir. In fact, this is exactly what occurred; the result was a family feud that began in the thirteenth century and did not end until the middle of the fourteenth century, in large part because most of the family died out.

Thus, the significance of the change in tenure from Welsh to English was directly responsible for about a hundred years of warfare in Southern Powys. Efforts by the king to adjudicate the conflict resulted in only temporary respites from the hostilities. In addition, the polarization of the family influenced the broader political alliances they made, especially during the reign of Edward II—although the only significant break in intra-family strife did happen to occur as a result of the entire family joining the anti-royal side during the rebellion of Thomas, earl of Lancaster.

The roles played by the women in the family—wives, widows, mothers, and sisters—and the families into which the de la Poles married make this feud even more interesting. In particular, the issue of ethnic alliances along Welsh and English lines became a significant one both for the women who married into the de la Pole family and for those who were born into it. In many ways, the experiences of the de la Pole family and its allies and marriage partners can serve as a paradigm for the ways in which Welsh and English ethnic identities became increasingly stratified in the period between the Edwardian conquest of Wales and the rebellion of Owain Glyndwr. For this reason, I will look at both the general behavior and activities of the family as a whole from 1250 to 1350 and the specific behavior of the women in the family in order to demonstrate the ways in which marriage ties could both engender and perpetuate ethnic conflicts.

A number of Anglo-Norman families frequently associated themselves with the lords of Upper Powys, among them the Lestranges of Knockyn and the Corbets—both the principle branch, the lords of Caus, and the cadet branch of Morton Corbet.[25] In the thirteenth century, most of the important marriage alliances for all three families involved strengthening and solidifying those associations. Gruffud ap Gwenwynwyn, whose mother was Margaret Corbet of Caus, married Hawise Lestrange (daughter of John Lestrange of Knockyn and Lucy Tregoz).[26] Hawise's sister, Catherine, was married to Robert Corbet of Morton Corbet. In the next generation, the family reinforced these associations: Joan, daughter of Catherine and Robert Corbet, married Owain, eldest son of Hawise and Gruffud. These three families—the de la Poles, the Lestranges, and the Corbets—seem to have designed these deliberate connections in order to form a power-bloc to replace the vacuum left in the twelfth century by the demise of the Montgomery earldom.[27] The fact that this bloc developed between families of Welsh *and* Anglo-Norman extraction was a significant step in the assimilation of the two populations in the region, at least with respect to the elite families. This blending of ethnic associations must have been one of the intentions of the architects of these alliances, one that was not shared by either the princes of the Welsh royal houses (despite their own active marital associations with marcher barons and the English Crown) or by collateral members of the de la Pole family. It is probably doomed from the start.

Part of the problem the family of Upper Powys faced by associating itself with the neighboring marcher families of Corbet and Lestrange (and Tregoz and Pantulf and fitzWarin) had to do with the notoriously bellicose character of those very families. Gwenwynwyn's initial foray into Anglo-Welsh marital alliances created its own fracas after his death, since it pitted his son, Gruffud, against his uncle, the belligerent Thomas Corbet, and his own mother, Margaret. Janet Miesel relates:

> The longest and most complex of all of Thomas's legal battles began in 1241 with a suit between him and his sister, Margaret, who by then was the widow of Gwynwynwyn [sic], prince of Powis [sic], and the mother of Griffin [sic] ap Gwynwynwyn. At first the only issue involved was Margaret's dower,[28] but by 1247 Griffin became involved in the dispute and the quarrel quickly grew to include such matters as alleged breaches of the peace by both men in several counties and a variety of land disputes ranging from Derbyshire in the east to Wales in the west. By 1255, the dispute had grown so large that the king appointed a special commission to investigate the various contentions of Thomas and Griffin, but this commission [including Fulk Lestrange—Gruffud's brother-in-law—who also quarreled with Thomas]... appears to have met with little success.[29]

The quarrel ended only with Thomas's death.

Thus, as early as Gruffud ap Gwenwynwyn's succession to Upper Powys, the volatility that had characterized the family's relations with its Welsh neighbors and Anglo-Norman opponents appeared as well between the family and the Anglo-Norman families to which they were connected by ties of marriage and blood.

Gruffud ap Gwenwynwyn and Hawise Lestrange developed marriage strategies for their children that were wholly focused on building powerful alliances around Upper Powys. The political motivations for these arrangements are obvious. What will never be known is the degree to which this "faux Englishness" was carried through to family life, education, and associations outside the marriage alliances designed by the family. Were the women who were brought into the de la Pole household expected to encourage the development of an "English" sensibility in their children?

Five of the seven children of Gruffud and Hawise married. Owain married Joan Corbet, his mother's niece—and his own first cousin. Since this marriage was well within the proscribed degrees of consanguinity, papal dispensation must have been required before the two could marry.[30] Llewelyn, next in line, married Sibyl, widow of Grimbald Pauncefot, another local marcher baron.[31] Margaret, Gruffud's and Hawise's only daughter, married Fulk fitzWarin, yet another marcher baron. After these three marriages, Gruffud and Hawise might have exhausted the "stock" in the local marriage mart. William married a woman named Gwladus (Gladys)—parentage unknown—and, although it is clear that Gruffud ap Gruffud (known as Gruffud Vaghan) married, his wife is not named in any record.

There were comparatively fewer children in the next generation, especially since John and David both became priests. Owain and Joan had two children, Gruffud, who married (as a teenager) Ela, daughter of Nicholas de Audely and Katherine Giffard,[32] and Hawise—known as "Gadarn" (the Hardy)—who eventually married John de Cherleton, a landowner and royal administrator in Shropshire. Llewelyn and Sibyl had at least one child, but it died in infancy. Gruffud Vaghan's line continued for a generation and then disappeared. William's and Margaret's lines, however, continued into the fifteenth century and beyond.

The marital strategy for the eldest children was thus to connect them as much as possible to local Anglo-Norman marcher baronages. This pattern of "Anglicization" might have worked efficiently had a series of disasters not befallen the family. Owain died in 1293, Llewelyn in 1295, both leaving very young sons whose minorities were destined to be protracted. The king, in recognition of the youth of Gruffud, Owain's heir (who was about two years old at the time of his father's death), granted guardianship of him to Joan, Owain's widow, as well as an annuity of twenty marks for his maintenance.[33] Wardship of the lands of Powys, however, was divided between the two dowagers. Hawise, the children's grandmother, was granted wardship of all of the late Owain's lands, including the castle of La Pole the family's *caput*, while Joan received wardship of her nephew's inheritance.[34] In addition, both women controlled substantial portions of Powys in dower. Thus, for the first time in the history of Wales, lands that had been in the control of a Welsh family were either held by or controlled by two Anglo-Norman women. Moreover, Llewelyn's widow, Sibyl, had received a nominated dower, despite the fact that Llewelyn did not hold by English tenure.[35] The establishment of a form of common law dower for Sibyl seems to have transformed those properties effectively from Welsh tenure into English tenure. It was therefore in Sibyl's best interest to maintain a connection with her sister-in-law, Joan, who was better placed to protect her dower properties, especially since she was the guardian of Sibyl's and Llewelyn's child and its inheritance.[36]

The family fortunes thus resided in the persons of two women: Hawise, the dowager lady of Upper Powys who held a third of the barony in dower and had wardship over the young Gruffud's inheritance; and Joan the dowager lady of Upper Powys who held another third of the barony in dower, had guardianship both of her children—Gruffud and his sister Hawise—and of her young niece or nephew, the child of Llewelyn and Sybil de la Pole, and wardship of its lands. It is unclear as to when this child died, but its existence after 1300 is highly questionable. Ultimately, Llewelyn's property devolved to Owain's heir.

In the space of one generation, the situation in Upper Powys had changed drastically. Where formerly there had been at least a Welshman as head of the family, all control over family property now rested in two women, both of them of Anglo-Norman parentage. The brothers of Owain de la Pole were not only disempowered, they easily could have seen themselves as disinherited as well. Certainly, their actions—and those of their offspring—for the next fifty years suggest that this was, indeed, the case.

What is even more significant in this story is the reaction of Hawise, Gruffud ap Gwenwynwyn's widow. Although Hawise herself had been dowered, in English fashion, in lands held of the barony and, moreover, held the wardship of the lands of the heir, she does not seem to have considered herself sufficiently empowered, perhaps because she did not have guardianship of her grandson. She could have allied herself with her daughter-in-law Joan—who was, after all, her niece as well—for the mutual benefit of each other and the young Gruffud, as Margaret, countess of Lincoln and Pembroke, allied with her daughter-in-law, Alice of Saluzzo. Instead she chose a different path: Hawise became "Welsh" and joined with her surviving sons to try to oust her dead son's widow from the lands she held quite legally by Common Law tenure.

Commissions of oyer and terminer were called as early as 1295 to investigate complaints by Joan de la Pole that her mother-in-law and brothers-in-law—William, John, and David—and their followers were trying to deforce her of her dower in Wales, had ejected her from her common pasture, and had stolen her cattle.[37] By the end of 1298, the skirmishes between Joan and her late husband's kin had escalated into all-out war.[38] The dangers Joan faced thus compelled her to make a significant change in her status: she remarried sometime between 1295 and 1298. Moreover, her choice of marriage partner is telling: Roger de Trumwyne was a knight with a career in royal administration who could give her the protection of the Crown should she require it. Competing commissions of oyer and terminer were sent out from Westminster in late 1298 and early 1299 because of complaints, on the one hand, of Hawise de la Pole and her sons—William, John, and Gruffud Vaghan—attacking Joan's dower lands and, on the other, of Joan and Roger's attempt to gain control of the castle of La Pole (which had remained in Hawise's hands), using as their excuse their guardianship of the lands and heir of the late Llewelyn de la Pole.[39]

The stresses of these events must have been tremendous for Joan, who was also having to cope with a new husband, trying to keep her children, Gruffud and Hawise, safe, and probably having to deal with at least one pregnancy.[40] Money must have been scarce as well, given the disruption in her dower properties. In 1305, Prince Edward of Caernarvon, to whom Joan had evidently petitioned, requested that the king release her from the "distress" of having to pay the balance on the 300 marks she owed as the fine for controlling her remarriage: she had managed to pay £120, but was being threatened with distraint by the sheriff of Staffordshire for the remainder.[41]

The success of Joan in being able to engage Prince Edward's interest might have motivated Joan and her husband to make another appeal to him in 1308, soon after he had assumed the throne. The parliamentary petition they introduced appeals to the king for redress against the depredations made against them in Joan's dower lands, which were causing "tremendous damage and threatening to disinherit the heir."[42] King Edward's solution was to release the custody of the castle of La Pole and the lands that had been held in life tenure by Owain's brothers, John and David (who were now dead) to the heir, whom he calls his "beloved valet," and who was still a minor.[43] This transfer of property might have, in fact, removed the very tool Hawise had employed to torment her daughter-in-law: her control of the castle. Joan's invocation of her "Englishness"—and her imparting of it to her son, Gruffud—was thus, for a time, victorious over Hawise's "Welshness." Unfortunately for Joan and Roger, the respite would be brief.

The year 1309 brought two connected, but equally calamitous (at least from the Welsh perspective), events: Gruffud de la Pole, the only son of Owain ap Gruffud ap Gwenwynwyn, died without progeny and the barony of Upper Powys devolved to his sister, Hawise "Gadarn", and her new husband, John de Cherleton. Like Roger de Trumwyne, John de Cherleton was a knight with ties to Shropshire and a career in royal administration that would eventually lead to his becoming the sheriff of the county. Although John had purchased Hawise's marriage through a grant from the king, the similarities between his and Roger's positions suggest that they, too, had encouraged the connection. All control of the barony was thus in the hands of two Anglo-Norman knights—not even noblemen—whose status was dependent entirely on their Anglo-Norman or Anglo-Welsh wives.

The death of Hawise Lestrange in 1310[44] might have deflated her sons to some extent, but it also might have spurred them to greater action, since all of Owain de la Pole's property now devolved entirely both to Hawise Gadarn and her husband and to Joan and her husband.

Hawise had not even figured in the records of the dispute until her inheritance of Upper Powys following the death of her brother in 1309. Between that date and her death sometime in 1345 or 1346, however, Hawise earned her sobriquet, Gadarn—"Hardy." This Hawise was no more Welsh, in reality, than her mother or grandmother: the product of the intermarriage of Corbets and Lestranges, married to a career administrator, probably raised in the English household of her mother and stepfather, she must have viewed the ongoing attempts of her Welsh uncles and cousins to take away her patrimony as astonishing.

After the death of Hawise Lestrange de la Pole in 1310, what had begun largely as a family dispute escalated into a full-scale political battle. Although by late 1311 the only brother of Owain de la Pole to survive was the youngest, Gruffud Vaghan, his longevity was enough to perpetuate and inflate the war.[45] The behavior and activities of both parties came to involve not only the king and his commissioners of oyer and terminer, but also Thomas, earl of Lancaster, and Roger de Mortimer of Chirk, justicier of the Principality of Wales, as well. In a pattern reminiscent of Gwenwynwyn and his son, Gruffud, the political alliances of all the parties seem to have shifted a number of times, which suggests that all the parties subscribed to the "hold and retain by any means necessary" philosophy of the earlier generations of the Upper Powys family.

Gruffud Vaghan, in 1310, was a supporter of Thomas of Lancaster; both Roger de Trumwyne and John de Cherleton were royal officials and, thus, adherents of the king. These political affiliations provided some of the rationale behind their behavior, but the actual motives were most probably the same ones that had compelled the Welsh brothers all along.

Joan and Roger tried to maintain a protective alliance with Hawise Gadarn and John, but the two couples were so busy defending themselves they did not have many opportunities to defend each other.[46] Gruffud Vaghan proved to be a most effective adversary. He was assisted, oddly enough, by his cousin—his mother's nephew—Fulk Lestrange of Knockyn, who took the side of the Welsh branch of the family against the English.

The bellicosity began in earnest in 1312 and did not abate until nearly all the antagonists were dead—some thirty-odd years later. This year also marked the high point in the power of the Lords Ordainer, led by Thomas of Lancaster, which might have benefited Gruffud Vaghan quite considerably.[47] In fact, the Ordinances included a stipulation for a commission to be sent to Powys to investigate the rights of Gruffud de la Pole because of incursions into the region being made against him.[48]

In 1312 alone, at least six different commissions of oyer and terminer were sent to investigate all the competing claims to the castle of La Pole and the multiple charges of trespass both parties brought forward: Hawise and John against Gruffud Vaghan; Gruffud against the Cherletons and the Trumwynes; Joan and Roger against Gruffud; the Trumwynes and Cherletons against Fulk Lestrange; Fulk and Gruffud Vaghan against the royal administration. Another complication developed: Gruffud and Fulk Lestrange were among the adherents of Thomas of Lancaster who received complete amnesty, pardon, protection, and safe conduct for their acts of aggression in Wales and the Marches, which gave them *carte blanche* to engage in any form of violence with impunity. Consequently, whenever a royal commission or the justiciar "interfered" with Gruffud Vaghan, he complained that this was in violation of his orders of protection. He must have felt invulnerable as long as Earl Thomas was in power.[49]

One commission of oyer and terminer was sent to the region to investigate the charges of Joan and Roger that Gruffud Vaghan and his followers had broken into their manors and had caused vast destruction, including the opening of their prison and the release of all the prisoners.[50] The inclusion of the last statement suggests that Joan and Roger had been using their prison as a repository for rebellious Welsh subjects. Certainly, there seems to have been no love lost between the Trumwynes and the people over whom they ruled.

The major campaigns in the Powys war in 1312 occurred around the castle of La Pole. Gruffud Vaghan, along with "a great multitude of armed men on horse and foot,"[51] laid siege to La Pole castle, where Hawise Gadarn and John were residing. King Edward II dispatched the justiciar Roger de Mortimer of Chirk to break the siege, which is described in detail:

> [T]he king understands that they lie in wait for the (king's) men garrisoning John de Cherleton's castle of La Pole [which an earlier entry claims that Hawise Gadarn acquired as heir to her uncle, Llewelyn de la Pole][52]...and that they hinder the garrison from issuing from the castle and providing it with food and other necessaries, and that the said Griffin [sic] goes armed with a multitude of malefactors in the parts of Powys that pertain to the said castle and there commits many evil deeds.[53]

Roger was apparently able to lift the siege; in gratitude, Hawise Gadarn and John ceded some of her inheritance to him.[54]

The force arrayed against the Trumwynes and Cherletons early in 1312 might have been led by Gruffud Vaghan and have included Fulk Lestrange, but by the middle of the year, yet another member of the family became involved on the Welsh side. John Goch, illegitimate son of Margaret de la Pole's son, Fulk fitzWarin, attacked La Pole. The king ordered Roger de Mortimer to arrest him.[55] John Goch was not the only one to enter the fray at that time, however. Edmund fitzAlan, earl of Arundel and lord of Oswestry and Clun (a neighboring marcher baronage) lent safe-harbor to Gruffud Vaghan and his companions; he was ordered to desist and to round up the malefactors, but he apparently never did so.[56] His support of Gruffud against the Trumwynes and Cherletons earned Edmund their unmitigated enmity. In 1326, after the Powys family had turned to the baronial party, John de Cherleton captured Edmund—who had always been an adherent of Edward II—and turned him over to Roger de Mortimer of Wigmore and Queen Isabella; they executed him immediately.[57] Nearly twenty years later, John, his son, John de Cherleton the younger, John de Trumwyne (son of Joan and Roger), and John, son of Richard of Leighton, agreed to grant an advowson to Haughmond Abbey to pay for three chaplains to pray for Edmund's soul.[58] Probably at around the same time, Edmund's daughter, Alice, was married to John de Cherleton the younger.[59] This episode demonstrates that the politics of the March were far from transparent: Edmund's support of Gruffud Vaghan served his interests because it kept Powys in disarray and occupied the energies of the Mortimer family, clearing the way for Edmund to expand his power in the March.

The king attempted to cool tensions in 1313 by proclaiming a general amnesty for *all* the antagonists in the Powys war.[60] This attempt at diplomacy failed utterly. The war, in fact, only escalated. Spurred on by his presumed protection under Thomas of Lancaster's umbrella, Gruffud Vaghan intensified his attacks, all the while complaining that any defense against his incursions abrogated the terms of his amnesty. In addition, he was able to use Hawise Gadarn and John de Cherleton's entry into other lands he claimed as his own—especially Mechain Iscoed—as yet another excuse for complaint, despite the fact that the grant of Mechain Iscoed, as outlined in the original dispersal of land by Gruffud ap Gwenwynwyn, was to be only for the life of Hawise Lestrange de la Pole, after whose death it was supposed to devolve to David and John for their lives, and thence back to the main lineage of Owain ap Gruffud ap Gwenwynwyn.[61] Thomas of Lancaster even gained a parliamentary decision ordering the release of all of Gruffud's adherents whom Roger de Mortimer of Chirk had arrested on the basis that "Gruffud and Fulk [Lestrange] and their accomplices should not be appealed, arrested, or molested on account of the premises."[62]

In 1313, it would have seemed to Hawise Gadarn and Joan that the "Welsh" part of the family had won. If Gruffud Vaghan could invade their holdings at will and with Lancastrian protection at his beck and call, then Upper Powys was destined to return to Welsh gavelkind tenure. The inclusion of Fulk Lestrange and John Goch ap Fulk fitzWarin into the dispute reinforced Gruffud's unassailable power: these two opportunists used their connections to the "Welsh" part of the de la Pole family to advance their own acquisitive interests, which might have had some marginal legitimacy in a hybrid gavelkind tenure. If the power of Hawise Gadarn and John de Cherleton—and by extension, the power of Joan and Roger de Trumwyne through Joan's dower properties—could be broken by the Welsh faction, then the whole structure of English-style tenure would crumble. If that were to happen, then Gruffud Vaghan would become the "legitimate"—that is Welsh—heir of Upper Powys, with a need to provide only minimal rewards to his related coconspirators, Fulk Lestrange and John Goch. The only hope for Hawise Gadarn and Joan and the continuity of Common Law tenure lay in the death of Gruffud or the curbing of Thomas of Lancaster's power. Unfortunately for the two women, neither would occur for several years.

Thomas of Lancaster's involvement in this dispute had absolutely nothing to do with Welshness or Englishness. His followers merely used the Powys war as a convenient opportunity for advancing Thomas's political allies at the expense of anyone else. This, indeed, might be the reason for the dispute taking a bizarre turn in 1314. John de Cherleton demanded a commission of oyer and terminer at that time against Philip de Middelton and Hugh de Audeley, constable of Montgomery Castle,[63] who had attacked his properties in Shopshire. Moreover, he proclaimed that anyone who arrested any follower of John de Cherleton and confiscated his goods would receive as bounty one-third of the goods confiscated, thus committing acts "to the great loss of John de Cherleton, his men, and tenants, and to the terror of the people in those parts."[64]

Between 1316 and 1322, Thomas of Lancaster's power was dimmed by a resurgence of the royal party. During this period, King Edward II worked hard to adjudicate the dispute in Powys without damaging his reputation with both parties. He allowed Mechain Iscoed to remain in Gruffud Vaghan's hands, but reinforced Hawise Gadarn's claim to La Pole and reiterated strongly the rights of Joan and Sibyl (Joan's sister-in-law, widow of Llewelyn ap Gruffud ap Gwenwynwyn) in their dower properties. Edward also instructed John de Grey, who replaced Roger de Mortimer of Chirk as justiciar of North Wales, and the sheriff of Shropshire to keep abreast of the conflict in Powys and to prevent any further outbreaks of violence between Gruffud and the Cherletons and Trumwynes. Gruffud, for his part, seems to have retreated somewhat in the wake of Thomas's political decline: he disappeared into the Welsh parts of Powys, making it impossible for the sheriff to find him.[65]

Hawise Gadarn and John de Cherleton took advantage of this respite in hostilities to ensure unequivocally their claim to Upper Powys. The king granted them a license, in 1319, to rearrange Hawise's inheritance, including the properties held in dower by Sibyl and by Hawise's widowed sister-in-law, Ela de Audeley. Hawise and John were able to grant her estate in fee tail to her three sons: John (along with Maud his wife), Owain, and Edward. The person who effected the transfer was destined to have a significant impact on Welsh and Irish relations with the English Crown in the reign of Edward III: John's brother, Thomas de Cherleton, who was at the time a royal clerk, but who eventually became the bishop of Hereford and chancellor of Ireland.[66]

Matters came to a head in 1322, when all the parties involved were suspected to be, or proven to be, allies of Earl Thomas of Lancaster. In particular, Joan and Roger de Trumwyne and Hawise and John de Cherleton were under suspicion and their lands were confiscated temporarily.[67] After giving sureties for their loyalty, the king directed his keeper of the confiscated lands of Powys to return the lordship to them. This seemed to provide the impetus for an all-out declaration of war against the Trumwynes and the Cherletons. Gruffud Vaghan and his followers attacked Robert de Sapy, the king's representative, assaulted Roger de Trumwyne's men who were conveying Joan to a place of safety, and abducted Joan, herself. In the letter patent, Robert describes his problems in delivering Joan's lands to her:

> Roger has replied that he has not been able to deliver the lands...to Roger and Joan on account of the resistance and malice of Llewelin ap Tudor, Owen ap Griffud ap Gwen, Philip ap Llewelin, Madoc ab Tudor Loyt, Madoc ap Tudir ap Madoc, Llewelin ap Howel, Griffin Cragh, Cadegan ap

Llewelin, Griffin Penbras, Owen his brother, Griffin ap Griffith ap Gwen, Griffin Whith ap Tuder Loit, Yevan Tor, Yevan Duy, Yevan ap Tuder ap Madoc, Griffin Loid Rouka, Houwel Cragh, David Duy ap Eynon, Griffin ap Edeneuet, Madoc ap Edeneuet, Edenewen ap Gwyn, Madoc ap Griffith ap Eyneon, Madoc ap Griffith ap Gliwys, Llewelin Gigh ap Griffith, Griffin ap Oweyn Gogh and his son Howel Gogh ap Nest, and Yevan Hyr, who with the entire commonality of the counties of Keveillok and Kereignen came to Lannurvel and answered in common that they would not attorn to the said Robert [Sapy] and Joan or to any other person for the king's mandate, or at the command of any person until they had order by word of the king's mouth at his Parliament; and that he could not without a great posse attach such disturbers of the peace on account of their numbers and malice...[68]

According to the reply sent by Edward II to the beleaguered Robert de Sapy, he was "not unjustly perturbed" by this episode, and instructed a massive force to be organized to assist Robert.[69] Joan was not freed until Roger was able to raise her ransom, but she in fact had been liberated by the time Edward's letter reached Robert de Sapy.

Although the Trumwynes and the Cherletons might have become adherents of Thomas of Lancaster in his last rebellion, the king pardoned them for this one lapse. He was not so forgiving to Gruffud Vaghan, who lost his claim on Mechain Iscoed at this time, although the king pardoned him for his adherence to the Lancastrian party.[70] John de Cherleton, after enduring fifteen years of chaos, was not in any mood to forgive anyone. He refused to return the lands of Hawise Gadarn's Welsh tenants who had allied with Gruffud Vaghan: they were forced to petition the king. Edward II established another commission to investigate, but also associated it with a jury comprised not only of Powys residents, but those of Montgomery, Oswestry, Knockyn (under the control of Isolda Lestrange), and Clun (under the control of Beatrice Corbet), as being adjacent to Powys. The Lestranges and Corbets thus were able to intervene yet again in the fortunes of Upper Powys.[71]

The years between Thomas of Lancaster's execution and Roger de Mortimer's and Queen Isabella's successful deposing of Edward II in favor of the young Edward III were not happy years for anyone in the Welsh Marches other than the Despencer family, the fitzAlan earls of Arundel, and the Warenne earls of Surrey—Edward II's favorites. Gruffud Vaghan and his erstwhile enemies might well have been compelled to endure the hardship together, especially since Edmund, earl of Arundel, seems to have abandoned his support of Gruffud for his own self-aggrandizement. It thus stands to reason that the Cherletons and Trumwynes would support Mortimer and the queen; the added incentive to procure the downfall of their hated neighbor, Edmund fitzAlan, must have also played a part in their decision. Faced with the likelihood that no strategy would regain the support of any powerful faction—and apparently unwilling even to contemplate forging an alliance with his "English" kin, Hawise Gadarn and Joan—Gruffud Vaghan lay low and did not reappear until shortly before his death, when a last opportunity arose for him to achieve his goal of preventing Hawise and her family from enjoying peaceful seisin of her rightful inheritance.

John de Cherleton's capture of Edmund fitzAlan and his surrender of the latter to Mortimer and Queen Isabella guaranteed their patronage. For the first time since he married Hawise Gadarn, the couple could begin to act more like typical Anglo-Norman marcher barons. They organized a marriage between their elder daughter, Isabella, and John, son and heir of John and Margaret de Sutton, another local marcher family. The transactions for this marriage precipitated an episode that serves as comic relief after the horrors of the previous years: John de Cherleton, who seems to have negotiated this marriage in order to gain a substantial release from a massive debt he owed John de Sutton, appeared in chancery with 500 marks in cash—it was loaded into five canvas sacks—complaining that John de Sutton refused to accept the money, and asking the exchequer to hold it for him, so that someone would be a witness to his attempt to repay John de Sutton.[72] John de Cherleton was also able to enjoy a little revenge upon his enemies, Hugh de Audeley and Philip de Middelton, when he was named to an inquisition to investigate the negligence of those constables in maintaining Montgomery Castle.[73] Gruffud's supporters seemed to have been thoroughly quelled.

The relative peace in Powys during the first years of Edward III's reign was shattered in 1330, when Roger de Mortimer and Queen Isabella were overthrown by Edward III and Roger was executed. A protracted suit between the bishop of St. David and Hawise Gadarn and John over the advowsons for the churches of the barony of La Pole, which the Cherletons had tried to introduce before the justices of the Bench, was stymied when Edward III agreed to investigate the bishop's claim that the king's court had no jurisdiction in this case, the advowsons being in Wales.[74] More importantly, Gruffud Vaghan seized his opportunity—made even more imperative by the death of Roger de Turmwyne, which made Joan a somewhat more vulnerable target—and reintroduced his claim to Mechain Iscoed and Dender. Unlike Gruffud's earlier claims to property in Powys, such as La Pole and the *caput* of the lordship, this new one stipulated that Gruffud held these territories in chief of the king, and that he had been disseised unjustly of both of them; he also demanded £4000 in damages. Thus, Gruffud assumed the mantle of Englishness he had rejected twenty years before: he claimed to hold both properties by Common Law tenure and for Common Law services.⁷⁵ This ploy initially succeeded—Gruffud was granted everything he claimed—but John and Hawise Gadarn refused to release the property, until an exasperated Edward III demanded that they identify the reasons for their recalcitrance. Gruffud's plot failed when the king learned from John "that there was an error in the record" and ordered the transactions regarding the dispersal of property and the assessment of damages to halt.⁷⁶ Just before his death in 1332, Gruffud Vaghan did succeed in foiling what seemed to be Hawise Gadarn's total victory in their long-lived conflict. He deeded his lordship of Dender—which he still claimed he held in chief—to Richard fitzAlan, earl of Arundel, to hold in fee.⁷⁷ Not only did that remove that portion of Powys from the control of Hawise and John, it also placed the heir of one of the Cherleton's worst enemies in the midst of their lordship.

Nevertheless, Gruffud's last act was more of a parting shot than a cannonade in the long battle between the Welsh and English factions of the de la Pole family. By 1332, Joan was living in comfortable widowhood on her dower properties from both Owain de la Pole and Roger de Trumwyne. Her children from her second marriage were sufficiently devoted to her that they were the executors of her will after her death, which occurred in 1348. Joan's daughter, Hawise Gadarn, died a few years before her mother, in 1345; she was buried in a monastic foundation, the Grey Friars of Shrewsbury, to which she had been a significant benefactress and where both her father, Owain, and her grandfather, Gruffud ap Gwenwynwyn, were buried.⁷⁸ Hawise had been able to guarantee the succession of her patrimony to her three sons and had, along with her husband, secured stable marriages for both her daughters, Isabella and Cecily.⁷⁹ Hawise Gadarn's cousin, Gruffud ap William de la Pole, was content to retain his control over Moutho, the original grant from Gruffud ap Gwenwynwyn.⁸⁰ It would remain separate from the main portion of Upper Powys thereafter.

The last significant player in this drama of the de la Pole family was Hawise Gadarn's son, John de Cherleton the younger, who entered his mother's inheritance after his father's death in 1354.⁸¹ He was declared of full age, performed his fealty, and received his inheritance: the castle and manor of La Pole; the manors of Botiton, Talgarth, Mathrawell, and Wallewern; the commotes of South Strata Marcella, South Llanverghudel, Caereinion, Cyfeiliog, Mechain Ughcoed, Mechain Iscoed, Trefwern, Teirtref, and Mochnant; half the cantred of Arwystli; as well as his paternal inheritance of the manor of Cherleton, Shropshire, which he did not hold in chief. It thus becomes clear that, by the middle of the fourteenth century, Gruffud ap Gwenwynwyn's dream of a united Upper Powys had been more or less realized, but in a way that he could never have predicted or, probably, desired. The transformation of Powys from a Welsh principality to a Welsh marcher barony had preserved Gruffud's patrimony, but the transformation did not end there. Instead, the Welsh marcher barony, beset with internecine strife for more than one hundred years, evolved into an Anglo-Welsh marcher barony and, ultimately, into an English marcher barony. Powys had been preserved, but at the cost of its "Welshness."

The roles played by the women in the de la Pole family—Hawise Lestrange, Joan Corbet, and Hawise Gadarn (to which one could also add Sibyl and Ela)—and the Lestrange family from which they all had, in some fashion, sprung contributed to this transformation. Hawise Lestrange's adoption of "Welshness" in supporting her younger sons against her granddaughter and daughter-in-law could have compelled Joan and Hawise Gadarn to adopt their stringently "English" stance.[82] The powerful nature of land hunger, in addition, might have been underestimated by Gruffud ap Gwenwynwyn, but Hawise, Joan, and Hawise cannot be accused of a similar lack of vision. All three women recognized that their power resided in the amount of land they and their factions controlled; all three women knew that the dangers inherent in wielding such power were worth the risk because the rewards would be great. It is possible that, without Hawise Lestrange's support, Gruffud Vaghan's initial foray against his brother's widow would have failed and his bid for a greater share in the Powys patrimony aborted. It is possible that Joan's perseverance acted as both a model and a goad for her daughter, Hawise Gadarn. Finally, the transformation of the women from "Welshness" to "Englishness" spurred the transformation of Upper Powys from Welsh principality to English barony, not only because of the accidents of birth, marriage, and death, but because of their own peculiar agendas and familial—even political—ambitions.

CHAPTER 6

MURDEROUS MAUD? THE CASE AGAINST MAUD MORTIMER OF RICHARD'S CASTLE

This is something of a medieval murder mystery, the basic facts of which are these. In the summer of 1304, Hugh de Mortimer, lord of the Welsh border fief of Richard's Castle, was found dead, apparently by poison. Six months later, in January of 1305, another death by murder occurred: that of a person called Hugh de Kyngesmede who was staying at the time in the Thameside, London residence of Walter de Haselshawe, the bishop of Bath and Wells. The linkage between these two seemingly unrelated deaths was Hugh de Mortimer's Ponthievan wife, Maud, a cousin of the late queen, Eleanor of Castile, who was charged with complicity in both.

Now here is a situation that King Edward I must never have anticipated: a member of the royal family accused of killing her husband and of conspiring to murder someone apparently totally unconnected to the family. Although the murder of one's wife was a serious offence, reckoned as homicide at the very least, the killing of one's husband was a much more heinous action. In medieval English law (and in the laws of other kingdoms as well, such as the Norman-derived laws of the kingdom of Sicily), husband-murder was considered a form of "petty" treason and the punishment was that reserved for female traitors: not hanging, drawing, and quartering but burning at the stake. Second, conspiring to murder someone—even someone who was not a member of her family—was also a very serious charge against Maud. It suggests, at best, that she was engaging in a form of dispute resolution, euphemistically termed "self-help" by some historians, rather than going through more appropriate channels such as the royal courts. At worst, the accusation against Maud suggests that she was mentally unbalanced or out of control in some way. Following in the wake of the apparently suspicious death of her husband, Maud's involvement in the murder of Hugh de Kyngesmede must have seemed to the Crown to be even more worrisome, not only because of its unfortunate timing but also because of the potential damage it could cause to the reputation of the royal family.

Maud was arrested and placed in the Tower, although "honorably and without danger of death" according to the gaol delivery roll.[1] There was only one problem: she refused to speak. She did not deny the killings, but she did not admit to them, either. She simply refused to have anything to do with the court officials charged with interrogating her. In addition, since English Common Law forbade the use of torture to extract confessions, the officials had no real means to compel her to speak.[2] If such a circumstance had occurred with a more typical defendant, the result would probably have been a relatively quick conviction and a public execution. But in this circumstance, with the royal family involved at the very highest level, such a quick and easy solution was clearly impossible.

Indeed, the outline narrated above indicates just how murky the case against Maud Mortimer is from the perspective of a modern-day historian. What is the connection between the death of Hugh de Mortimer and that of Hugh de Kyngesmede, other than Maud's alleged involvement with both? What possible motivation could Maud have had for such a course of action? Was Maud, indeed, guilty of these crimes or could her silence be construed as an expression of outrage at being charged with them? Why was she imprisoned, but without "danger of death," if she did, in fact, commit these crimes? What sort of trial would Maud have had, given the fact that she was a member of the royal family (albeit through marriage and cognate ties) and one who was married to an important marcher baron?

Indeed, this narrative has all the elements of a good mystery story: unexplained deaths, the accused a person of significant social status, the facts of the cases unclear. Moreover, the alleged actions of Maud took place within the context of the last years of Edward I's reign, a period in which there was considerable political disruption, in particular over the disputed throne of Scotland, which involved the highest levels of the baronage and that paved the way for the disastrous reign of Edward II. Thus, one would think that the charges against Maud de Mortimer of Richard's Castle would have interested other historians, especially those who focus on the political and legal conflicts of the late thirteenth and early fourteenth centuries. Yet historical references to the two deaths are extraordinarily minimal. Robert C. Palmer includes an anecdotal reference to the poisoning of Hugh by Maud in his book, *The Whilton Dispute*, in which he makes it clear that he believes Maud to have been guilty of the deed.[3] Hilda Johnstone deals with the murder of Hugh de Kyngesmede in a little more depth in the introduction to her edition of the letters of Prince Edward of Wales as an example of the ways in which "the interference of powerful friends could affect the ordinary judicial machinery."[4] I would never have even encountered the story had I not been researching widows in the Mortimer families and come across the laconic entries in the *Calendar of Patent Rolls* that outlined the cases in brief.[5]

I believe that the story of Maud de Mortimer of Richard's Castle is more than an interesting example of the ways in which the Crown could manipulate the legal system, although its significance might be more relevant to discussions of local economic, political, and family considerations than to discussions of national concerns. The charges against Maud of responsibility for these two deaths, and the ways in which the cases were played out "behind the scenes" rather than in the glaring light of a public trial, can serve to illustrate that private and local issues in the later Middle Ages had public consequences and that membership in the royal family did not necessarily make a person exempt from calumnious accusation, although it might well have been a useful connection when it came to saving one from the executioner's block.

What I hope to accomplish in this case study is the following. First, I will provide a chronology of events, from Maud and Hugh's marriage to the end of Maud's life in 1308. This chronology will direct attention to the important participants in the suits, those named in the documents pertaining directly to the two murder charges and those unnamed. I will then offer some possible (and highly speculative) reasons for the concatenation of events as described in the sources and will discuss why I believe these reasons might be legitimate. Finally, I will place this episode in the context of the disputes that were so common to the medieval nobility—those over land—which I believe to be the connection between the deaths of Hugh de Mortimer and of Hugh de Kyngesmede.

It is impossible, given the sources now available, to know if Maud was guilty or not. Her apparent protection from death mentioned in the gaol delivery roll does not necessarily mean that she was innocent of either deed. Neither is it an indication of guilt. Maud's refusal to speak, no matter how profound her reasons for it, have rendered her guilt or innocence moot. Second, analysis of the available sources—most of them related only obliquely to the actual deeds of which she is accused—suggest that Maud might well have been little more than a useful pawn in a continuing conflict within Hugh de Mortimer's maternal family. It is possible that she was forced into action after his death, perhaps in order to protect her children and her own future prosperity. In fact, the most important actors in this series of events might have been those who seem most tangential to them: the bishops of Bath and Wells, the family of Hugh de Kyngesmede, and the cognates of Hugh de Mortimer of Richard's Castle, none of whom are central to the "facts" outlined in the charges against Maud.

Let us go back to the putative beginning: Maud's marriage to Hugh de Mortimer in 1290. Maud was the daughter of one William le Marshal, a cousin of Queen Eleanor of Castile.[6] Queen Eleanor had developed a strategy of arranging marriages between her cognate kin and members of the English baronage. These connections provided her with intimates and familiars as ladies-in-waiting and also linked certain baronial families much more closely to the Crown. More politically significant examples of this were the marriages Eleanor arranged for several members of the de Vescy family to her cousins and intimates.[7] Maud seems to have been a more distant cousin and her marriage, perhaps understandably, was to a somewhat less significant peer. The Mortimers of Richard's Castle were important barons of the March of Wales that ran alongside the English counties of Shropshire and Hereford, but their influence did not extend very far beyond that area. In fact, the marriage of Hugh de Mortimer's parents, Robert de Mortimer and Joyce la Zouche, had been designed to move the family's nexus of power into the western counties of Wiltshire and Devon in order to promote the combined interests of both families.

At the time of his marriage, Hugh de Mortimer was a royal ward; he did not attain his majority until five years later. This connection to the royal household was a situation that appealed to Queen Eleanor's matchmaking sensibilities: she tended to marry her female cousins to royal wards whenever possible, perhaps because they were more available for such arrangements. Hugh was the heir not only of his father, Robert de Mortimer, but of his mother, Joyce la Zouche, as well. She was a main protagonist in the dispute over the manor of Whilton that Palmer has detailed in his book. As her heir, Hugh was also involved, even during his minority, in the dispute. In June 1290, sometime just before or just after his marriage, Hugh endorsed an agreement between Robert Burnel, bishop of Bath and Wells and chancellor of England, and Philip and Felicia de Montgomery (Felicia was Hugh's half-sister) in which Felicia and Philip granted the manor of Whilton to the bishop, who granted it back to them in perpetuity, with reversion to himself and his heirs. Hugh's endorsement was designed to enable him to put forward his own claim to the manor when he came of age.[8]

The marriage between Maud and Hugh seems to have been more or less successful.[9] About two years after the wedding, Maud gave birth to a daughter, Joan, and four years later to another daughter, Margaret. There were no surviving sons and the girls were married off to members of the minor nobility at quite young ages, since Joan was already married at the time of their father's death, when she was reckoned to be twelve years old, and Margaret, who was only eight at the time, was married before her mother's death in 1308.[10]

This lack of sons might have led to the establishment of a much more significant landed stake in the family's holdings for Maud. In a writ patent dated August 20, 1297, Hugh received a royal license to enfeoff William de Marchia, bishop of Bath and Wells and king's treasurer, with seven manors in Essex, Worcestershire, Devonshire, Hampshire, Northamptonshire, and Shropshire and for Bishop William to regrant all of the manors back to Hugh and Maud *jointly*.[11] This agreement was subsequently enrolled in the Common Pleas roll for the Hilary term of the following year. The chyrograph was prepared by (and perhaps one or both of the parties were represented by) one Adam de Kyngesmede.[12]

The plot thickens. This one dilatory mention of Adam de Kyngesmede in the plea roll of Hilary 1298 is the only one that links the Kyngesmede family both to the Mortimers of Richard's Castle and to the bishop of Bath and Wells.[13]

The agreement that created Maud's jointure not only guaranteed her a larger share of the Mortimer patrimony if Hugh predeceased her; it also demonstrates a connection between another bishop of Bath and Wells and one of the parties involved in the dispute over the manor of Whilton. Indeed, the use of Bishop William as the conduit for the creation of the jointure was probably a deliberate move on Hugh's part to promote a connection between them. The usual procedure among the baronage for the creation of jointures in the late thirteenth century was to return the lands in question to the king and for the king to regrant them in joint tenancy. Since William's predecessor, Robert Burnel, had become involved on the side of the Montgomerys, Hugh very probably reasoned that an alliance between the Mortimers of Richard's Castle and the present bishop would have political benefits, especially in the disposition of the Whilton case. William de Marchia would have been a valuable ally in any case. As king's treasurer he had enormous influence on exchequer and chancery procedures and he was a notably popular individual. In fact, his reputation was so pristine that, in 1324, the bishops of England and the Crown presented him to the pope as a candidate for canonization.[14]

Sometime before June 1302, Bishop William de Marchia died. His successor, Walter de Haselshawe, received royal assent to his election in August and, by September, was invested with the temporalities of his office.[15] This meant that Hugh de Mortimer's connection to the diocesan office of Bath and Wells, made so painstakingly just five years before, did not avail him any lasting benefit. Nevertheless, the period between 1302 and Hugh's death in 1304 seems to have been relatively peaceful: no documents exist that suggest the development of a dispute among any of the relevant parties—the Mortimers, the Kyngesmedes, or the bishops of Bath and Wells.

Hugh de Mortimer of Richard's Castle died sometime around August 5, 1304, the date of both the escheator's order to take Hugh's lands into the king's custody and of the writ ordering the inquisition *post mortem*.[16] The inquisition lists Hugh's lands, those that he and Maud held jointly, and the distribution of lands to the heirs. Notably, the king granted the wardship of the heirs' lands to Queen Margaret (his second wife). She, in turn, granted half of the lands on the marriage of Joan, the elder daughter, to Thomas de Bykenore, Joan's husband, and sold the remainder of the wardship to Walter Langton, bishop of Coventry and Lichfield, who had succeeded William de Marchia as king's treasurer.[17] No mention is made of the manner of Hugh's death in the inquisition.

This is where the story becomes very interesting. Between the summer of 1304 and January 1305, Maud does not seem to have been charged with *any crime*. A series of entries from the Close Roll of October 1304 demonstrate that Maud's dower was assigned and her jointure returned to her within the mandated forty days of her husband's death.[18] It seems unlikely that such assignments would have been made had Maud been under suspicion of murdering her husband. Thus, there was apparently no particular disturbance over the manner of Hugh's death for at least a few months. Moreover, in an entry in the Ancient Petitions (undated, but probably sometime soon after October) Maud requests terms for the payment of £121 8s 2d of Hugh's debts to the Crown out of her jointure.[19]

Similarly, although the murder of Hugh de Kyngesmede, according to the gaol delivery roll, was alleged to have occurred with Maud's connivance in January 1305, there is no indication in other documentary sources that any comment was made on this supposed murder for some months. The only official activity with respect to Maud was the granting, in April 1305, to Queen Margaret of the fine should Maud remarry without the king's license and two acknowledgments of debts owed to two clerks, Adam de Osgodby and William de Thorntoft, in April and June, respectively.[20] Both clerks were members of the royal chancery; Adam also held a prebend in Bureford, Shropshire, from Maud.[21]

The first evidence that accusations as to Maud's alleged homicidal activity had been made appears in a collection of letters of the Prince of Wales, Edward of Caernarvon. Although Edward was at the time estranged from his father because of their conflict over Piers Gaveston, in June 1305, he began a campaign designed both to free Maud from imprisonment in the Tower and to secure the most reliable royal justices to hear the case. But what case?

The suit that had compelled Prince Edward to act was the conspiracy to murder case against Maud claimed by the Kyngesmede family. Significantly, Edward is absolutely silent about the (earlier?) accusation that Maud had caused the death of her husband.

Prince Edward's letters and other public documents provide the outlines of the story. According to the writs sent to the justices of oyer and terminer charged with investigating these crimes, one Walter de Kyngesmede appealed Maud and William de Billebury (according to Hilda Johnstone, Maud's chamberlain[22]) for the death of his brother, Hugh. Walter subsequently also appealed William de Billebury for robbery and breach of the peace.[23] Maud was accused not only of sending William de Billebury and her men-at-arms to the bishop of Bath and Wells's residence at Thameside, London, in order to murder Hugh de Kyngesmede, she was also charged with harboring the murderers afterward.

Edward's letter-writing campaign began in late June, when he wrote to the mayor and sheriff of London in order to secure Maud's release from prison on the grounds that she was falsely accused. He states that her imprisonment is causing her very great duress that she does not deserve and asks, "for the love you have for me," that her duress be alleviated and that she be treated in a more courteous manner.[24]

Prince Edward followed this letter with one to Adam de Kyngesmede rebuking him for bringing the suit against Maud.[25] Why did Edward write to Adam rather than to Walter? What role did Adam, presumably another brother of the murdered Hugh, play in the accusations against Maud? These are key questions and they do not have easy answers. Possibly, Adam was the elder brother and, so, Edward directed his correspondence to him rather than to Walter. It is more probable, however, that Edward knew Adam de Kyngesmede personally. As his participation in the agreement between William de Marchia and the Mortimers attests, Adam was employed in the royal administration. In fact, in March 1305, Adam was a witness to an agreement over rents in Worcestershire; one of his fellow witnesses was the chancery clerk, Adam de Osgodby, who held a prebend from Maud.[26] In December 1305, Adam would be associated with justices of oyer and terminer investigating a series of trespasses in Ludlow.[27] Adam de Kyngesmede was also a landholder of some consequence: in an enrollment of debt in which he agreed to pay a royal clerk, Robert de Harewedon, £20, he pledged lands in Herefordshire, Shropshire, and Buckinghamshire as his sureties. Elsewhere, Adam styled himself Adam de Kyngesmede of Northampton.[28] All of these indications of Adam's status and position suggest that he was the important family member, that he had connections to the bishops of Bath and Wells as well as to the Mortimers of Richard's Castle, and that he might have been the instigator of the charges directed against Maud and her men. Thus, the appeal of Walter de Kyngesmede listed in the writ to the justices of oyer and terminer might have hidden the more politically powerful person behind the accusation: Adam de Kyngesmede. By writing to Adam rather than to Walter, Prince Edward might have gone directly to the source of the problem.

For the remainder of the summer, Edward wrote letters to everyone involved in the case. On July 18 he sent a request to Peter Malorre that the men whom he held in his prison and who belonged to the "lady de Mortimer" be treated gently.[29] A month later, he sent a request to the sheriffs of London and Middlesex that a special commission be established to investigate the charges.[30] Prince Edward's efforts bore fruit: in August 1305, a commission of oyer and terminer—led by Ralph de Sandwich, John de Bakewell, and Stephen de Gravesend (all of them handpicked by Prince Edward)—was sent to Middlesex to inquire into the charges.[31] This was, of course, in the Crown's best interests as well as Maud's. A commission devoted to investigating the accusations had more time to concentrate on particular problems of the case; by appointing justices associated with the royal family to lead the commission the Crown guaranteed that the end result would be as favorable to royal interests as possible.

Once the commission was established, events proceeded rapidly. Edward sent letters to John de Bakewell urging a speedy conclusion and also sent a thinly disguised request to Roger de Appleby, the sheriff of Middlesex, that the jury be packed with royal supporters so that "[Maud's] deliverance should be to the honor of herself and of her lineage."[32] Throughout the months, it is unclear as to whether Edward was successful in securing Maud's release from the Tower. It is also unclear whether the husband-murder case against her was moving forward, as there is no direct documentary evidence of an investigation into Hugh de Mortimer's death. Perhaps Edward also directed his energies to securing his stepmother's support for his cousin. It appears that at the same time as charges against Maud were dropped in the Kyngesmede case, Queen Margaret secured a pardon for Maud in the case of her husband's death. The writ patent, dated September 16, 1305, grants Maud a pardon at the behest of Queen Margaret for the poisoning of her husband, Hugh de Mortimer, and instructs the justices of oyer and terminer in Hereford and Worcester to supercede the execution of the "exigents" (writs of outlawry) directed against her and to restore to her the goods that had been distrainted on account of the exigents.[33] By mid-September, Maud was free and Edward was sending thank-you letters to John de Bakewell—and asking him to continue acting as Maud's confidante in the coming months. He also instructed John to give Maud a kiss and tell her it was from him![34]

One would think that the case would end there, but there is an odd postscript to the proceedings. Presumably, when Maud was freed so, too, were William de Billebury and the other men-at-arms accused of participating in the attack on Hugh de Kyngesmede. Nevertheless, a little over a year after Maud's pardon, in December 1306, King Edward granted a pardon to William de Billebury respecting the proclamation of his outlawry, on the condition that he surrender immediately to the justices of oyer and terminer in Shropshire. What makes this entry so peculiar is that the crime for which William de Billebury was apparently outlawed was the death of Hugh de Mortimer of Richard's Castle, *not* Hugh de Kyngesmede.[35] Upon being freed of the one charge, did William then flee in anticipation of being charged with the other crime? Did the clerk enrolling the pardon make an error and substitute "Mortimer" for Kyngesmede? Was William the culprit all along, first killing Hugh de Mortimer and then killing Hugh de Kyngesmede without Maud's connivance?

What to make of this interesting, but mystifying, chronology of events? What was the connection between Hugh and Maud de Mortimer and the bishops of Bath and Wells? How did the Kyngesmede family factor into the relationship?

In fact, the ongoing relationship among several successive bishops of Bath and Wells, Hugh de Mortimer, and members of his family—especially those on his mother's side—and possibly several generations of the Kyngesmede family might be the connective tissue among this disparate collection of people. In 1286, one Simon de Kyngesmede of Hereford acted as a pledge of law for Hugh's niece, Alice, and her husband, Nicholas del Lee.[36] The manor of Kyngesmede was contained in the temporalities of the bishops of Bath and Wells, which might help explain that family's level of interaction in the business of the diocese. Adam de Kyngesmede had acted either as attorney or as the preparer of the chyrograph in the concord between William de Marchia and Hugh and Maud de Mortimer that resulted in Maud's jointure, as mentioned previously. Later, Adam would be assigned to two commissions of oyer and terminer taking place in Ludlow in December 1305 and his fellow justices included Roger de Mortimer and William de Mortimer.[37] Moreover, although he tended to locate himself for official purposes in Northampton, Adam also held lands in the marcher counties. If Simon de Kyngesmede was a relation, then the connection to Herefordshire, where the lordship of Richard's Castle was in part located, was made twice over.

If one also recalls that Hugh's half-sister, Felicia, and her husband, Philip de Montgomery, included William de Marchia's predecessor, Robert Burnel, in a transaction involving the manor of Whilton, then three successive bishops and possibly two generations of Kyngesmedes had become involved with Hugh or his maternal family. Significantly, aside from William de Marchia, none of these people seem to have been clear allies of Hugh de Mortimer or of his wife, Maud. The Kyngesmedes appear in the records as supporters of Hugh's half-sister and her kin in the suit over the manor of Whilton. Hugh de Kyngesmede was staying at the London residence of Walter de Haselshawe, the incumbent bishop of Bath and

Wells, at the time of his death. The chyrograph outlining the land transaction between William de Marchia and Hugh and Maud de Mortimer was prepared under the eye of Adam of Kyngesmede. All of this suggests the complicity of the Kyngesmedes with Hugh's maternal half-kin, their connection to the bishops of Bath and Wells, and, possibly, antagonism between the Mortimers and these other parties. Certainly, Hugh's relationship with his half-sister and her children was tense because of their disagreements over the manor of Whilton. Securing William de Marchia's support had been an important step for Hugh and Maud: by doing so, they probably hoped to enhance their position in the dispute once Robert Burnel and his heirs had become involved as allies of the Montgomery faction. The association of Hugh de Kyngesmede with the new bishop of Bath and Wells might have indicated that Bishop Walter was intending to side against the Mortimers in the ongoing suit over Whilton.

After Maud's release from the Tower of London and her exoneration and/or pardon, she did not entirely disappear from the scene, although she seems to have directed her attention almost entirely toward the maintenance of her lands. Almost immediately after her release, during the Michaelmas term of 1305, she sued the coexecutors of Hugh's will, John Saumesyn and Robert la Zouche (the latter his maternal cousin), for money (£22 10s) they owed her.[38] This suit apparently connected to another suit introduced in the Hilary term of 1306, in which she was sued by Richard the Mercer of Worcester for the same amount: he claimed Maud owed this amount because of purchases she made at his shop in September 1305 and for which she promised to pay by All Saints Day.[39] Her difficulties with the coexecutors might have prevented her from paying her cloth bill because in Easter term, 1306, she was distrained for failing to pay it.[40] Maud also might have been out of the country during this time because she received a simple letter of protection in December 1305 until Michaelmas of the same year, necessitating the appointment of attorneys to represent her, since her letter did not include protection from prosecution.[41] Maud received another letter of protection, this one more comprehensive and including protection from prosecution for both herself and her men, from June 1306 until the king's return from Scotland.[42]

Maud's longest course of litigation involved her elder daughter, Joan, and her husband, Thomas de Bykenore, whom she sued over the advowson of the church of Farnebarewe, Warwickshire. They defaulted twice and the court awarded her the advowson, but she was unable to have damages assigned until nearly eighteen months later, in Michaelmas term, 1307, because of their persistent failure to respond to the sheriff's summons.[43]

The business surrounding Hugh's death did not entirely go away, however. In 1306 Maud pursued a suit against John de Drokenesford for return of the manor of Farleye, Hampshire. This manor had been one of the properties that formed part of her jointure. John, a royal clerk who happened to be on the king's business abroad, did not have to answer Maud's charges; it is unclear why and how he had acquired the manor, but it is perhaps significant that he eventually succeeded Walter de Haselshawe as bishop of Bath and Wells. John might have been able to trespass upon the manor because the agreement that had been made long before to establish Maud's jointure had passed through the hands of the earlier bishop, William de Marchia. This transaction could have provided him with this opportunity to interfere with Maud's seisin.[44]

Maud died soon after the completion of the suit against her daughter and son-in-law, shortly before February 15, 1308. Her inquisition *post mortem* identifies her daughters, Joan and Margaret, and their husbands, Thomas de Bykenore and Geoffrey de Cornwayle, respectively, as her heirs. The stresses of the murder charges made against her in 1305 might have shortened her life; certainly, they must have contributed to the circumstances that compelled her to sue both John de Drokenesford and her own daughter for her rightful property upon being released. Unfortunately, the records cannot reveal whether Joan and Margaret blamed their mother for their father's death. Both John's acquisition of Farleye and Joan and Thomas's appropriation of the advowson could have been examples of taking advantage of an opportunity, so typical among medieval people when property was at stake. Maud's lack of reticence, however, in staking her various claims during her brief widowhood might suggest not only that she was possessed of a strong character, but also that she suffered no long-term disadvantage from the ordeal of accusation and imprisonment she had suffered. She does, nevertheless, seem to have been careful to steer well clear of Bishop Walter de Haselshawe, the Kyngesmede family, and the dispute over the manor of Whilton. For example, she never claimed dower from Whilton, although she could have done. This suggests that the intimidation tactics of the Kyngesmedes, the bishop, and perhaps her late husband's maternal kin did have an impact on her activities after her pardon.

I repeat a question I raised earlier: what to make of this extraordinary series of events, both bizarre and pedestrian? Although any conclusions have to be entirely speculative, it is nonetheless possible to suggest ways to evaluate the significance of this tale of suspicious death, family conflict, and individual complicity in both. First, there might be no direct connection at all between the deaths of Hugh de Mortimer and Hugh de Kyngesmede beyond the circumstantial. It is entirely possible that Hugh's death by poison was accidental. Maud, as manager of the household, might have been held responsible for what went on in her kitchens and, if anyone died from food poisoning in her home the connection might have been made between her management abilities and the death of the unfortunate diner. Similarly, William de Billebury, as Maud's chamberlain, could have been held equally responsible for many of the same reasons, but his safety would have been less assured (he was not a cousin of the prince of Wales, after all) and he might have believed that flight, even if it meant outlawry, was the safest course of action. These, indeed, might have been the circumstances surrounding Hugh's death. In the absence of an extant coroner's inquest, we will never know. But this scenario would make sense of the total absence of charges against Maud until after the Kyngesmede incident had occurred. Perhaps no one had really thought anything about the suspiciousness of Hugh's death until another death—and one far more violent than Hugh's—had been laid at Maud's door.

Hugh's death, in fact, could not have come at a worse time for Maud and their daughters.[45] Although Maud's dower in Richard's Castle was secure and she and Hugh had taken steps to enrich her traditional widow's portion with a jointure, the conflict over Whilton was still very much in evidence. The last thing either Hugh or Maud would have desired was another protracted minority that would delay further the progress of the suit. In 1304, the eldest Mortimer daughter was twelve, the younger was only eight. Hugh would certainly have preferred to live long enough to see both his daughters grown to adulthood and married; this would have been Maud's preference, as well. Moreover, the political gambit that Hugh and Maud had attempted, that of involving Bishop William de Marchia in the establishment of Maud's jointure, did not succeed: William died and the new incumbent in the diocese harbored the Kyngesmede family, perhaps thereby tacitly placing himself on the side of the Montgomerys and the Lees against the Mortimers.

In terms of the domestic life of Hugh and Maud, there is no evidence (other than the pardon) to suggest that their marriage was conflicted, although there is also no evidence to suggest that they were blissfully happy together. In the absence of specific evidence of spousal abuse, it is reasonable to assume that the material considerations of protection, prosperity, and security would have outweighed—especially after fifteen years of marriage—the possible benefits accrued by Hugh's early death. Consequently, I find it very difficult to believe that his death was a deliberate homicide perpetrated by Maud or, with her approval, by William de Billebury.

The only people, it seems, who might have benefited from Hugh's death were, in fact, his maternal half-kin. The family's dispute over the manor of Whilton would have been put into abeyance during the minority of Hugh's heirs. This breathing space would have been welcome to the litigants, as delays in common pleas suits tended to favor the possessors both financially, in that they continued to enjoy the revenues of the disputed property, and practically, as records of the dispute could easily be mislaid or destroyed in the intervening years. I would not go so far as to accuse Hugh's maternal kin of complicity in his death (again, there is no evidence to suggest anything of the kind) but I believe that his untimely end did provide them with a perfect opportunity to capitalize on the misfortunes of the Mortimers.

The death of Hugh de Kyngesmede is a much more complicated issue than that of Hugh de Mortimer. Unlike the poisoning charge, which appears for the first and only time in Maud's official pardon, the accusations against Maud and her men in the death of Hugh de Kyngesmede are comparatively well documented. No documents, however, provide adequate information about Maud's involvement. While possible witnesses might have been able to place William de Billebury and Maud's men-at-arms at the scene and while Maud seems to have harbored the murderers after the deed, there is no apparent purpose to the violence directed against Hugh de Kyngesmede. The connections among the Kyngesmedes, the bishops of Bath and Wells, and the relations of Hugh de Mortimer outlined above are never explicitly addressed in the documents pertaining to Hugh de Kyngesmede's murder. Those connections, however, might have been the reasons for his death. Was Hugh staying with Bishop Walter de Haselshawe as a liaison between the bishop and the Montgomerys and/or Lees in order to gain the bishop's support in their land dispute with Hugh de Mortimer? Were plans afoot to deprive Maud of her jointure; was this to be attempted through the machinations of the designated successor to the diocese, John de Drokenesford? Was Hugh's brother Adam the "real" power in a conspiracy designed to render the Mortimers helpless against the combined power of the bishops of Bath and Wells, the Montgomerys, and the Kyngesmede family's other affines and allies? Did Maud and William de Billebury decide that, under the circumstances, some form of "self-help" was appropriate, leading them to make the unfortunate decision to confront the Kyngesmedes in a location to which they had reasonable access: the residence of the bishop of Bath and Wells in London?

Unfortunately, these questions are unanswerable. They do, however, illustrate quite clearly that the deaths of Hugh de Mortimer of Richard's Castle and of Hugh de Kyngesmede were significant in the contexts of local authority and local disputes over that authority in which the nobility of England typically engaged. All of the connections among the participants in this story—the Mortimers, Hugh's maternal kin, the bishops of Bath and Wells, the Kyngesmede family—involve land, much of it confined to the region between the Welsh March and the western counties. Control of land was important to the baronage for several reasons including the obvious one of wealth. Land conveyed authority over people; it created the context for political, social, and military alliances; it provided a physical manifestation of one family's power. Land embodied the social and political ideals of the medieval noble class and people were willing to do *anything* to preserve it, to increase their access to it, and to diminish others' ownership of it. They were even willing to commit murder for it.

Although a landed widow after fifteen years of marriage, Maud de Mortimer of Richard's Castle was nevertheless in a relatively precarious position in terms of local authority and influence. She had begun her married life as a virtual stranger, not only to her husband but also to her home and surroundings. The death of her cousin, Queen Eleanor, soon after her marriage deprived Maud of the most powerful ally she could have commanded. The tangled legal affairs of her husband, especially those involving Whilton, led Maud and Hugh to take steps to defend their interests, which might have, in fact, backfired on them because of the early deaths of William de Marchia and of Hugh himself. Maud's allies in widowhood were two underage daughters, one (and, eventually, two) relatively unimportant son-in-law, and the highly unpredictable and volatile prince of Wales. Is it any wonder, faced with such a horrifying array of charges and so few resources at her disposal, that Maud refused to speak? The fact that she was able to marshal her forces, to gain the patronage of the royal family—even those unrelated to her—and to secure not only her freedom but also the security of a landed position for her daughters is a testament to the woman's perseverance, as well as a testament to her understanding of the importance such a position signified. Perhaps Maud's silence was truly golden, for it gave her life, wealth, and a relatively powerful and thoroughly independent position for the few years she had left in the world.

CHAPTER 7

ISABELLA DE VESCY AND THE LORDS ORDAINER: MARITAL POLITICS AND THE CROWN, 1272–1327

The reigns of Henry III and Edward I were marked by significant tensions between the baronage and the kings' wives, queens Eleanor of Provence and Eleanor of Castile. These tensions also tended to influence baronial relations with the Crown because of the support these women received from their husbands. Moreover, both Eleanors were perceived by commoners as grasping and acquisitive, using their position to advance unfairly the careers of friends and relatives while lining their pockets with the spoils of the exploitation of landholder, merchant, peasant, and Jew. Doggerel verses about Eleanor of Castile's acquisitiveness survive to this day; Eleanor of Provence's influence on her husband created some of the most acrimonious exchanges between the Crown and the baronage.[1]

The reign of Edward II can be seen in some ways as a direct result of these previous royal relationships. Although Edward and his queen, Isabella of France, did not have the kind of devoted partnership that his parents and grandparents seem to have enjoyed, his fondness for relatives of his mother and other "foreigners" contributed significantly to the disintegration of political stability that characterized his reign.

Isabella Beaumont, lady of Vescy, was one of the most notorious of these collateral royal relatives: the daughter of Louis de Brienne and Agnes *suo jure* countess of Beaumont, she was Eleanor of Castile's first cousin.[2] The hostility directed toward her was more virulent than any, with the exception of that directed during the Barons' War to the least popular semi-royal, William de Valence, half-brother of Henry III, and, later, one of Edward I's most trusted advisors.[3] Like William, Isabella figured prominently at court, as one of Eleanor of Castile's favorite ladies-in-waiting. Eleanor arranged her marriage to the long-widowed John de Vescy, one of Edward I's closest friends.[4] Isabella was also instrumental in ensuring the success of her brother, Henry Beaumont, who became the earl of Buchan by marrying Alice Comyn, the niece and heir of Earl John Comyn. Both Henry and Isabella were seen by the followers of Thomas of Lancaster, cousin of Edward II and leader of the first major rebellion against him, as interlopers whose power in the north of England and in Scotland interfered with the power of the "rightful" English baronage in that region—that is, of the earl of Lancaster, himself.[5]

For someone whose royal associations put her at such risk, however, Isabella was remarkably capable in the face of adversity and she was also a remarkably able manager of the delicate political situations in which she so often found herself. Unlike Earl Thomas and many others, Isabella survived a remarkable number of hostile assaults on her power and lived to a grand old age as the beloved elderly cousin of the esteemed Edward III. Surprisingly, her story has never been told in its entirety; when mention is made of her, the tone is highly critical.[6] Isabella succeeded in doing things that few men could have accomplished: she survived three volatile reigns, switched sides during the endemic conflicts of the reign of Edward II with ease, returned from exile with her estates still intact, solidified political relations between northern England and Scotland, and kept the memory and reputation of her famous and apparently beloved husband intact—despite the fact that she had no children to survive her and her brother-in-law, who had inherited the Vescy lordship, was evidently a wastrel whose incompetent, possibly criminally negligent behavior as justiciar of Ireland resulted in the forfeiture of most of his estates to the Crown.[7] Isabella thus demonstrated the kind of political acuity that would have been labeled as masterful if she had been male, but her sex has rendered her accomplishments historically negligible until now.

Isabella's story begins in her youth, sometime between 1278 and 1280, when she arrived with a gaggle of other female cousins at the court of Edward I and Eleanor of Castile. Eleanor was determined to outdo her mother-in-law in establishing members of her family in positions of prominence in England. To that end, she negotiated a series of marriage alliances that joined her cousins to a number of important baronial families, especially those who controlled the volatile Marches of Wales and Scotland.[8] This marriage between John de Vescy, lord of Alnwick and heir to his mother's share of the Marshal earldom of Pembroke (which included the county of Kildare in Ireland), and Isabella Beaumont in 1280 (a good fifteen years after the death of his first wife) not only benefited the young royal cousin, it also solidified the already close relationship between John and the royal couple. According to John Carmi Parsons, John and Isabella were among the closest associates of Queen Eleanor, outside her own household.[9] Isabella and John received valuable grants of land from both the king and the queen to commemorate the marriage.[10]

The Vescy family's position in northern England and the March of Scotland—second only to that of the earls of Lincoln—combined with the personal fame of her husband, gave Isabella an enviable status in Yorkshire, Northumberland, and Cumberland, the counties from which her dower was, eventually, to come. John himself had been one of the possible candidates for the title of king of Scotland (through his Vescy grandmother) but it would have been gross favoritism for Edward I to choose him over his cousins, John Balliol and Robert Bruce, both of whom had better claims to the crown.[11] The Vescys and the Lacy earls of Lincoln also had very close and long-standing connections. The Vescys started as the principal sub-feofees of the Lacy lords of Pontefract; indeed, they did not achieve independent tenant-in-chief status until the early thirteenth century, despite the fact that the first Eustace de Vescy had accompanied the Conqueror to England in 1066. These connections were at their most intimate when Edmund de Lacy and John de Vescy were married as children to the Saluzzo sisters, cousins of Queen Eleanor of Provence. The real political relationship, however, developed between John de Vescy and Edmund de Lacy's son, Henry: both were among King Edward I's closest friends and advisors and Henry maintained the friendship he enjoyed with Isabella after John's death until his own in 1311. Some of the political problems experienced by Isabella in the fourteenth century could, in fact, be attributed to this relationship: Henry de Lacy's son-in-law, Thomas of Lancaster, did not share the same attitude toward the Vescy–Lacy connection and seems to have resented the power Isabella wielded as the Vescys's senior member.

Isabella demonstrated her affection for the family of her husband early in their marriage. She seems to have had a good relationship with her mother-in-law, the notorious Agnes de Vescy (who died in 1290), as there was no litigation prosecuted between them either during her marriage or during the brief time between John's and his mother's death. Isabel also supported the young James de Mohun (John's maternal cousin) in his clerical career—just as his female cousins and aunts did.[12] She might have done much more, had John not died in 1289 while on royal service in Gascony, a situation that did not bode well for the future of the Vescy family. The position of head of the family and the family's estates devolved to John's younger brother, William, who was a very different figure from his brother. Isabella, although she was one of the executors of John's will, seems to have opted out of family politics during the years immediately following her husband's death. She secured her dower in short order, despite having to sue her brother-in-law for her share of the family lands that had been granted to sub-feofees.[13] Isabella evidently spent the next few years traveling with members of the royal family, as she received letters of protection for much of the time between 1291 and 1295.[14]

Isabella's political authority as leader of the Vescy family in the north did not develop until after the disastrous career of her brother-in-law, William, had destroyed the family's position in Ireland. His outrageous exploitation of the populace during his term as justiciar of Ireland—a position he received in 1290 because of the control of the county of Kildare by the Vescy family—resulted in his removal from the position by Edward I in 1294 and the forfeiture of his Irish lands as repayment for the moneys he embezzled.[15] Although William seems to have been able to gain Edward's patronage after the Ireland disaster—for example, he gained permission to grant his English estates to his illegitimate son, William de Vescy of Kildare—he never attained the status that he had achieved before the debacle of the justiciarship. After William's death in 1297, it became necessary for Isabella to step in as "materfamilias" to recoup the family's prestige.[16]

The dowager "lady de Vescy" was by this time a more or less permanent fixture in the royal household. In 1296 she suggested delicately that the elderly and feeble royal tailor be replaced as head of the assize of cloths because the rigors of the position were proving to be too much for him.[17] The following year saw her travelling with the countess of Holland and the duchess of Brabant.[18] The years between 1297 and 1305, despite the disgrace and death of William de Vescy, saw a marked rise in the fortunes of the Vescy family through Isabella's access to royal patronage. Her mother, Agnes, was, by 1297, the sole heir to the vicomital honor of Beaumont and chose that moment to quitclaim the Scottish honor of Caral [Crail] in Fife to her daughter.[19] Edward I gave Isabella a house in Leeds Castle so that she would have a place to stay at his pleasure.[20] After the first successful phase of the Scots War ended in 1300, Edward granted to Isabella extensive lands from those forfeited by one of the Scottish adherents, Nicholas Graham, "in consideration for her service to Queen Eleanor." More grants appeared in 1303.[21] By this time, Isabella had yet another ally: her younger brother, Henry, who had appeared in England sometime after 1300 and who clearly associated himself with his illustrious sister. Isabella, in 1305, managed to secure for him the remainder to lands that, first, John de Vescy and, then, she had received for life from Queen Eleanor of Castile.[22] Thus, as a result of Isabella's connections to the royal court, what had once been a life-grant became a part of the Beaumont patrimony. The association of Isabella and Henry Beaumont would prove to be one of the most politically significant alliances of the early fourteenth century.

The greatest political coup for Isabella occurred in 1304/1305, at the height of the conflict in Scotland and following the murder of John Comyn by Robert Bruce. When the castleward of Bamburgh Castle, one of the most important defenses along the Scottish–English border, became vacant upon the death of John de Warenne in 1304, Edward I chose Isabella for the position.²³ This move was unprecedented: no woman had controlled a royal castle in such a volatile and politically significant region (although women routinely controlled family castles in the Welsh Marches and kings had placed women in control of royal castles before). Edward was already organizing another invasion of Scotland at the time of Isabella's appointment, so it is likely that he was guaranteeing a loyal warden in the most important fortification in the north.

According to Michael Prestwich, Isabella's appointment was irregular in a number of ways. The original grant, made at the king's pleasure in 1304, was not appended by the great seal, thus lending a note of informality to the appointment. However, the entry in the Fine Roll in 1305 did identify the writ as being under the great seal, and at that time the grant of the castleward was made to Isabella for her life, not merely at the king's pleasure, with the stipulation that she may not remarry while she held the wardenship. Prestwich associates the latter change with the problems Isabella experienced a few years later in the reign of Edward II, but admits that her competence as warden of the castle cannot be faulted. Nevertheless, he cannot identify any particular reason for Isabella to be chosen for this position during such a politically charged period.²⁴

Why choose Isabella as the warden of such an important castle? There were other northern barons who could have been chosen: Henry Percy, Henry de Lacy, earl of Lincoln, and Thomas, earl of Lancaster all come to mind. Nevertheless, Isabella got the job—and no one seems to have been distressed by this arrangement, at least in 1304. Quite a number of possible reasons for the appointment come to mind if one puts aside the issue of Isabella's sex. It is entirely possible that Isabella's position at court, combined with the fact that, upon William de Vescy's death, she had assumed materfamilial status in the Vescy family, made her the best possible candidate.²⁵ The stipulation that she remain single while she held the position might have been a move designed to protect the king from the entry of a political opponent into the custody of such an important defensive post; Isabella seems to have been unlikely to remarry in any case. The caveat might also have been designed to protect Isabella herself, since it would have discouraged an ambitious man from abducting and raping her in order to gain control of the castle. Isabella's status as a competent manager of family business had been amply demonstrated and could have been a factor in Edward I's decision to appoint her to the castleward. For example, she seems to have been acting as a kind of attorney-in-fact for Clemencia, the widow of her nephew (Clemencia was also her cousin), an unusual move that no doubt had its basis both in their relationship and in Isabella's status in the realm.²⁶ The castle and its outbuildings were apparently in some disrepair at the time of the grant and she was ordered to oversee their restoration.[27] This suggests that John de Warenne might have been neglectful of his duties as warden of Bamburgh; Isabella's managerial competence could have been an important consideration in the appointment. Additionally, Edward I might have desired someone closer to the throne once it was possible to replace John de Warenne as warden.[28] The financial exigencies of the Scots War might have been yet another factor: because of the unusual nature of the appointment, Isabella might have been less inclined to complain about the payment of a farm of £110 per year for holding the castleward, although she would eventually be relieved of those payments as the situation in the Scottish March became more dangerous. She was also trustworthy, experienced, and was cloaked in the memory of her esteemed husband in the public eye. We will never know the king's motivations for choosing Isabella, but it is clear from the lack of protest in the sources that his decision was seen as an astute one (at least for the duration of Edward I's reign).

Isabella seems to have been a good warden. She had to be reminded occasionally to pay the man who was in charge of the castle gates, but, if the repayments of the exchequer are accurate, she seems to have cared well for the prisoners in the castle.[29] She paid the farm of the castle faithfully and there were no apparent conflicts in the region. When Edward I died in 1307, one of the first things Edward II did was to renew her appointment to the wardenship, an order that also accompanied one instructing her to release certain Scottish prisoners.[30] Isabella's position at court was also reiterated: she received a letter of protection to travel in the king's retinue overseas.[31] In 1308, when the gatekeeper of the castle resigned, Isabella managed to secure the position for herself, on the stipulation that she would be responsible for maintenance of the castle, the cost of which would be subtracted from the income derived from the position.[32]

Edward II, who was very attached to his mother's cousins in general and to Isabella in particular, was no doubt pleased to have such a loyal royalist in charge of Bamburgh. This period, between 1307 and 1311, was one in which the star of the Beaumonts was definitely on the rise. Isabella was probably instrumental in securing the marriage of Alice Comyn, niece and heir of John Comyn, earl of Buchan, for her brother, Henry in 1310. The marriage of Alice was in the king's gift and the political situation in Scotland was highly volatile: the late earl of Buchan had been stabbed to death by Robert Bruce and the Scots magnates were coalescing around two distinctly different political camps. The marriage of Henry and Alice must have been considered to be an astute political move on the part of Edward II in that it guaranteed a loyal subject settled in the midst of a political environment that was fraught with tension. It was also supremely useful for both Isabella and Henry because they could begin to develop

MARITAL POLITICS AND THE CROWN 99

their own political affinity through their connections in northern England and Scotland independently of the now-defunct Vescy affinity.

It is also clear that Isabella was maintaining necessary ties to old friends of her late husband. In 1310, at the request of Earl Henry de Lacy, she received remission of the farm for Bamburgh castle, on account of the expenses Isabella had incurred accompanying Queen Isabella in her position as senior lady of the chamber.[33] Although the remission of payment was a fairly typical act of royal generosity, the fact that the request had come from the highly esteemed earl of Lincoln demonstrates Isabella's ability to secure the support of the most prestigious familiars of Edward II for her own benefit. Earl Henry's death the following year would alter the political climate irrevocably.

Isabella and Henry Beaumont were thus among the significant beneficiaries of the last years of Edward I's reign and the first years of Edward II's. This situation probably drove the ambitious Earl Thomas of Lancaster to focus his energies on toppling them. Unlike Isabella, Thomas was a relative parvenu in the north of England. He had achieved his status there only by marrying Alice de Lacy, the heir to the earldoms of Lincoln and Salisbury (through her mother, Margaret Longespee) and to the constableship of Chester. Although Thomas was the son of Edward I's younger brother, Edmund, earl of Lancaster, he was a relatively untried young man surrounded by older, wiser, and more experienced men and women: not only Isabella Beaumont de Vescy, but his father-in-law, Earl Henry de Lacy, and Henry's cousins Aymer de Valence, earl of Pembroke, and Gilbert de Clare, earl of Gloucester and Hertford. Nevertheless, Thomas's ambition and energy became the fulcrum around which a baronial party coalesced. This party—and perhaps Thomas, in particular—resented the success of Isabella and Henry Beaumont in attaining royal patronage. As a result, when the baronial party gained power in 1311, Isabella and Henry were targeted as exemplars of Edward II's lack of political acuity.

Thomas spearheaded the first of the rebellions that plagued Edward II's troubled reign. As the main architect of the Ordinances, Thomas seems to have focused on punishing his enemies and those who jeopardized his position in the north of England. Along with a condemnation of "foreigners" in general, he singled out two people specifically: Isabella Beaumont de Vescy and her brother, Henry Beaumont.

The Ordinances identify Isabella as one of the principle culprits of the corruption of Edward II:

> It is determined by the investigations of the prelates, earls, and barons that the Lady of Vescy petitioned the King to give to her brother, Sir Henry de Beaumont, and others, lands, franchises, and baillies to the damage and

dishonor of the king and to the disinherison of the Crown. Moreover, she has procured letters of privilege contrary to the law and the intentions of the King.

The Lords Ordainer then required that she depart from her house no later than the quinzaine of Michaelmas and not return to court, and also demanded the immediate relinquishing of her wardenship of Bamburgh Castle.[34]

Thomas of Lancaster thus engineered the immediate exile of both Isabella and Henry and, in a Fine Roll entry, also tried to guarantee that Isabella would turn Bamburgh Castle over to his handpicked candidate, Henry Percy.[35]

Isabella, her brother, and her sister-in-law did leave the court, at least for a short time, and repaired to their estates in the north. Queen Isabella sent her favorite lady of the chamber gifts of venison, wild boar, and Brie cheese during her exile.[36] What Isabella did not do, however, was immediately turn over Bamburgh Castle—because the king sent her a letter under his privy seal telling her not to turn the castle over to Henry Percy, and to delay as long as possible.[37] Isabella was apparently in a powerful enough position to be able to demand recompense for the loss of Bamburgh and she apparently refused to relinquish her control of the castle until she had been satisfied. In the end, she received a number of manors in Lincolnshire and Dorsetshire in exchange for the castleward, which she then obediently turned over—not to Henry Percy, but to a royal clerk named John de Esshlyngton.[38]

Isabella might have gone into exile for a while, but she soon returned. It is clear that, despite Thomas of Lancaster's hostility toward her, she was too valuable to the queen—and, at the time, probably to Edward as well—for her to be banned for long. By 1313 she was receiving letters of protection in order to accompany the queen overseas.[39] A letter patent of the same year abrogated the clauses of the Ordinances that referred to her and to Henry.[40] When the Ordainers tried to sue her for failure to pay the farm on the castleward, she received formal acquittals of the payments and remissions on the rents she was supposed to pay for the manors she received in exchange.[41] Nevertheless, it seems that Isabella's political astuteness led her to make some changes in the direction of her loyalties after the incident with the Lords Ordainer. Her ties to the queen became deeper; her associations with her brother more obvious. Isabella and Henry Beaumont both bided their time, but their sympathies seem to have belonged to the queen in the increasingly dysfunctional court life of Edward II's household. This sympathy was developed in a dangerous strategy that seems to have made Isabella a "silent partner" in the furthering of what would eventually become the queen's political alliance against Edward II.

After the failure of the Ordinances, Isabella and Henry took steps to consolidate their hold on certain lands in the north, near the border between England and Scotland. Between 1316 and 1320, Isabella and Henry purchased a number of manors, exchanged properties, and established Henry as Isabella's heir.[42] Henry's wife, Alice, was almost never involved in these transactions (with one exception, when they granted a manor from Alice's inheritance to Isabella for her life);[43] the Beaumonts seem to have been engaged in a strategy of property consolidation that would lessen their vulnerability should political turmoil in England or Scotland get worse. Earl Thomas of Lancaster made one lackluster attempt to impinge on this strategy in 1319 by trying to interfere with Isabella's life tenure in a number of manors she held from John de Eyvill of Aldingfleet, Yorkshire. Thomas purchased the manors from John but was unable to eject Isabella from her tenure.[44]

The earl of Lancaster rebelled against the king one last time in 1322. His rebellion failed; he was captured, taken to his wife's castle of Pontefract, tried, and summarily executed.[45] Like other royal favorites, Isabella benefited from the destruction of the man who seems to have been her most tenacious opponent: she was awarded, in 1322, with lands forfeited from the earldom of Lancaster.[46] Nevertheless, after 1322, Isabella's activities, in both the acquisition of manors and in the daily movements of the queen's household, seem to disappear. Both Isabella and Henry are unusually silent. Such silence, however, might easily indicate marks of unusual favor on the part of the king, since virtually all of Isabella's friends and neighbors were soon to find themselves at the mercy of the extraordinarily rapacious Hugh le Despencer the elder and Hugh, his son. That Isabella, whose vulnerable position could have made her an easy target and whose wealth would have been an attractive prize, did not experience the horrors of the Despencer juggernaut (as, e.g., Alice de Lacy and Elizabeth de Burgh did) suggests that the queen was able to protect her from the ravages of Edward's new favorites.

The end game of Edward II's reign was about to begin, and Isabella must have been quietly preparing for it for a number of years. This is the point at which her strategizing was transformed from the merely competent to the masterful: Isabella seems to have been involved in the growing movement in favor of the queen and Roger de Mortimer, earl of March, but she was a silent partner. When, in 1326, the king ordered the arrest of all the adherents of the king of France (who was supporting his sister against Edward II), Isabella was one of the people specifically excepted from the order.[47] Although an intimate of the queen and one, moreover, whose brother was under suspicion, Isabella nonetheless maintained the illusion of loyalty while, as her experiences in 1327 attest, she plotted with the leaders of the coup.

When Isabella did appear again, in the final rebellion that ended Edward II's reign, she did so alongside Queen Isabella, Earl Roger de Mortimer, and the young Prince Edward. Isabella and Henry Beaumont (who might have been partly responsible for the death of Edward II, as he apparently prevented him escaping from Berkeley Castle[48]) had switched sides: they rejected the man whose encouragement of their ambitions had led to their exile and allied themselves with the party they thought would benefit them the most, that of the queen whom Isabella had served so faithfully.

The ease with which Isabella and her brother effected this change of loyalties is breathtaking. Not only did they receive no censure for this about-face, they were amply rewarded for it. When David de Strathbolgi, earl of Athol, died in 1326 the king acquired the wardship of David, his teenaged son. One of the first acts of Edward III's reign (probably orchestrated by the queen mother) was to grant the wardship and (probably) the marriage of the youngster to Isabella.[49] Thus, in the space of a single act, the Beaumonts managed to gain control of two of the five Scottish earldoms. Isabella was an intelligent and gracious guardian—she seems to have been very generous in his maintenance—but she was also determined to continue the political agenda of her natal family. She arranged a marriage between young Earl David and one of her nieces, Catherine, daughter of her brother, Henry, and Alice Comyn.[50]

What happened to Isabella and her brother, Henry, in the first years of Edward III's reign demonstrates how thoroughly they had learned the politics of intrigue. Henry Beaumont had become an elder statesman of the Scottish Marches by that time: he was virtually the only one left of the group that had included Aymer de Valence and Henry de Lacy. Thomas of Lancaster was dead and his estates had been absorbed by the royal family. David de Strathbolgi, Isabella's young ward, although he had not yet reached his majority, had entered into his inheritance, had married Isabella's seemingly handpicked bride, and seemed destined to maintain the associations with the Beaumonts and their allies that she had established at the time of her assumption of guardianship. There were no tensions apparent between the Beaumonts and the queen, who acted as unofficial regent for the young king. However, appearances can be deceiving.

Queen Isabella and her lover, Roger de Mortimer, earl of March, are castigated in the chronicles as being little better than exploitative and vengeful jackals: no improvement over their predecessor, Edward II. That their (albeit unofficial) rule was unpopular is evident almost from the beginning of Edward III's reign. The first of the former allies to declare against the dowager queen was none other than Henry Beaumont, who rebelled against Isabella's and Mortimer's rule in 1328 and was outlawed in

1329. Edmund, earl of Kent, even implicated Isabella Beaumont de Vescy herself after the palace coup of 1330, claiming that she and Henry had participated together in an anti-Mortimer conspiracy.[51] Despite this accusation, she suffered no forfeitures or, indeed, any apparent harm at all from this episode. Reading the signs as astutely as always, Isabella fell in with the young king and his adherents and succeeded in transferring her loyalties so completely that there is not even a hint of censure concerning either her or Henry's behavior in the aftermath of the coup. In fact, her brother became one of Edward III's most trusted advisors, especially in the wake of the growing tensions in Scotland that ultimately led to another war, the devastation of the Scots baronage, and the imprisonment of many Scots nobles. Isabella received her usual rewards for good service and good behavior: a grant of land, this time in North Wales.[52] She was to have only a few years left of her long and adventurous life, but she made good use of them. Isabella arranged for her burial in her favorite foundation, the Gilbertine Black Friars at Scarborough, to which she had earlier given one of her urban properties that abutted their chapter house.[53] In 1331, she received a papal indulgence granting that her confessor should give her plenary remission at the hour of her death.[54] In 1332 and 1333, she and Henry leased out some of the manors they had amassed during the reign of Edward II.[55] Although she never regained control of Bamburgh, she was amply compensated until the end of her life.

Isabella Beaumont de Vescy died in 1334. Her life had been played out in the thick of political action; I believe that it can tell us a great deal about the intersection of family associations and political life that characterized the medieval centuries. Isabella could have had an entirely uneventful life. As a foreigner, married for less than a decade and widowed for forty-six years, the circumstances of her career would discourage even the most independent individual: she was virtually alone, often friendless, and almost completely isolated from the familiar connections of parents, siblings, and close kin. It would not have been unusual had she retreated from public life, or even to have returned home—which her cousin, Clemencia, who married her nephew, John de Vescy, seems to have done after his death. Cousin of a queen she might have been, but such associations do not usually imply close emotional ties and often could suggest avenues of royal exploitation that might have rendered Isabella little more than a tool of royal ambition. Isabella, however, neither retreated nor went home. She stepped boldly into the frenetic center of the royal household and never left. While it is clear that Isabella's social and political connections expanded rapidly after the arrival of her brother, Henry, on English soil, he seems initially to have been more dependent on her than vice versa, a scenario that becomes more explicit in 1311, when the Ordainers settled on Isabella rather than Henry as the cousin most closely allied to the throne. She might have been vilified by Thomas of Lancaster and his followers, but that suggests that she had some real power, publicly displayed, and that it threatened them and their ambitions.

One could also speculate that Isabella might have pursued an agenda, especially after the arrival of Henry Beaumont, that involved sacrificing herself for the sake of a more politically ambitious younger brother. The medieval world was hostile to women in positions of overt power. At least in theory, Isabella's progress through her career might have been viewed more positively by people such as Thomas of Lancaster had she been motivated more by a desire to be the "power behind the throne" than to be the person in the center of the arena. In this, too, Isabella broke the mold: not only did she fail to eschew power for herself, she embraced it, sought it, fought to retain it, and used all her considerable gifts to guarantee that she would never lose it. After the exile of 1311, Isabella's methods became subtler; the rewards she gained, however, while less overtly political than the custody of Bamburgh Castle, might have brought more satisfaction. She was able to amass considerable personal wealth; she guaranteed the financial security of herself and of her brother and his family; she remained at the center of the queen's household; and she never again lost the status she had worked so tirelessly to maintain. Finally, at the end of a life very well lived, she even had the security of knowing that, through the grace of a papal indulgence, she would go to Heaven when she died. The responsibility for the many successes and the few failures of the rest of her life, however, had been hers alone.

CHAPTER 8

MARTYR TO THE CAUSE: THE TRAGIC CAREER OF ALICE DE LACY

Alice de Lacy, *suo jure* countess of Lincoln and Salisbury and dowager countess of Lancaster and Leicester had the kind of extraordinary life of which films starring Mel Gibson are made. Unlike Gibson's portrayal of William Wallace, however, Alice's career can be reconstructed with relative accuracy from an unusually rich collection of sources and chronicle commentary that emphasize her importance in the political schemes that characterized the period between 1300 and 1350. Despite the facts that Alice's life spanned the reigns of three kings, connected her in myriad ways to the royal family and their adventures, and located her at or near the center of the major political events of the time, however, historical eyes have consistently overlooked her or, even worse, dismissed her as irrelevant, except as a conduit through which wealth, land, and power passed from her parents to two generations of other men.[1]

In order to address all of these issues, this case study will not only focus on the documentary evidence of Alice's activities, but will also assess depictions of her in roughly contemporary (fourteenth- and early fifteenth-century) chronicles, both anonymous and authored. Finally, I will discuss Alice's career in the contexts of the changing nature of the political community and definitions of political action that typify the reigns of Henry III to that of Edward III; that is, from 1216 to 1377.

Act One

Alice de Lacy was born on December 25, 1281, the daughter of Henry de Lacy, earl of Lincoln and constable of Chester, and his first wife, Margaret Longespee, *suo jure* countess of Salisbury. Alice's family history abounds in images of powerful, intelligent, and successful women who, despite the strictures against female activity in the public world, spent much of their adult lives as independent and active widows. Henry, Alice's father, was actually raised in a female-centered household. After his father's death, his mother, Alice (daughter of Manfredo, marquis of Saluzzo), and grandmother, Margaret de Quency, *suo jure* countess of Lincoln and dowager countess of Pembroke, gained custody of both his lands and his person. His marriage might have been arranged by his grandmother, who also gave him an allowance of £300 a year to help defray his expenses: his mother, Alice, was paying a substantial sum to the exchequer every year for the guardianship of Henry's person and the wardship of his lands. Henry's mother never remarried after the death of Edmund de Lacy, his father. She lived as a widow for some fifty-three years, dying the same year as her son and apparently bequeathing a legacy of longevity to her granddaughter.[2]

Alice's maternal female kin were just as formidable as those on her father's side. Ela Longespee, *suo jure* countess of Salisbury and the founder of Lacock Abbey (Alice's great-great grandmother), had been appointed sheriff of Salisbury for a number of years. She also undertook the patronage of Salisbury's new cathedral and ensured that her husband, William Longespee, one of Henry II's illegitimate sons, would be entombed splendidly within it.

A spirit of conjugal partnership seems to have been characteristic of Lacy family alliances. Margaret de Quency's marriage to John de Lacy was a well-planned arrangement that seems to have worked effectively, not only in linking illustrious lineages (the earls of Chester and Winchester to the constables of Chester and lords of Pontefract), but also in establishing the family's position at the royal court and guaranteeing its continued success. The marriage of their son, Edmund, to Alice of Saluzzo was abbreviated, but could have been a significant boon to the family fortunes had Edmund lived longer. The marital arrangements of Edmund and Alice's two children, Henry and Margaret, were equally significant. Henry's marriage to Margaret Longespee linked two of the most important nonroyal earldoms in the kingdom, while Margaret's marriage to George de Cantelou (a distant cousin) would have resulted in her achieving the position of countess of Pembroke, if they had had surviving children: George's nephew, Henry de Hastings, inherited both his estates and those of his uncle, Aymer de Valence. The family's agenda thus suggests a deliberate policy by which they solidified their current position, but also made concerted efforts to advance both socially and politically. On the whole, these efforts were successful. At the time of Alice's betrothal to Thomas, nephew of King Edward I and earl of Lancaster and Leicester,[3] in 1292, this arrangement must have seemed ideal for advancing the family's fortunes. No doubt Henry and Margaret would have planned equally brilliant marriages for their sons, Edmund and John, had they not died before 1292.[4]

Alice thus was destined to follow in the footsteps of her illustrious female ancestors, at least with respect to her first marriage. Henry and Margaret's sons were both dead, making Alice likely to be their sole heir (Margaret was still alive at the time of Alice's betrothal; Henry's remarriage to Joan Martin would produce no children). The betrothal between the eleven-year-old Alice and the fourteen-year-old Thomas represented the pinnacle of the family's social ambitions. Their marriage took place two years later, in 1294.

Henry made sure that the royal family would be happy with the arrangement: he guaranteed that the earldom of Lincoln would pass into the Plantagenet family should Alice die without heirs of her body. Henry released the bulk of his inheritance to the king, who regranted it to Alice and Thomas and their heirs, with the remainder to Thomas's right heirs, rather than those of Alice. The king also released Henry's estate back to him for the term of his life.[5] Alice received lands from her mother's estates as her *maritagium* (of which she was, in any case, the direct heir), thereby guaranteeing that, should she have children, the vast majority of the family property amassed over four generations would pass to the house of Lancaster—which would be blended with the house of Lacy.

King Edward I would have found such a series of arrangements particularly pleasing, especially because they benefited his nephew without undue strain on his own treasury. Nevertheless, Henry's maneuvering succeeded in disinheriting not only his own immediate family—if Margaret, his sister, had had children they would have suffered from the situation—but also his collateral relations. Ironically, if Henry had not granted his own earldom to Thomas of Lancaster through his wife, the ultimate heir to the earldom of Lincoln would have been the three sisters of Earl Gilbert de Clare, who were well acquainted with Alice during the reign of Edward II.[6]

Henry's and Margaret's arrangement for their daughter was a brilliant move, which should have had equally brilliant consequences. Unfortunately, Alice and Thomas apparently hated each other. There is little material evidence about Alice's personality, especially at thirteen; Thomas's reputation is described as heroic, even saintly, in the chronicles that were critical of the reign of Edward II.[7] He has been characterized more recently by historians such as Michael Prestwich as ambitious without being diplomatic, cunning but unintelligent, vainglorious but lazy—in short, everything one would never wish for in a son-in-law.[8] Even if he were as splendid as the chronicles make him out to be, such a paragon would have been hard to live with; contemporary sources, such as chancery documents, seem actually to depict an ambitious and acquisitive person, rather than a saint. The arrangements made to turn over Alice's inheritance to Thomas and the house of Lancaster suggest that the financial incentives were an overwhelmingly significant factor in the marriage. Even though one could argue that this was the case with most marriages among the medieval elite, the events following the marriage, especially after the death of Earl Henry de Lacy, suggest strongly that this marriage did not work, and probably never had.

In contrast, Alice had significant examples of marital success and individual excellence among her own relatives—both male and female—to measure against her own husband. Henry, her father, is notable in having the kind of reputation to which few noblemen could aspire: chronicles, chancery sources, and modern-day historians agree on Henry's *gravitas* and reputation. He was considered both wise and politic; sagacious and shrewd; and he was numbered among King Edward I's greatest friends.[9] Henry's criticism of King Edward II might have spurred the activities of his son-in-law,[10] but his magisterial presence might also have served as the brake on Thomas's ambitions, as Henry's protection of Isabella Beaumont de Vescy (discussed in chapter 7) suggests. More importantly, as long as Henry lived, Alice's marital situation could be moderated: Thomas could neither abuse her nor repudiate her with impunity. But Henry could not live forever.

In 1311, in the midst of the first major crisis of the disastrous reign of Edward II, Earl Henry de Lacy died. The escheator almost immediately delivered his vast estates to Thomas, who performed homage for Alice's inheritance. Joan, Henry's second wife, also received her dower with unusual rapidity.[11] Thomas and his adherents soon began escalating their attacks on royal authority, especially in Wales and the Marches. Thomas worked strenuously to consolidate his position between 1313 and 1316: he was able to procure amnesty for the depredations committed by his adherents in Wales; he and Alice received both royal and tenants' grants and privileges; his influence at court was at its peak.[12] He was also incredibly extravagant. The only extant account roll of the Lancaster household is for this period; according to the keeper of the accounts, Thomas—the wealthiest man in England besides the king—was spending about twenty percent more each year than he was receiving in revenue. By this time, he and Alice were also maintaining entirely separate households. The same account roll sums up Alice's expenditure for the year at around £425—about six percent of what Thomas was spending.[13]

Edward II and his supporters apparently decided to undermine Thomas's authority by attacking him where he was most vulnerable, that is, his relationship with his wife. Alice, in 1316, was living at the manor of Canford, Dorset, a hunting lodge she had inherited from her mother, and she was evidently insufficiently protected. According to the most commonly cited chronicle source, Sir Richard de St. Martin, a knight in the household of John de Warenne, earl of Surrey—one of the principle supporters of King Edward II—abducted Alice from Canford and took her to the Warenne stronghold of Castle Reigate.

Intermezzo: Alice, the Chronicles, and the Historians

The chancery rolls are absolutely silent about the actual abduction, but the chronicles are full of information, gossip, and conjecture about this episode. They also vary widely in their assessment of this episode. Most are more or less neutral in their inclusion of the abduction, although almost all blame the Earl Warenne for the attack. A typical entry for the year 1317 includes a terse statement such as, "In this year the earl Warenne abducted (or raped—the Latin word *rapta* means both) the wife of the earl of Lancaster."[14] Thomas de Burton, abbot of the monastery of Melsa and author of the chronicle for the years around 1317, includes the statement that Earl Warenne's abduction of Alice was not because of adultery, but in order to discredit the earl of Lancaster.[15] The *gesta* of Edward of Caernarvon written by a canon of Bridlington, who does not mention Alice by name, but who does identify her as the daughter of Henry de Lacy, earl of Lincoln, suggests that Alice was, in fact, a voluntary contributor to her own abduction, although the language used does not necessarily condemn her for her actions:

> In that same year the wife of Thomas of Lancaster, namely the daughter of Henry de Lacy earl of Lincoln, left the household and power of her husband and the earl de Warenne took her into his custody [or, under his protection].[16]

Some chronicles, however, are detailed in their description of events, and many of these are vicious in their condemnation of Alice's actions.

Thomas of Walsingham's chronicle (one of the St. Alban's chronicles that continued Matthew Paris's history) is the most complete version of the events and the one that the majority of historians have used as their source. Walsingham, however, is not exactly an objective observer: he was a hack for Henry IV, who needed an historical apologist to disarm the critics who claimed that he had usurped the throne and murdered the rightful king, Richard II.[17] Henry IV, before he was king, was known as Henry of Bolingbroke—duke of Lancaster. According to Walsingham, the idea for the abduction was actually developed by the king himself in order to discredit Thomas.

> In this same year, on the Monday before the feast of the Ascension, the Countess of Lincoln, legitimate wife of the nobleman Lord Thomas, earl of Lancaster, was abducted by a certain knight of the household and affinity of John, Earl Warenne, at Canford, Dorset; as it is said, the organization of these detestable events occurred with the assent of the king of all the English. She was carried away, moreover, in contempt of the earl of Lancaster, by the instructions of Earl Warenne to his castle of Reigate. And while the lady was

being taken thus, Lo! while on the path between a hedge and a grove of trees, between Alton and Farnham, the abductors saw in the distance [what they took to be] standards and a troop of soldiers; it was, in fact, a group of holy men who approached with their folk, who were in the habit of making processions around the field. The abductors of the countess, suddenly struck with fear and dismay, supposing that the earl of Lancaster or someone else had sent the troops, decided to save themselves from the consequences of the abduction of the lady and fled with all speed, leaving her behind; but the truth was revealed when the procession and its attendants moved away in the other direction [and the abductors returned to Alice].

With this group had come a certain person of short stature [or lowly estate], lame and hunchbacked, Richard, called "of St. Martin," who always endeavoring evildoing and fixing upon a great benefit for himself, demanded—for shame!—the abovementioned mocked and wretched woman in marriage, fortifying his demand by means of the claim that he had known her carnally before she was betrothed to the earl; that furthermore the lady remembered him clearly and recognized him in front of everyone, and furthermore, she confessed it to be true—she was not abducted in fear. Thus, she who during the whole of her life had been considered the noblest of noble ladies, suddenly by a turn of the wheel of fortune, by this shame is acclaimed by the whole world to be the foulest whore.

Accordingly, Richard, raising himself above his station, presumed in the king's court to lay claim to the earldoms of Lincoln and Salisbury in the name of his wife; but in vain, as the information following will make clear. The scandal came to the ears of the Supreme Pontiff; the pope chose two cardinals for the purpose of making peace between the King and the Barons, and especially Earl Thomas, in order to solidify his position. [Translation is mine][18]

Walsingham's version is the one used by G. E. Cockayne in his *Complete Peerage*; it therefore has become the account most commonly appropriated by historians of the last century—those who bother to mention the incident at all.

The Malmesbury author of the *Vita Edwardi Secundi* describes an extraordinary confrontation between King Edward II and Earl Thomas, which he claims occurred when Edward chastised Thomas for failing to appear when summoned to court. Thomas's reply (i.e., his reply as constructed by the author of the *vita*) hardly exonerates the king:

> If it pleases the Lord, if the earl of Lancaster does not come to Parliament it is not to cause offense or to demonstrate a lack of esteem [toward the king]. He is incensed, in fact, by the abundant treasonous crimes [perhaps, criminals] that the royal court is harboring and nurturing. The enmity of the court is now clearly evident; now they disgracefully and scandalously kidnapped the wife of the earl, by which act the love that she bore him is now certainly

driven away. The earl therefore pleads that you hasten to expel the malefactors from your friendship, and then he will come to you anywhere you wish to choose. He pleads, moreover, that he be able, without your condemnation, to possess vengeance for the dirty injury done to him, and to obtain whatever satisfaction he may.

The king's reply in this *vita* reinforces the author's contention that Edward was to blame for the episode: "I will avenge the contempt of the earl when I am able; I do not wish to expel my familiars; concerning the rape of his wife, he can merely plead the remedy of the lawcourt" (translation is mine).[19]

The author of the Westminster chronicle known as the *Flores Historiarum*, who consistently refers to Alice as "Avelina," is one of the most libelous accounts of the abduction. It also became immortalized by May McKisack in the Oxford History of England series.[20]

At this time, when God decided to visit vexations on everyone, the violent boiling anger of the king overflowed because of the wisdom and integrity of the lord earl of Lancaster, his cousin, and convening a malicious assembly, they all together cooked up a deceitful plot against the earl. In one of the meetings the evil council directed the Earl Warenne, one of the worst sycophants, to take to himself a band of strong soldiers for pursuing and swiftly bringing about the unhappy end desired.

When they drew near to the lands of the earl of Lancaster, a huge fear and trembling suddenly invaded their hearts, so that as they ventured into those parts, looking around fearfully, they could scarcely go any further. But returning to their madness, they attacked speedily the place where they were going to fashion the dishonor of the countess of Lancaster. And they captured her, whose whole heart's desire was bent favorably to their will, and they hastened with her, celebrating, to the castle of Reigate. In this way, the countess, besmirching the nobility and honor of her family, clinging to the lame knight, transformed her name from countess to ignoble adulteress. [Translation is mine][21]

There are a number of items in these accounts that are sufficiently bizarre as to call them entirely into question—and by extension to reject the claim to their veracity made by historians who have appropriated them.

There is a certain ring of truth to the exchange between Thomas and the king in the *Vita Edwardi Secundi*: in Thomas's outrage, in his attempt to garner sympathy for the abduction, as it were, of his wife's love (for which, it must be mentioned, he does not blame her at all), and in Edward's careless reply. The sheer volume of detail in the *Flores Historiarum* and Thomas of Walsingham's *Historia Anglicana*, however, while entertaining, scarcely reassure the historian as to their accuracy. They are discussed one at a time.

The author of the *Flores* purports to be an enthusiastic supporter of both Henry de Lacy and Thomas of Lancaster, to the extent of describing Henry's funeral and burial.[22] He also mentions an episode many years before, when Henry de Lacy and John de Warenne engaged in a lengthy, public, and violent dispute over some plot of land: a contest that Henry won when a jury empanelled by commissioners of oyer and terminer awarded him the lawful tenure.[23] On the other hand, the author of the chronicle clearly cannot identify the "lame knight" and he fails even to provide Alice with a *correct name*—calling her in other contexts, Avelina, daughter of Earl Henry de Lacy.[24] The remainder of the account, while entertaining, is nonetheless conventional in its claim of Alice's (or, rather, Avelina's) decline into ignominy.

Walsingham's account is a wonderfully cinematic tragicomedy: the malevolent, limping, hunchbacked Richard de St. Martin, who brings to mind Tudor depictions of King Richard III; the ludicrous terror-driven flight away from the innocent religious procession; and the even more ridiculous mental picture of Alice left abandoned by the hedgerow and the sheepish return of her abductors. This wealth of detail makes his story even less credible, however. Walsingham, writing nearly one hundred years after the events he describes, is the only one who names and describes Richard de St. Martin[25] and is certainly the only one to describe the silly episode on the path between Alton and Farnham. Moreover, he is the only chronicler to include the story of Richard's pre-betrothal seduction of Alice and his claim, thereby, to her inheritance. This apparent motive for the abduction, however, simply makes no real historical sense. Alice was eleven when she was betrothed to Thomas. It is highly unlikely that any unknown knight, let alone one of the household of John de Warenne, would have had the opportunity to meet her, convince her to marry him, have sexual relations with her, and then be abandoned by her for the material joys of marriage to Thomas of Lancaster. Finally, if these events had indeed occurred as Walsingham outlines, the evidence of them would appear somewhere: in a Parliamentary petition, a papal letter, a chancery writ, litigation in the courts, or a commission of oyer and terminer. Nothing, however, appears. There is no evidence.

This leads to an important question: why were these chronicles so determined to associate Alice with John de Warenne and his abduction, and to blame the king for the plan and Alice for its success? There is ample reinforcement of the claim that Alice was abducted by John de Warenne, either directly or through the mechanism of his men-at-arms: this we can safely take as fact. It is also easy to connect the war that ensued between Thomas and John after 1316 to have been motivated by the abduction.

Unfortunately, *before* 1316, there are two almost insurmountable problems for the chronicler intent on fleshing out a very thin story: first, there was no obvious enmity between Thomas of Lancaster and John de Warenne and, second, *Thomas apparently never demanded Alice's return.* Whatever happened between 1316 and Thomas's death in 1322, Alice was not an overt participant in it. The fifteenth-century chroniclers, especially, must have felt compelled to blame Alice for her abduction because they could find no other reason for its occurrence, other than the obvious enmity of the king, and they could not find an excuse for Thomas's effective abandonment of his wife, except for a putative act of adultery.

In order to reconstruct a reasonably accurate narrative of these events, it is necessary, unfortunately, to remove all the entertaining additions that make the later accounts so memorable. This leaves us with the following: sometime in the spring of 1316, Alice was living at the lodge of Canford, Dorset, from which she was abducted by John de Warenne, earl of Surrey—probably by a chosen band of his *familiares*—and taken to Castle Reigate. This abduction was probably organized by John and King Edward II in order to discredit Thomas of Lancaster. Alice, who was not living with Thomas, anyway, and who had been separated from him for some time, was apparently a passive participant, neither willing nor unwilling; Thomas was more interested in using the abduction as an excuse to wage war on John than in facilitating the return of his wife.

It is easy to understand why Edward II would connive at such a deed, but where does John de Warenne fit into this scheme? Only one possible reason for this episode to have occurred comes to light: Thomas's own possible involvement against John de Warenne between 1314 and 1316, when John was trying to obtain a divorce from his wife, Joan of Bar, in order to marry his mistress, Maud de Neirford, and legitimate their children. King Edward II had already given his blessing to the divorce and had agreed to the transfer of part of John's estates to his Neirford sons, even though Joan of Bar was his niece.[26] Edward and John had gained the support of William Greenfield, archbishop of York, as their advocate in the papal court. Nevertheless, Thomas's control of the chancery as the principle Ordainer might have been instrumental in "discovering" the extant papal dispensation of Clement V to John and Joan's marriage, which made a divorce nearly impossible.[27] John de Warenne, seeing his hopes for a divorce dashed, might simply have wanted revenge on Thomas; the abduction of Alice by John might have been planned as a diabolically appropriate revenge on Thomas for interfering with John's marital affairs. Such a scenario might even legitimize part of Walsingham's tale: what fitter vengeance could John have invented for Thomas than to have one of his minions claim to be Alice's lawful husband?

End of Intermezzo: Act Two

Even if the motivations for the abduction are murky—as well as the degree of Alice's involvement or collusion in it—it is clear that the already tense relationship between Earl Thomas and Earl John had deteriorated, by late 1316, into outright war. Thomas invaded John's lands in Yorkshire and Wales, prompting the king to intervene and to use the opportunity to regain control of his kingdom.[28] By 1319, Edward II had reaped enough power from Thomas's clearly obsessed behavior to demand a settlement. John de Warenne agreed to enfeoff Thomas with the reversion of his lands, which he would continue to hold for life.[29] In exchange, Thomas granted John 1000 marks worth of land—taken from Alice's Lacy inheritance—for his life.[30] While the enfeoffment by John of Thomas with his own estates suggests his culpability in the abduction of Alice, Thomas's relinquishing such a large amount of land to John suggests that his political star was beginning to wane.

Thomas spearheaded a rebellion against Edward II, but he was not the leader that his father-in-law had been. The result was disaster: a massacre of the rebels in the Battle of Boroughbridge in 1322 and Thomas's arrest and execution for treason at Alice's family home of Pontefract Castle. In a move both ironic and deliberate, Edward II sent John de Warenne and Robert de Ferrers (another noble with a grudge against the Lancaster family because they held the earldom of Derby, with which he should have been invested) to arrest Thomas and to bring him to Pontefract.[31] Who knows what sorts of humiliations Thomas endured on the trip to his wife's family's most ancient holding?

Edward II moved against his enemies rapidly. The Lancaster and Leicester estates were forfeited to the Crown; although most of these properties demised to Thomas's heir, his brother Henry, many estates of the rebellious baronage were absorbed by the king's favorites: Hugh le Despencer and his son, Hugh, John de Warenne, Richard fitzAlan, earl of Arundel, and Robert de Ferrers were the most visible of this group. Alice, herself, was arrested and imprisoned in March 1322, along with her stepmother, Joan, whose second husband, Nicholas de Audeley, had just died. She was not released until she had agreed to pay a staggering indemnity of £20,000 to the Crown, a move that effectively disinherited her from the bulk of both parents' estates. Only then was she permitted to make fine to marry whomever she wished (or not to remarry at all) and was granted those lands that remained from her inheritance.[32]

Alice must have been convinced that she would soon follow Thomas to the executioner's block. In July, at the time when most of the property alienations were being organized, she received royal permission to alienate the manor of Swaveton, Lincolnshire, in mortmain to Barlings Abbey.[33] The deed for the grant specifies its use to provision thirteen paupers, to pay for Alice's and her father's obsequies, and to pay for a mass every year on the anniversary of her death.[34] Fortunately for Alice, the king seems to have been interested in her wealth more than her life, and he satisfied his interests by extortion rather than execution. The monastery at Barlings would have to wait some twenty-six years for their acquisition of Swaveton.

This extortion perpetrated by the king involved forcing Alice to release the honors that predated the Lacy family's acquisition of the earldom of Lincoln (the honors of Builth, Bolingbroke, and Pontefract[35]). The honors were released to Hugh le Despencer (now titled earl of Winchester) and to Hugh the younger (alleged to be the king's lover).[36] In return, she was permitted to hold some of the estates in life tenure by the king's "special grace."[37]

These arrangements were scarcely completed before Alice was faced with another threat: the king instructed the royal officials in Lincolnshire "to be attendant upon and aiding Alice...with the *posse* of the county if necessary, the king having heard that certain men with armed force are marching to where she is staying awaiting an opportunity to abduct her."[38]

What men were these? No further mentions of this alleged plot appear, so it is not clear whether the vigilance of the county constabulary thwarted the would-be abductors or whether the king applied such a rationale as a means of preventing Alice from being able to *leave* the county. The latter reasoning might be more likely than the former. Thomas's actual base of power lay in Wales and the Marches. Alice seems to have been more or less under house arrest at this time, probably on one of her smaller manors in Lincolnshire.[39] Events of the following year suggest that the Marches were rising against Edward II and his favorites as early as the autumn of 1322; moreover, Alice's remarriage in 1324 to a Welsh-marcher baronial supporter of her late husband indicates that she, too, felt the center of power to be in Wales and among the marcher baronage. Alice was, however, confined to a county on the opposite side of England, a virtual prisoner at the pleasure of the sheriff and his "posse." It seems likely that the armed men galloping to Lincolnshire might have been interested in rescuing her, might even have included her future husband, Sir Ebulo Lestrange. What better method could Edward II employ in order to keep her under the watchful eye of his sheriff than to claim it was for her own protection? Moreover, the earlier abduction provided a perfect excuse for the king's concern at this time.

The king and his supporters cemented their power during the next year. Alice was again compelled to dispose of more of her inheritance, this time many of the estates that had comprised the comital inheritance of her mother. John de Warenne received a life grant of many of Alice's manors in the West.⁴⁰ Hugh le Despencer the younger acquired one of her Lincolnshire manors.⁴¹

Although Alice's life seems to have been relatively quiet during the spring and summer months, the autumn brought new stresses. The antiroyal movement coalescing around Roger de Mortimer of Wigmore was gaining strength and again Alice was to feel constrained because of it. In October, Edward II demanded that the clerk serving as the keeper of Pontefract scour the castle to identify and secure the strongbox containing the muniments of the Lacy family.⁴² A few weeks later, Alice, under the titles countess of Lincoln and "lady of Clifford," was singled out among all the landholders in Wales and the Marches in a royal mandate forbidding anyone from aiding Mortimer and commanding them to pursue him and his adherents "with hue and cry."⁴³ A month later, Alice's unlicensed mortmain grant to the chapel of St. Peter, Kyrkeby upon Wrethk, was discovered and she had to secure a pardon for the chapel.⁴⁴ On a more positive note, the king conceded Alice's right, as *suo jure* countess of Lincoln, to the "third penny" of the county, although he standardized it to a rent of £20 per year to be drawn from the profits of the county court. Unfortunately, the sheriffs were reluctant at best to relinquish that sum and Alice had to petition for the arrears owed to her at least once a year.⁴⁵

The uncertainties of the two years following Thomas's execution must have contributed to Alice's decision to marry again, but it was probably only a contributing factor: Alice seems to have married for love the second time around. Sir Ebulo Lestrange, brother of Roger Lestrange, lord of Knockyn, had been mentioned as one of Thomas's adherents in the Marches in 1314; he and Alice must have become acquainted before the debacle of her abduction by John de Warenne. He might even have been connected to her own household, although no documents survive that attest to this. Nevertheless, all evidence points to a loving, happy union between devoted spouses. In many deeds Alice is described as Ebulo's "dear and loving companion," even though he apparently eschewed the title of earl to which he was entitled, *jure uxoris*.

Most of the documents of Alice's private administration date from this marriage. All of the estates that Alice had relinquished before it had to be confirmed, lest Ebulo make a claim on them by right of his wife. A plethora of these "quitclaims" were generated between 1324 and 1325, all in the form of final concords. The purpose of these documents is clear: by requiring all of the releases to be in the form of chyrographs, the king and the Despencers (who received the largest number of these concords) guaranteed that Alice could never claim entry into the property on the grounds that she could not "gainsay" her husband. The fiction of choice is reinforced by a stunningly cynical maneuver by King Edward II: he "pardoned" the Despencers for having acquired Alice's inheritance by chyrograph "without royal licence," thus suggesting that the transfers of property were made without his connivance and with Alice's willing agreement.[46] As a reward for their cooperation, the king also confirmed the life grants made to Alice and discharged Alice and Ebulo from responsibility for Thomas's debts.[47]

The king had another method of ensuring Alice's cooperation. In January 1326, he appointed Ebulo as a supervisor of the array in Lincolnshire, charged with encouraging the levying of troops and punishing defaulters.[48] As this levy was being arrayed in order to quell the uprising against the king—and Ebulo had been a member of the anti-royal faction ten years before—this appointment was probably part of a strategy described by the advice "keep your friends close but your enemies closer." Neither this approach nor any other availed Edward II, however. The invasion of Queen Isabella and Roger de Mortimer, who had control of the young Prince of Wales, ended his reign and his life. The two Despencers were also summarily tried and executed; Hugh the younger's son, Hugh, was imprisoned. Alice and Ebulo should have been convinced that their difficulties were over, but in fact it was only after the overthrow of Mortimer and his lover, Queen Isabella, in 1330, that they benefited significantly from the destruction of the Despencers and their power.

Roger de Mortimer of Wigmore was in many ways little better than Hugh le Despencer, especially with respect to his tendency to prey upon those who were powerless to resist him. Roger had quickly taken over the honors of Oswestry and Clun, which belonged to Edmund Fitz Alan, earl of Arundel, whose lands were forfeited because of his support of the late king. In a sleight of hand that would have done his enemies, the Despencers, proud, Roger "agreed" to surrender these honors if he could instead gain control of Alice's honor of Denbigh and the three Welsh cantreds that formed a significant portion of her inheritance in Wales. These had been among the lands gained by the Despencers; they were destined to go to the reconstituted earldom of Salisbury that Edward III gave to William de Montacute. In a letter to the Parliament, Edward stated his willingness to pay 1000 marks per year to William de Montacute, while Roger agreed that reversion of the estates should be held by William should Roger die without heirs of his body.[49] Alice and her husband, Ebulo, however, were conspicuous by their absence in the documents discussing the transfer: it appears that they never officially warranted the grant of the estates to Roger, which made the whole process illegal.[50] This would rebound to their advantage in 1332, when they made a chyrograph with William de Montacute releasing Denbigh and the cantreds to him for £200.[51]

Even if Roger de Mortimer coveted Alice's land in Wales, he seems to have left the couple alone elsewhere in the country. This is particularly evident in Lincolnshire. When John Talbot, Alice's "dear esquire," to whom she had entrusted the constableship of Lincoln Castle around 1324,[52] died in 1327, she and Ebulo were not prevented from taking control of the bailey themselves. The sheriffs of the county, however, continued to fail to pay them the issues arising from the third penny and, in fact, the mayor of Lincoln apparently opposed their control of the constableship, bailey, and the law court attached to them.[53]

Alice and Ebulo were even rewarded for their patience in 1328: a grant of 500 marks worth of land that had been granted to them for Alice's life was extended in chancery through Ebulo's life as well, should he outlive her.[54] Queen Isabella seems to have been an important patron, as well; she oversaw an exchange of land they made in 1329 with Ralph Basset of Drayton.[55]

Other than these transactions, Alice and Ebulo appear to have been keeping well away from public view in the years between Edward II's death in 1327 and the removal of the queen mother and her lover, the earl of March, in 1330. This appearance of distance, however, might well be deceiving, because Ebulo was evidently involved in the young king's plot to overthrow his mother and her lover. Certainly, he became one of Edward III's most trusted officials after the coup and the distinctions began as soon as he took control. Ebulo was one of the men ordered to bring Queen Isabella from Berkhamstede to Windsor for Christmas in 1330.[56] A vacated entry in the Charter Rolls of 1331 concerning confirmation of the transfer of Denbigh from Alice and Ebulo to William de Montacute connects the transfer with Edward III's desire to reward William, to whom he had revealed "his secret design touching the arrest of Roger de Mortimer."[57] At the same time, the king granted a portion of the honors of Bolingbroke and Pontefract to Alice and Ebulo more permanently than by the life tenure that Alice had been forced to accept after Thomas's death.[58] Later that year, Ebulo was appointed to be a mainpernor for Geoffrey de Mortimer's good behavior and was charged with guaranteeing his appearance before the king.[59] He also received orders that same year, as mainpernor of Hugh le Despencer III, to deliver Hugh from prison to Bristol Castle.[60] Such responsibilities demonstrate not only the young king's confidence in and reliance on Ebulo, but also his growing respect for Alice's husband's abilities and loyalty. These must have been heady days for both of them, especially since Ebulo had been destined for a life of obscurity before marrying Alice. More responsibilities were heaped on Ebulo between 1331 and 1335, but they were largely focused on Lincolnshire as the center of his activities. He was appointed as keeper of the peace, chief commissioner of oyer and terminer, and justice of gaol delivery in 1332, retaining these positions more or less continuously until his death, except for a couple of months in 1333, when he was overseas on royal business. Upon his return, Ebulo also took up the duty of receiver for the collection of the tenth and the fifteenth in Lincolnshire.[61] This focus on Lincolnshire probably had something to do with Alice's preference for the castle of Bolingbroke. Ebulo's duties in the county did not require that he and Alice be separated for long periods of time, as was more typical of noble couples. Thus, the king seems to have been unusually sensitive to the closeness of their relationship, a possibility reinforced amply in the years that followed.

Ebulo was not merely the recipient of royal patronage in exchange for extensive labor, however. He and Alice were recipients of significant honors from the Crown. Alice, apparently permitted to act as a *feme sole* in this transaction (for which she also received Ebulo's assent), was able to lease some land to Roger Lestrange, Ebulo's brother, whose son, Edmund, would eventually be Ebulo's heir.[62] The two of them used the benevolence of the monarch to reorganize their property holdings, for example quit-claiming lands to Geoffrey le Scrope.[63] The most significant benefits from Ebulo's tireless service, however, were the return of the castle and honor of Builth, Wales, and Bustlesham, Berkshire, in double life tenure: they would not pass out of their control until both of them had died, "in consideration of [Ebulo's] charges, risks, and labours in the king's service."[64] Perhaps most importantly, Edward III pardoned Ebulo of the charges laid against him by the previous king, on account of the service he had rendered in the Scottish war.[65]

By the end of 1334, Alice and Ebulo had succeeded in regaining a significant portion of her estates, albeit almost entirely in life tenure. Bolingbroke and much of Pontefract were in their hands; Builth and a large number of smaller holdings in Wales and the western and midland counties were also theirs. The price had been high—the bulk of the earldoms of Lincoln and Salisbury—but the estates they did control were prosperous, well-placed, and represented some of the earliest Lacy family holdings. The king was also generous with small rewards of wardships, pardons for amercements, and ready assistance in the adjudication of disputes with tenants.[66] Neither Alice nor Ebulo were young any longer—both were in their mid-fifties—but their ages and their childlessness were not impediments to a future that must have looked comfortable, secure, and happy. Thus, Ebulo's death in the late summer or early fall of 1335 must have been devastating for Alice, not only for the loss of security that it ensured, but also because of the genuine devotion they both enjoyed. Alice was one of the executors of his will, along with the abbots of Barling and Revesby and their trusted clerk, Henry de Halton (he was their official at Builth

Castle).⁶⁷ She also arranged for Ebulo's burial at her favorite monastic foundation of Barling, where she, too, was to be interred. King Edward III quickly ordered the escheators to surrender Alice's own lands and her jointure from Ebulo's estates into her hands.⁶⁸ Finally, Alice deliberately took a vow of chastity before the bishop of Lincoln, thus indicating both her devotion to Ebulo's memory and her fears for her own safety.⁶⁹

These fears were justified. In February or early March, 1336, a royal official, Sir Hugh de Frene—who must have known Alice and Ebulo because of his appointment as steward of Cardigan Castle⁷⁰—entered her castle at Bolingbroke (he evidently bribed the servants) and seized her in the hall. Alice tried to fight off this abduction, even going so far as deliberately to fall off the horse that Hugh and his grooms had forced her to mount. She was put back on the horse, with guards surrounding her; they rode to Somerton Castle and, there, Hugh raped her.⁷¹

Michael Prestwich, with a callousness only too typical in political historians' discussions of women adds:

> Since she was by then in her mid-fifties, it is likely that Hugh was attracted more by her vast estates than by her physical charms. As frequently happened in medieval cases of rape, the couple soon married; it is possible that she was not a wholly unwilling victim. With few exceptions, marriage for the medieval aristocracy was a matter of business and politics. Alice de Lacy was fortunate to have loved one of her three husbands...⁷²

I beg to differ. Although Common Law considered rape to be a felony punishable by castration, it was rarely prosecuted as such. Instead, rape cases were usually adjudicated under Canon Law, which virtually required that a rapist, if unmarried, marry his victim, if unmarried: this was considered his punishment. Alice's vow of chastity did not benefit her; indeed, there is a suggestion in a papal letter that she was taken to task for "allowing" herself to be raped—certainly an unfortunate instance of "blaming the victim." Finally, business arrangements they might have been, but medieval marriages were supposed to be based on mutual respect, not mutual antipathy. This episode, after the happy years with Ebulo, could have shattered Alice, were she not so resilient.

After this episode, nevertheless, Alice was compelled to marry again. King Edward III's response to this turn of events was also interesting. As soon as news of Alice's abduction occurred, the king ordered her lands taken into royal hands and kept "safely until further orders." He did not release them until after the marriage had taken place, perhaps waiting until he could both confirm that Alice was still alive and secure her safety by sending Sir Hugh immediately to Scotland to join the royal forces there.⁷³

Fortunately for Alice, Sir Hugh died the following year, in February, 1337. Alice immediately renewed her vow of chastity (the bishop of Lincoln was commanded to compel her to renew the vow, as she had been unable to keep it earlier), and, for what remained of her life, settled into her estates, usually living at Bolingbroke.[74] During her uninterrupted widowhood, she called herself either "countess of Lincoln" or "widow of Ebulo Lestrange" (or both), but never countess of Lancaster or widow of Hugh de Frene. It was as if those portions of her past were deliberately excised from her recorded memory.

Alice's final years as a widow was not uneventful, however, although she might have wished it so. Hugh de Frene was scarcely cold in his grave when, sometime in April or early May, Ebulo's brother, Roger Lestrange of Knockyn—accompanied by the abbot of Roucestre and thirty men-at-arms—invaded Bolingbroke, imprisoned her there, stole twenty of her horses, and assaulted the residents.[75] This unprovoked attack by someone to whom Alice had shown a more than gracious generosity must have been, emotionally, one of the lowest points in her life; the reason for it becomes clear when, in June, the king granted Roger license to enfeoff Nicholas de Cantelou with the remainder to the lands that Alice and Ebulo had held jointly, and of which Roger was the putative heir. Roger must have decided that threatening Alice would ensure his perpetual tenure in the land, despite Ebulo's death. It is perhaps the final irony that the jointure in question was, in fact, property that she had originally inherited from her parents, including Clifford, Herefordshire, and Halton, Lincolnshire; thus, Roger's claim to the property was solely by reason of Ebulo's marriage to Alice.[76] Roger's determination to establish his claim, by any means necessary, to anything that Alice still held in fee (rather than by life tenure) is amply demonstrated by their ongoing interactions over the next few years. Roger established his legitimacy by requiring Alice's approval of a mortmain grant of some of her property to the convent of Burnham and by associating himself with a number of suits in which Alice was involved.[77]

Alice was not bereft of defenders and supporters, however; neither was she without resources of her own. She and Edward III seem to have been in regular contact, since she appears in chancery roll entries as having "spoken to" (that is, written to) the king herself. These sorts of interactions involved both defending Edward's interests in her lands—such as in two *novel disseisin* cases that she feared would prejudice the Crown were she to be found guilty—and defending her own interests—as in the situation in which the king demised the reversion of Alice's Welsh lands to Thomas de Bradeston, an act that threatened to de-legitimize her tenure.[78]

King Edward III was also a little more deliberate about compelling the sheriffs of Lincoln to pay Alice the arrears for the third penny every year.[79]

Further, the several commissions of oyer and terminer that Alice requested be sent in the last ten years of her life seem to have been appointed promptly and their investigations pursued thoroughly.[80]

Alice had other defenders and supporters besides the king. Henry, earl of Lancaster (Thomas's brother), appears as a petitioner in a request for a commission of oyer and terminer just a few months before her death.[81] Although his motives were by no means altruistic—the trespasses occurred in Kingston Lacy, Dorset, which he was due to inherit after her death, and involved the wholesale destruction of her park and the poaching of her game—Henry's assumption of responsibility can be seen as a mark of respect for the woman wronged so shamefully by his family.

Despite the poaching on her property, which is understandable in this period of recurring famine, livestock murrains, and climatic disaster, Alice's relations with her subordinates seem to have been profoundly sympathetic in both directions. This reflects the relationship that she and Ebulo had apparently established with tenants, dependents, and estate officials: they participated in generous transfers of property and reciprocal financial arrangements.[82] Alice rewarded her loyal esquires soon after Hugh de Frene's death, endowing John de Wormeleye with a pension of 20s a year and William de Castre with a croft and forty acres of land.[83] She also assisted the prior of Spalding in establishing the priory's immunity from payment of royal taxes and the common summons on the basis that it was founded by and remained in the gift of the Lacy family as lords of Bolingbroke.[84]

The appearance of sympathy on Alice's part seems to have been reciprocated by her tenants and dependents. First of all, an unusual number of women seem to have been named Alice in Lincolnshire and Yorkshire, an encomium not only to her but to her grandmother, Alice of Saluzzo.[85] Other marks of gratitude and appreciation were more obvious. Edmund de Aete quitclaimed his right to sue Alice—and also quitclaimed this right for his executors and heirs—from "the beginning of the world" (i.e. from the time of his birth) to the time he made his feasance to her.[86] Robert de Silkeston the younger, Alan de Kirkeby (Alice's chaplain), and the prior of Malton all received royal licenses to alienate lands in mortmain in part to pray for the souls of Henry de Lacy, Margaret Longespee, and their daughter, Alice.[87]

Thus, although there were anxious months immediately following Hugh de Frene's death (in large part because of the covetousness of Roger Lestrange), Alice spent her last ten years in pursuits more typically within the provenance of noble widows: protecting land, rewarding loyal followers, and trying to maintain a life of quiet retirement.

Alice died in 1348, at the age of 67 and in the midst of the worst outbreak of the Black Death in England. Although there is no way to determine the cause of her death, plague is not unlikely. She was buried in Barlings Abbey, the monastery that received most of her pious attention, next to her second husband, Ebulo Lestrange. Her inquisition post mortem illustrates how little of the massive inheritance she had received from her parents she managed to retain (although extensive in comparison to other widows' estates, it represents only a fraction of her Common Law inheritance): only the lands that had been settled on her at her marriage to Thomas of Lancaster, a small dower from Thomas's estate, and the jointure she shared with Ebulo Lestrange (which, in fact, she had already released to his heir, Roger Lestrange, lord of Knockyn). Her life had been long, eventful, and ultimately tragic. But why could she be considered a Martyr, and to what "Cause"?

The famous historian K. B. McFarlane once asked the question "Had Edward I a 'Policy' Towards the Earls?"[88] which has raged as a subject of controversy ever since. Another question worth pursuing is, "Had the Earls a Policy Towards Edward I?" The second half of the thirteenth century witnessed a number of significant marriage alliances between the royal family and some of the most powerful nonroyal earldoms. Alice's marriage and the settlement arranged by her father, Henry, share some similarities with the arrangement made at the marriage of Gilbert de Clare, earl of Gloucester and Hertford, to Edward I's daughter, Joan of Acre (Gilbert's inheritance was returned to the crown and regranted to Gilbert and Joan jointly). These marriages, which combined important noble families and the royal family, had political implications beyond Edward's supposed desire to limit and control the highest levels of the baronage. Alice's marriage was designed to place her close to the pinnacle of marital achievement: in 1292, Thomas of Lancaster was third in line to the throne, after his cousin Edward and his father, Edmund (Thomas of Brotherton and Edmund, earl of Kent, had not yet been born). It was not beyond the realm of possibility that he would find himself much closer than that. As young as Alice was, she must have known why she was destined to marry Thomas of Lancaster, despite the fact that her father had to have been aware that Thomas suffered from a surfeit of all of the bad traits of the Plantagenets— from an inability to control his temper to an arrogant sense of entitlement. Thus, she was made a martyr to the family cause of upward mobility.

A second issue is the rather significant difference between Alice's career and those of other women in her family, especially her paternal grandmother Alice, great-grandmother Margaret, and her maternal ancestor, Ela of Salisbury. The period between 1215 and 1307 seems to have been one of burgeoning opportunity for independent action among English noblewomen, especially those who were widowed at fairly young ages. Women such as Ela and Margaret were able to retain both huge inheritances and huge dowers without strenuous interference; they also seem to have enjoyed quite active widowhoods. This does not seem to have been possible for Alice. It is possible that the particular characters of the reigns of Henry III and Edward I (a rather benign torpor on the one hand, and a keen and, usually, protective oversight on the other) have more to do with this situation than perhaps the specific legal changes that historians usually refer to as significant. Despite the existence of Magna Carta and the statutes of Westminster, Edward II was able to extort, threaten, and terrorize widows and heiresses with seeming impunity—just as his great-grandfather, John, did. In fact, arguments made by rebellious subjects against Edward II parallel closely those made by rebellious subjects of John. Although the situation was moderated during the reign of Edward III, the protections against rape embodied in Westminster II do not seem to have helped Alice in her abduction and rape by Hugh de Frene. Thus, Alice became a martyr not only to the cause of her family's social and political mobility, but also to the troubles of Edward II's reign and their resolution in the reign of his son. In fact, Alice could almost be used as an example of the political impact of female inheritance in the fourteenth century: rather than enjoying the protected status of widowhood, Alice had to relinquish her estates and her independence in order to survive.

While her father lived, Alice seems to have tried to maintain her role in family responsibilities. After he died, however, she apparently found the situation unbearable: the activities of the year 1316—or what we can know of them—have a pronounced flavor of desperation. Alice's choice of Ebulo Lestrange as her second husband, moreover, suggests that she wanted no more part in the family's ultimate plans. Of course, by that time, she had placed herself beyond the pale: a reluctant martyr apparently stripped of her respectability as a result of the political machinations of a husband she detested, a father she respected, and two kings she could not afford to trust. The succeeding events of her life must only have reinforced this sense of reverse entitlement. Instead of being protected by Crown and Church, Alice's reputation made her vulnerable to further abuse and exploitation. Only at the end of her life, with her family's ambitions in ruins, was she able to achieve some measure of peace.

CHAPTER 9

THE RISE AND DECLINE OF THE MEDIEVAL ENGLISH NOBLE WIDOW?

Noblewomen in medieval political and social culture during the 150 years between 1200 and the Black Death were remarkably forthright, effective, and flexible actors within a culture that placed them in a rigid ideological category but nonetheless provided significant practical outlets for female power to be exercised: the seven case studies attest to the abilities of such women to manipulate and navigate this labyrinthine relationship between ideology and practice. Although a very small and specialized sample, the experiences of the women who figure in this study can suggest a number of conclusions as to the impact of changes in the law, the influence of specific monarchs, and ideologies of gender on the ability of women to achieve their ambitions. While it is not possible to know definitively how effective women actually were—or to identify definitively their motives for action—it is possible to suggest the ways in which all three issues—law, politics, and gender—served to define the parameters of female activity and thus their public careers.

Political historians tend to use royal reigns as boundaries. It is easy to look at the political life of a region and see its dynamism and proclivities for change. It is also easy to see—at least in hindsight—where it all goes wrong. Legal historians, on the other hand, are more interested in looking at long-term trends in which reigns matter little. Kings are among those responsible for change and growth in legal institutions and theory, but the legal system seems to take on a life of its own and a rhythm that is not dependent on the personality of a particular monarch. Social historians often reject both the reign-driven structure of the political historian and the idea-driven structure of the legal historian. They see society as developing outside the realm of the political, which has an impact but is not the engine. The legal intersects frequently, in the sense that the law court is one of the most visible places where social interactions occur and the tools of the law courts—the charters, deeds, plea rolls, writs, summonses, and so on—provide the fodder for many social historians' work. Nevertheless, the social historian considers the activities of individuals and groups to be what drive culture to develop, not the particular ideology of an elite class of intellectuals.

It is obvious that all three systems—the political, the legal, and the social—affected women's lives significantly in medieval England. The difficulty comes in teasing out the relationship between the three, in order to determine what issues might have driven women to make the choices they did. It is clear to me that women of the nobility (and probably women further down the social ladder as well) were well aware of the advantages and limitations of their legal status and did everything in their power to make use of those advantages and to stretch those limiting boundaries to their fullest extent. There were times in the thirteenth and fourteenth centuries when women could engage in activity that might have been unthinkable to the legal theorist. The jurist Henry de Bracton, for example, would scarcely have countenanced the idea of women legally engaging in the activities that war, rebellion, and necessity foisted upon Maud de Mortimer of Wigmore. The inflation in the number of widows after the Black Death prompted Rowena Archer to comment on the abundance of "rich old ladies"; their dominance in certain comital families might well have encouraged legal innovations late in the century that limited the amount of land a widow could retain.[1]

What is not clear is the degree to which changes in the law actually benefited or disadvantaged women further. The few references to claims deriving from Magna Carta in the plea rolls, for example, suggest that some women—or their lawyers—were aware that the legal definition of reasonable dower had changed in the 1225 version of the Charter and they were determined to take advantage of it. After the promulgation of Edward I's *De Donis* statute in 1290, medieval English noble people quickly saw the advantages of granting land in fee tail, especially to younger sons, in order to guarantee that, should a cadet branch fail, the main branch of the family would regain control of the property. This suggests, simply, that the laws overseeing the distribution of the *maritagium* had been transferred into a system of tenure that could be used to endow younger sons—as the *maritagium* endowed daughters—but would nevertheless maintain the stability of the family holding. It is not clear whether the intention of the original *De Donis* statute included a limiting of female access to family property, but it came to be interpreted in a way that made this happen.[2] After the Black Death, the number of grants in "tail-maile" began to exceed that of grants in gender-neutral fee tail that served simply to secure a limited tenurial relationship between the donor and the donee.

Nevertheless, medieval women tended to push the limits of whatever system they experienced: in legal terms, they adapted to changing circumstances rapidly and quickly identified the "gray areas" into which they could intrude. Thus, it could be said that, although they were all too aware of the restrictions placed on them by the legal system, noblewomen, in particular, managed to reap the maximum benefits from the law at any given time by means of their determination, perseverance, and stubborn refusal to give in. For example, the tenor of women's behavior in the law courts of the later fourteenth century did not undergo a significant change despite the increasing use of grants in tail-male. If women had more limited access to family land, they nevertheless were careful to preserve and maintain the property to which they were entitled. The long-term effects of statutory innovations, however, might have contributed to the worsening of women's economic independence in the following centuries.

Political events also had an impact on the ability of medieval women to function effectively both within the milieu of their families and as independent actors. Kings of the thirteenth and fourteenth centuries had radically different styles of ruling. The legal system might have been developing rationally into the sophisticated and organized complex of Common Law, Parliament, and other institutions and innovations designed to defend the interests of free English people from undue interference by the king or each other, but the differences in royal careers owes more to personality than to an ideology of kingship imperfectly realized. Five reigns occupied the period between 1200 and 1350. It is instructive to point out the contrasts in personal rule, especially those that might have had the greatest impact on medieval noblewomen.

The rapaciousness of King John is legendary: it is revealed in the payment of huge reliefs and double reliefs heirs had to suffer; the extortion of similar payments from widows before they could receive their dowers; the forced marriages of widows and heiresses; the manipulation of wardships in the king's gift. All of these examples of John's deficiencies as a ruler were highlighted in the Great Charter of 1215. They comprise some of the most important clauses of the charter and they had some of the most long-lasting effects.

Henry III's personality, on the other hand, was characterized by his contemporaries as being deficient in determination: he was seen as "weak" or "ineffectual." His preference for the relatives of his wife and mother, his uncertain temper, his effete religiosity, his petulance, his ineffective political and military leadership, his financial extravagance: all seem to have contributed significantly to the crises of the thirteenth century. Not even his father had suffered so many baronial rebellions. Nevertheless, Henry's longevity might have been beneficial. Not only was the kingdom saved from another protracted minority, but Henry's successor was an experienced and mature man who had worked hard to develop a positive relationship with his barons well before attaining the throne. Moreover, Henry's focus on projects such as the rebuilding of Westminster Abbey church meant that the quotidian business of the realm was often overseen by administrators more competent than he.

Edward I is usually characterized as embodying all of the beneficial attributes of the previous two monarchs and few of their deficiencies. The "Justinian of the North" shared his grandfather's penchant for rationalizing and systematizing the institutions of law founded in the twelfth century; he advocated and oversaw changes in the process of law, including the professionalization of the overseers of litigation. Like his father, he was a devoted husband but a rigid parent; unlike Henry, he was devout but not extravagant, a superb military strategist, and an active participant in the everyday doings of the royal court. If Edward's animus against the Celtic portions of the British Isles led him to respond vengefully to their continuous efforts to establish their independence, his apparent success in Wales and Ireland and temporary success in Scotland serve to heighten the differences between himself and his immediate predecessor and successor.

The contrast between the successes of Edward I's reign and the disasters of that of his son, Edward II, could not be more marked, especially in the realm of politics and law. Unlike his father, Edward II seems to have embodied many of the worst traits of the Plantagenets with few of their moderating attributes. His twenty-year reign was marked by the return of three of the four horsemen of the apocalypse—war, famine, and death (plague would come later)—but Edward seems to have done little to ameliorate the problems and crises that arose.[3] Apparently less interested in statutory innovation than any of his predecessors, Edward II nonetheless used the legal system to his own advantage and to the advantage of his court favorites.

The violent overthrow of Edward II and the succession of Edward III was problematized by the mayhem of the regime change itself: the unofficial regency of Queen Isabella and Earl Roger de Mortimer was perceived as little better than the reign of the king they deposed. Nevertheless, Edward III was able to establish his authority before the kingdom was plunged entirely into disarray. His personal charisma has informed much of historical opinion, but Edward's political and legal innovations—the expansion of Parliament's role, the establishment of Justices of the Peace, the improved relations with the baronage, the dramatic increase in the professionalism of the royal courts of law—all served to reinvigorate the monarchy and to provide it with a new legitimacy. Nevertheless, Edward III was not a monarch in the mold of Edward I: the latter's innovations were directed toward a standardization of practice and greater and more transparent access to justice. By the time Edward III succeeded to the throne, the patronage-based system that characterized his father's reign might have become so deeply ingrained that the personal motives of the ruler comprised a more significant component of the political system than it had during the previous century. Hence the establishment of specific venues for royal patronage, such as the Knights of the Garter, was apparently designed to institutionalize such patronage. A perhaps unlooked-for effect was the reduction of female access to the king and his royal generosity.

These brief portraits are, admittedly, designed to highlight the differences between the Plantagenet monarchs, but the characterizations are not thereby groundless. They are also designed to highlight two issues that could form the grounding of a debate about the relative advantages and disadvantages that women experienced during the reigns of specific monarchs—the independence of the legal system, on the one hand, and the effects of royal patronage or enmity and their reputations on the other. Historians of women typically assumed—like other colleagues in nonpolitical history—that legal innovations had effects that were consistent over time; that the benevolence or tyranny of a particular monarch might have very little effect on the longer-term development of social systems and conceptions of gender, race, and class that ultimately had a greater impact on people's lives; and that the topos of the Good versus the Bad monarch is not all that useful when looking at the ways in which women experienced their lives, families, and society. I suggest that the two issues might be more interconnected than has been assumed.

For example, women during Henry III's reign—and not just those who occupied the rarified air of the magnate class—seem to have benefited from the expansion of the central law courts and the relative ease with which they could gain their dowers, pay relief for the lands they inherited, and achieve control over their own marriage, in spite of Henry's apparent fecklessness about other matters. Women could acquire guardianship of their children, although they paid a premium for it. They were also more visible in the queen's entourage and in the larger world. Eleanor de Montfort's unceasing travel from manor to manor during the rebellion of her husband, as outlined in Margaret Wade Labarge's book,[4] was not unique; what is unique is the survival of her accounts for that year. There is evidence to suggest that women other than Eleanor de Montfort and Maud de Mortimer of Wigmore also engaged in quite extensive activity on behalf of their husbands during the war—Joan de Valence, for example, who becomes the object of Matthew Paris's wrath because she outwitted Simon de Montfort and managed to smuggle money out of the country to assist her husband, William.[5]

In some ways, Edward I's 1290 *De Donis* statute, which established the principle of land held in fee tail, could be seen as an attack on female control of land. Nevertheless, he also codified a more generous definition of what constituted "reasonable" dower by enrolling the 1225 definition in the 1297 Statues of the Realm and developed the process by which property could be held "jointly" by the wife and the husband. Moreover, Edward I seemed determined to use anyone available—man, woman, or child—if they proved their effectiveness and loyalty. He was unafraid to reward women for the work they did; he was unafraid to rely on women in situations that were not typically within the female sphere. He was also unafraid to punish women who supported or participated in political and military campaigns against him, as Cynthia Neville has pointed out.[6]

Did women, however, experience these reigns differently? Political historians, if they consider the issue of female status at all, would probably reply in the affirmative to this question; other historians might be more equivocal. I believe that there were enough similarities between the agenda of Henry and that of his son, Edward, to suggest that women who lived during both reigns might well have experienced one as an extension of the other, albeit with greater responsibilities in the latter reign than the former. The opportunities for amassing power in both reigns were remarkably similar, despite the radical differences in styles of rule. If I were to base my conclusions on these two reigns alone, I might conclude that the legal and sociocultural systems were, by the end of the thirteenth century, independent enough of the monarch to diminish radically the king's influence on the day-to-day lives of his noble subjects. In theory, Edward's legal innovations should have reinforced this impression and should have guaranteed that, with the exception of disasters such as plague, famine, war, and death, women's careers in the first half of the fourteenth century would continue to develop as they did in the thirteenth—toward greater autonomy, a larger role within the family, and a more important role to play in the public world.

The reigns of Edward II and Edward III, however, do not bear this out. In fact, it could be said about the former that his reign was an unmitigated disaster for most women. Edward II's reign is an excellent illustration of how precarious women's status and safety were, even when they were protected by wealth and by powerful families. Alice de Lacy was not the only prominent noblewoman to be abducted, manipulated, and exploited by Edward II and his *familiares*. It might be true that Edward exploited anyone he could, but women seem to have been among his favorite targets—unless they were related to his mother, such as Isabella Beaumont de Vescy and Maud de Mortimer of Richard's Castle. If she were a cousin, Edward could prove to be remarkably benevolent, protective, and forgiving: one possible reason for the Ordainers' hostility toward Isabella Beaumont could have been Edward's generosity toward his female relations in contrast to his rapacious acquisitiveness directed against other vulnerable noblewomen. The legal system, although on paper seemingly identical to that which Edward I bequeathed to his son, broke down from above to such an extent that markedly fewer pleas were introduced into the royal courts by the end of his reign than had existed in the beginning (although the number of suits is still huge). The social fabric of the realm also seems to have become frayed during this reign, although the alliances that developed within and among noble families resembled strongly those that had developed during the Barons' War of the mid-thirteenth century. Unlike the rebellions during Henry's reign, however, women in Edward II's reign did not benefit from their participation in these rebellions. They found themselves imprisoned (like Alice de Lacy and Margaret de Mortimer, mother of Earl Roger de Mortimer), stripped of their possessions, abducted, and forcibly married.

While the relative status of women during the reign of Edward II seems to demonstrate that "bad" rulers were usually bad to women, too (as in the juxtaposition of John and his treatment of widows and heiresses), the association breaks down during the reign of Edward III. For, indeed, Edward III was not much better with respect to women and their status than his father had been. Edward III's restructuring of the itinerant court system, with the inclusion of the peace justices, tended to localize political power more thoroughly into the hands of specific male-headed families who developed extensive affinities, primarily made up of single men who wore livery and dedicated themselves to the maintenance of their lord—the origins of so-called bastard feudalism. The expansion of grants in fee tail and tail-male—which barred women from the line of inheritance entirely—disadvantaged women, a situation exacerbated by the evident panic over the profusion of dowagers after 1350. The gradual deflation of the *maritagium* from a grant of land as well as moveables to one that was entirely cash-based provided young wives with no security at all, since their husbands controlled all of their moveable property. The establishment of the Order of the Garter, which was supposed to signal a return to chivalric sensibilities, identified and promoted a male-dominated network that removed women from the inner sanctum of royal contact. Edward's beneficence toward certain women, moreover, was just as idiosyncratic as his father's and his hostility just as dire. He might have had more of a conscience than his father, demonstrated by his protection of Alice de Lacy and his desire to return to her a part of what had been stolen from her. This conscience, however, did not deter him from assuming control over most of Alice's inheritance and giving it to one of his favorite courtiers, William de Montacute. It also did not deter him from imprisoning numerous Scots wives, mothers, and widows of "rebels" in the party of Robert Bruce—something that Edward I did, as well.

Women during the reign of Edward III might have found themselves less overtly threatened, but they also found themselves less empowered. The apocalyptic visitations of plague, famine, war, and death on the fourteenth century were disastrous for everyone, but in the end, the result included an equally drastic limitation of women's independence and a reduction of their already somewhat ambiguous status.

What to make of this complicated situation? The analysis suggests that the historical characterization of some kings as "Good" and others as "Bad" might not be an effective evaluative tool with respect to the treatment of women. What it does highlight, however, is the likelihood that the king did matter. Individual monarchs could have a tremendous impact on the lives of women during their reign. This impact, obviously, grows stronger the closer to the throne the woman is, but it is possible to extend the analogy over a broader field: it is likely that kings acted as exemplars; therefore, a particular monarch's treatment of women could have had "trickle-down" effects through the imitation of royal policy by the baronage. If a king, such as Henry III, showed marked patronage of women, especially widows, then it is possible that his behavior was mirrored—or deliberately contradicted—by the behavior of other men in positions of authority. The opposite could also occur: Edward II's depredations against vulnerable portions of the population were clearly emulated by his courtiers. It is therefore possible to view the informal, unsystematic influence of kings on their subjects as having an impact on the ways in which these subjects interacted. Women's status and their ability to achieve their goals could be altered by such influence.

In order to highlight this suggestion, I would like to return to Alice de Lacy, who died in 1348, and to her great-grandmother, Margaret de Quency, who died in 1266. Both women were *suo jure* countesses of Lincoln; both were married more than once; both lived through the most terrifying years of their respective eras; both had protective and dedicated parents; both lived for many years. Despite these similarities, Alice and Margaret had radically different careers. Why?

It is not enough to speculate that Alice's personality or agenda might not have been as aggressive or focused as Margaret's. For one thing, there is no evidence to support this speculation. Their legal situations were remarkably similar, as heiresses to earldoms whose marriages conveyed the estates to another lineage. The one significant difference—Margaret's first husband was not beheaded and his lands forfeited—certainly did have a positive impact on her life, but the precariousness of Alice's situation preceded her husband's death. On the other hand, the behavior of Henry III and that of Edward II toward these women did alter, radically, their autonomy, their effectiveness as landholders, their position in the family, and their position with respect to the larger world. Despite Henry's usual characterization as an ineffectual ruler, he was "good" to women, even those women who were not members of his family. Edward II's "badness" was more or less comprehensive. Therefore, the positive opportunities for independence and autonomy offered to Alice might have been far more limited in scope than those offered to her great-grandmother Margaret.

It is possible that the fourteenth century witnessed more than the all-too-obvious crises related to weather, agriculture, disease, and war. It also might have witnessed a gradual but deliberate hardening of gender categories that had a deleterious effect on women's access to power. The social structure of high medieval England and the degree to which conventional notions of gender and rank affected women's lives are indisputable factors that must be considered in order to understand the ways in which women operated effectively in the system. Noblewomen were so obviously the beneficiaries of the class structure in comparison to men of lower social status that it can be taken as a given that they enjoyed more (informal) power than did men "below" them. The status of noblewomen in the family could also encourage them to collect power and to disperse patronage from a family-based nexus that had larger effects in the political milieu. Noble widows not only enjoyed this higher status, their legal independence also rendered them formidable adversaries and significant allies within the larger family structure. Moreover, widows who were mothers carried more weight than those who had no children. Looking back at the preceding case studies, it is easy to see the degree to which a mother's influence in the family could affect the political and social lives of its other members: Margaret de Quency (de Lacy la Marshal), countess of Lincoln and Pembroke, Hawise Lestrange (de la Pole), Maud de Ferrers (de Kyme de Vivonia de Rochechouard), and Agnes de Ferrers (de Vescy) all achieved a level of authority within their families that would normally have been held by their husbands—had they survived.

Widowed dowagers of stature, these women in some ways transcended the gendered system that expected their subordination. This phenomenon, however, was not unknown to medieval people. The arbiters of the social structure and those who controlled the cultural architecture of society and gender even had a name for women such as these: they called them *viragos*. This term was loaded with both positive and negative connotations: on the one hand, the characterization of powerful women as having transcended their gender; on the other hand, the characterization of powerful women as having usurped the place of men. Loaded it might be, but the mere fact that the term virago exists at all and was used to describe living women, not just female saints and martyrs and "dangerous" women such as Joan of Arc, suggests that the culture of medieval society was aware of—if not entirely comfortable with—women who simply did not fit the conventionalized mold. Moreover, the description of women as viragos in chronicles, letters, and literary works can be found in every medieval period and in every region of the medieval world; thus the exigencies of political change or legal innovation did not alter significantly medieval conceptions of gender and the understanding of how those conceptions could be transcended by extraordinary people.

The term virago is significant in other ways because it informs the reader of a phenomenon not usually acknowledged in historical circles: for all the discomfort experienced by medieval male authors, they acknowledged that some women, in some ways, were able to "be like"—or, perhaps, even "better than"—men.[7] In ethnomethodological terms, this calls the entire notion of conventional dichotomized gender constructions into question. If medieval authors could posit the existence of viragos, then the activities of women for whom that designation was appropriate might not have "fractured" the reality of medieval culture's notions of gendered behavior.

Indeed, the conflict between cultural norms as to gender and social norms of human action might not be between historians' acknowledging of the reality of gender constructions and the need for historians to acknowledge that some women were capable of wielding power and therefore did so, thereby seemingly transcending those gender norms. The conflict might arise between competing cultural norms within a given society and historical analysis exterior to it. In other words, civilizations might have conflicting conceptions of gender embedded in their cultures; the historian might privilege one conception over another and thereby fail to acknowledge both the validity of the other conception and the prevalence of interior conflict.

The structuring of gender in a given society is one such notion open to inherent contradiction and conflict. Medieval society was peculiarly prone to such contradiction. The religious culture, although dominated by a male intellectual elite that expressed comprehensive suspicion and fear of women nevertheless approved of the canonization of female saints, welcomed lay female patronage, and admitted the possibility of female salvation and transcendence. The lay "feudal" culture, dominated by a male military elite, modeled an idealized society in which only men of proven military skill controlled land, made political decisions, and oversaw the legal and judicial apparatus. Yet this same elite was aware that their model was just that: a model. The legal and judicial systems, the political structure, and the practice of land tenure all allowed for the presence and active participation of women—as partners, as subordinates, and as independent actors.

A classic study of the ethnomethodology of gender suggests strongly that Western conventional modeling of gender as being limited to two might not be shared by other cultures—or perhaps not even shared within a current counterculture of transgendered relationships.[8] The "berdache" in Native American culture, as well as some self-defined alternatively gendered groups in contemporary American culture demonstrate that the limiting of gender categories to two fails to present a realistic picture of the ways in which people tend to categorize gender informally.

I suggest that this might have been the case to some extent in the use of the term virago—especially in its non-pejorative context—and in the status of widows in the thirteenth and early fourteenth century. Although the dualisms of the Old Testament became integrated into Christian conceptions of the world, the presence of the Virgin Mary, female saints, and Apocryphal Old Testament female figures such as Judith in popular imagination posits the possibility of women being capable of transcending their gender. In essence, certain saintly women—and perhaps certain wealthy widows—constituted a third gender, one that was unconsciously addressed in the legislation of the era but that had never been overtly categorized.

On a microcosmic level, this alternative to traditional femaleness could be seen in relationships between husband and wife, mother and son, father and daughter in which the "traditional" gender ideals are not present: relationships where conventional gender-based disabilities are overlooked for pragmatic ends. The wife who takes over military obligations, the mother who raises her male heir, the daughter who is destined to inherit her father's lordship: all were ubiquitous in medieval English society. On the macrocosmic level, such an alternative gender would be almost invisible to modern eyes: embedded in notions of filial piety, family dynamics, and social pragmatism, a third gender category of "virago" would be seen merely as anomalous femaleness. Nevertheless, it is possible that statutory developments from Magna Carta to Edward I's legal innovations might have addressed a popular but little-articulated conviction that women's social status and legal personality were not the only elements to be affected by their marital status: perhaps their very gender was affected as well. Although unarticulated, such a comprehensive re-visioning of femaleness in widowhood could have been a sufficient motive to address it legislatively and statutorily. Moreover, the late fourteenth-century development of intellectual movements such as humanism, the hardening of definitions of appropriate behavior and belief in the religious culture, and the growing influence of classical culture, in addition to a popular perception of the overabundance of empowered virago-dowagers might have reintroduced an emphasis on the essential dualism of the human condition. The rigid distinctions between male and female characterized by tenure in tail-male, for example, might have been influenced in part by a desire to see the reality of property tenure mirror more accurately the cultural ideal of two clearly defined genders. Such a hardening could be seen as accelerating in the fifteenth through the nineteenth centuries, as classical conceptions of political rule based on an enfranchised male citizenry instead of on lineage-based status came to be considered more desirable. The thoroughgoing "domestication" of middle-class women in the nineteenth century and the dichotomy of respectability versus unrespectability being defined increasingly as invisibility versus visibility in the "public" milieu could be the logical end result of such a self-conscious limiting of gender to a dualism.

A tri-fold division of gender into male, female, and virago that might have operated as an unarticulated but nevertheless more accurate description of gendered relations in early Germanic, early medieval, and central medieval Europe could have influenced legal changes that brought economic and social autonomy to greater numbers of women in the thirteenth century. Indeed, the tri-gendered model incorporates the conception of widowhood—with its emphasis on widows' autonomy—that seems to have become dominant by the time of Magna Carta far better than a more conventional dichotomized model can. Did the attempt to rationalize and pragmatize the inherent conflict between bi-gendered and tri-gendered models produce a "fracturing" of medieval "reality"? Was the realization of such trends toward pluralistic gender notions as leading farther away from traditional dualistic models encourage or even mandate the legal changes of the following two centuries, which by limiting female autonomy seem to have sought to bring the legal and economic structure more into line with assumed normative gender notions? Was this an attempt to prevent a further fracture of reality? It seems unlikely that medieval people were more sensitive to inherent cultural contradictions than modern people, but the legal steps taken to limit women's access to property and, hence, to power—which occurred in the fourteenth to the sixteenth centuries, times of significant cultural stress—might have been motivated in part by a desire to bring "reality" more in line with the "ideal." Therefore, if "reality" were fractured by the apparent increase in female activity, the strategy employed to repair the rift was apparently to alter the structure rather than changing the parameters of female-gendered activity.

Where does this leave the women in this study? Putting aside the relative merits of thirteenth- and fourteenth-century monarchs, these case studies demonstrate a resilience that pervades all their activities. All of these women could have been called viragos by medieval chroniclers: certainly, despite limitations placed on them by society, by culture, by law, and by politics, all of the women in these case studies were able to survive, even to thrive. They made the most of the circumstances in which they lived;

if those who lived in the reign of Henry III were somewhat more advantaged than those who endured the reign of Edward II, they did not apparently bewail their fate in public (although they might have done in private) and they did not leave any indications as to why their status had changed. The glimpses of their lives we receive through the sources available to us tantalize, but do not satisfy. Nevertheless, it must be enough: our imaginations must do the rest.

ABBREVIATIONS

SC8/	London. P. R. O. Ancient Petitions.
C 47/	———. Chancery Miscellanea.
C 53/44	———. Charter Rolls.
DL 25/	———. Duchy of Lancaster Ancient Deeds.
DL 36/	———. Duchy of Lancaster Cartae Miscellania.
DL 34/	———. Duchy of Lancaster Coucher Books.
DL 27/	———. Duchy of Lancaster Deeds.
DL/7; DL/ 41; DL 42; PRO 3/	———. Duchy of Lancaster Miscellanea
DL 10/	———. Duchy of Lancaster Royal Charters.
CP 25/1/	———. Final Concords *Pedes Finium*.
CP 40/	———. Rolls of the Court of Common Pleas.
E 13/	———. Rolls of the Court of Exchequer of Pleas.
E/ 159	———. Rolls of the King's Remembrancer, Memoranda.
JUST 1/	———. Rolls of the Justices Itinerant.
KB 26/	———. Rolls of the King's Bench Henry III.
KB 27/	———. Rolls of the King's Bench, Edward I–.
BL	British Library
Bracton	*Bracton on the Laws and Customs of England*. 4 vols. Ed. George E. Woodbine. Trans. Samuel E. Thorne. Cambridge, MA: The Belknap Press, 1968–77.
Brut	*Brut y Tywysogyon*. Ed. Thomas Jones. Cardiff: University of Wales Press, 1952.
Ancient Correspondence Concerning Wales	*Calendar of Ancient Correspondence Concerning Wales*. Ed. J. Goronwy Edwards. Cardiff, 1935.
Ancient Petitions Concerning Wales	*Calendar of Ancient Petitions Relating to Wales*. Ed. William Rees. Cardiff, 1975.
CChR	*Calendar of Charter Rolls*. 6 vols. London, 1903–27.
ClR/CClR	*Close Rolls/Calendar of Close Rolls*. Henry III–Edward III. 32 vols. London, 1900–38.
CDI	*Calendar of Documents Relating to Ireland*. Ed. H. S. Sweetman and Gustavius Frederick Handcock. 5 vols. London, 1875–86.

ABBREVIATIONS

CFR	*Calendar of Fine Rolls.* Edward I–Edward II. 3 vols. London, 1911–12.
CIPM	*Calendar of Inquisitions Post Mortem.* Henry III–Edward III. 14 vols. London, 1904–54.
CLR	*Calendar of Liberate Rolls.* Henry III, 1216–72. 6 vols. London, 1916–75.
Papal Letters	*Calendar of Papal Registers: Papal Letters.* 2 vols. London, 1893–95.
CPR	*Calendar of Patent Rolls.* Henry III–Edward III. 31 vols. London: 1891–1916.
GEC	G. E. Cockayne, *The Complete Peerage*, 2nd ed. 13 vols. London, 1910–40.
Excerpta è Rotulis Finium	*Excerpta è Rotulis Finium in Turri Londonensi Asservatis, Henrico Tertio Rege,* A.D. *1216–1272.* 2 vols. London: Record Commission, 1835–36.
Testa de Nevill	*Liber Feodorum. The Book of Fees Commonly Called Testa de Nevill.* 2 vols. London, 1920–23.
Monasticon	*Monasticon Anglicanum.* Ed. Sir William Dugdale. New ed., ed. John Caley, Henry Ellis, and Rev. Bulkeley Bandinel. 6 vols. London, 1817–30.
Matthew Paris 1	Paris, Matthew. *English History.* 3 vols. Trans. J. A. Giles. London: Henry G. Bohn, 1852. Reprint, AMS Press.
Matthew Paris 2	*Chronica majora*, ed. Henry R. Luard. 7 vols, Rolls Series. London, 1872–83.
RP	*Rotuli Parliamentorum; ut et Petitiones, et Placita in Parliamento.* Vol. 1. London: Record Commission, 1783.
Letters of Henry III	*Royal and Other Historical Letters Illustrative of the Reign of Henry III.* 2 vols. Ed. Walter Waddington Shirley. Rolls Series 27, 1862–66.

NOTES

Chapter 1 Introduction

1. Ethnomethodology has been developing as a theoretical method for nearly forty years. See, e.g., Harold Garfinkle, *Studies in Ethnomethodology* (NY: Prentice-Hall, 1967; reprt. Cambridge: Polity Press, 1984); H. Mehan and H. Wood, *The Reality of Ethnomethodology* (NY: Wiley-Interscience, 1975); and Suzanne J. Kessler and Wendy McKenna, *Gender: An Ethnomethodological Approach* (Chicago: University of Chicago Press, 1978).
2. *Gendering the Crusades*, ed. Susan B. Edgington and Sarah Lambert (NY: Columbia University Press, 2002).
3. All of which had to be housed somewhere: in the end they tended to be amassed in the Tower of London in a room called, appropriately, the "Rolls" Room. There was also an extensive archive at Westminster Palace. The royal treasury, the exchequer, and the county sheriffs also had to maintain archives.
4. Bracton 2: 178. The ability to alienate even unharvested crops developed from the statute of Merton, ch. 2.
5. *Maritagium* is the term used in English Common Law for the property the bride brings into the marriage, since the Latin word *dos* was used to refer to dower. *Maritagia* could take the form of land, moveable property, cash, or a combination of all three. It rarely equaled the property the widow could claim in dower from her late husband's estate, but the widow's "ownership" of the property was more secure and complete.
6. Germanic law usually stipulated that widows lost guardianship and dower rights if they remarried.
7. For a discussion of this, see S. F. C. Milsom, "Inheritance by Women in the Twelfth and Early Thirteenth Centuries," in *Studies in the History of Common Law* (London: Hambledon Press, 1985), 231–60. See, esp., 241–44. There is evidence that, although partible inheritance was always practiced in post-Conquest England, when females inherited initially the eldest female (sister, daughter, or cousin) was the main feofee with her younger sisters as subordinate tenants. This situation, called *parage*, had disappeared by the reign of King John.

8. See, e.g., Emma Mason, "*Maritagium* and the Changing Law," *Bulletin of the Institute of Historical Research* (1976): 286–89.
9. See T. F. T. Plucknett, *The Legislation of Edward I* (Oxford: Clarendon Press, 1962), 131–33.
10. The definition of what comprised one-third changed over the thirteenth century from that portion of the husband's lands he held on the day they were married to one-third of the lands the husband held at any time during the marriage. This was because of modifications made in successive redactions of Magna Carta; by 1225 the new definition was in place.
11. Bracton 2: 178–79. For scholarly discussions of wills, see Michael M. Sheehan, *The Will in Medieval England* (Toronto: Pontifical Institute of Medieval Studies, 1963), esp. 234–39; and Courtney Stanhope Kenny, *The History of the Law of England as to the Effects of Marriage on Property and on the Wife's Legal Capacity* (London: Reeves and Turner, 1879), 143.
12. Bracton 2: 180.
13. I have made use of—and comment on—the work of K. B. MacFarlane (*The Estates of the Higher Nobility in Medieval England*), Chris Given-Wilson (*The Nobility of Later Medieval England*), Anthony Woolgar (*The Great Household in Late Medieval England*), and many others who focus on the relationships between noble society, land, and family continuity. Please refer to bibliography.
14. Exemplified by the work of Natalie Zemon Davis (*The Return of Martin Guerre*) and Carlo Ginzburg (*The Cheese and the Worms*), both of whom derived their methodologies from Mikhail Bakhtin.

Chapter 2 Agnes and Her Sisters: Squabbling and Cooperation in the Extended Medieval Family

Earlier versions of this chapter were presented at the International Congress of Medieval Studies, Western Michigan University, at Trinity College, Washington, DC, and portions also appear in Linda E. Mitchell, "The Lady is a Lord: Noble Widows and Land in Thirteenth-Century Britain," *Historical Reflections/Réflexions Historiques* 18 (1992): 71–97.

1. Such as Michael Altschul's history of the Clare earls of Gloucester and Hertford, David Crouch's study of the Beaumont twins in the twelfth and early thirteenth century, and Mark Hagger's recent book on the Verdun family.
2. The sheer number of works critical of Ariés's thesis obviates their inclusion here, but exemplary texts include the collection, *Medieval Mothering*, ed. Bonnie Wheeler and John Carmi Parsons (NY: St. Martin's Press, 1996); Joel Rosenthal, *Patriarchy and Families of Privilege in Fifteenth-Century England* (Philadelphia: University of Pennsylvania Press, 1991); Barbara A. Hanawalt, *The Ties that Bound* (Oxford: Oxford University Press, 1986), and *Growing Up in Medieval London* (Oxford: Oxford University Press, 1993); and many others.

3. According to GEC 4: 197.
4. Isabella de Clare was *suo juris* countess of Pembroke and lady of Leinster and Striguil, being the only heir of Richard de Clare, son of Gilbert Strongbow. William le Marshal received the marriage of Isabella as his "reward" for the long years of service to the Crown he had performed.
5. It also forged another connection between the earldom of Pembroke and that of Chester, as William Ferrers's mother was the sister and coheir of Earl Ranulph de Blundeville.
6. According to Matthew Paris, Gilbert died in 1241 when he fell and hit his head after his horse tripped over a fallen tree. Isabel's young son also died that same year, "to the grief and dismay of his whole family." Matthew Paris 1: 323. Gilbert is also mentioned in a number of historical works, among them, R. F. Walker, "The Supporters of Richard Marshal, Earl of Pembroke, in the Rebellion of 1233–34," *Welsh History Review* 17.1 (1994): 41–65.
7. The Vescys and Kymes, as affines of the Lacys of Pontefract, were connected to the Marshals through all of their associations with Ranulph de Blundeville, earl of Chester, and would be connected more thoroughly in succeeding generations through both marriage and blood relations. The Bohuns were marriage partners of the Marshals and their other associates, including the Braose lords of Gower.
8. *CIPM*, Henry III: 1: 141 and *CChR* 1: 252–53. Interestingly, when Isabel remarried, her *maritagium* to Reginald de Mohun included lands in Wiltshire that William le Marshal had granted to his own daughter, Sibyl, as her *maritagium* at the time of her marriage to William de Ferrers. *Testa de Nevill* part II: 727, 758. The term *maritagium* refers to the Common Law version of dowry: the gift of the parents or relatives of the bride to her at the time of her "free marriage." It was often in the form of a combination of land and movable wealth, although women of lower social status usually had to content themselves with only cash. Inheritance of *maritagia* by the bride's family-by-marriage usually depended on her having surviving children: although she controlled her *maritagia* in her widowhood, a childless widow's marriage gift would devolve to her natal family should she die without progeny.
9. John de Bohun more or less took himself out of the family arrangements before 1276 by selling his share to the other Ferrers coheirs. He does so, unfortunately, without royal license. *CFR 1272–1307*: 65.
10. Incredibly, this was even the case with the marriage of William Ferrers's son, Robert, who married one of the Lusignan nieces of King Henry III—which also connected him to one of the other Marshal heiresses, Joan de Valence—and, second, a daughter of Humphrey and Eleanor de Bohun—yet another Marshal heiress.
11. Eleanor Ferrers eloped with her first husband, William de Vaux, while she was still in wardship to the king. William died in 1252, whereupon she immediately married Roger de Quency, earl of Winchester, without first securing royal license. Earl Roger died in 1264; Eleanor waited three years and gained royal permission before marrying Roger de Leyburn, who died in 1271. Eleanor herself died in 1274.

12. Maud's first husband, Simon de Kyme, died in 1248. She received permission that same year to marry William "le Forz," son of Hugh de Vivonia and Mabel Malet (*CPR 1247–1258*: 23). William died in 1259; Maud married Emery, viscount of Rouchechoard, who died ca. 1284. Maud lived another fifteen years after Emery's death.
13. Eudo la Zouche paid the king to marry Agatha in 1253, but he then sold it to Hugh de Mortimer of Chelmarsh in 1255. Agatha was staying with Agnes at the time: the queen and Richard, earl of Cornwall, had committed her to Agnes's keeping while the king and the court were in Gascony. *Excerpta é Rotuli Finium* 2: 166; *CPR 1247–1258*: 419.
14. Agnes and William de Vescy's eldest son, John, married, first, Agnes of Saluzzo, a cousin of Queen Eleanor of Provence, and, second, Isabella Beaumont, a cousin of Queen Eleanor of Castile. Their grandson by William, their second son, also married a royal cousin.
15. James Conway Davies mentions that the division of the Marshal lands "was a fruitful cause of protracted litigation and of frequent disorders." *The Welsh Assize Roll 1277–1284*: 23.
16. Margaret was the widow of John de Lacy and of Walter le Marshal. More on her in chapter 3.
17. The Ferrers sisters received it back upon Eleanor's death in 1275. *CClR 1272–1279*: 190–91.
18. *CLR* 4: 318, 372–73, 401; 5: 77, 89.
19. E 159/29 m. 1. Other references to the debts abound: *CDI* 2: 103–04, 112, 144, 193; *ClR 1254–1256*: 438–39; *ClR 1268–1272*: 472; *ClR 1272–1279*: 276–77; *Excerpta é Rotuli Finium* 2: 447; E 159/47 m. 8d; E 159/48 mm. 27, 279; E 159/49 mm. 31d, 129; E 159/51 m. 23; E 159/52 m. 12; E 159/55 m. 2d; E 159/56 m. 1.
20. *ClR 1247–1251*: 70–71, 156–57, 294, 366; *ClR 1251–1253*: 88, 89, 264, 350; CP 25/1/283/13 no. 285.
21. The case appears in 1290 (E 13/9 m. 4d) and various entries appear until 1300 (E 13/14 m. 7), at which time the last litigants, Gilbert de Clare and Maud de Kyme, were still litigating over Maud's failure to pay the debt.
22. For example, John of Hamme vs. Marshal heirs, *Civil Pleas of the Wiltshire Eyre, 1249*, ed. M. T. Clanchy (Wiltshire Record Society, 1971), 120; Walter de Baskervill vs. Marshal heirs: KB 26/142 m. 6; William de Ebroycis vs. Marshal heirs: KB 26/159 m. 1.
23. *CDI* 4: 14–18, 29–31, 50–51, 52–57, 67, 70–71. William de Vescy, younger son of Agnes, attacked the monastery, which complicated the issue considerably.
24. KB 27/1 mm. 3d, 19; KB 27/5 m. 16d; KB 27/7 m. 4; KB 27/9 m. 11d; KB 27/11 mm. 3, 26d; KB 27/15 m. 3d. See also, *CClR 1272–1279*: 50.
25. Joan, daughter of Joan Marshal and Warin de Munchesney, inherited one-fifth of the Marshal estates. She married William de Valence, uterine brother of King Henry III, and their son Aymer was named earl of Pembroke after her death.
26. Arrangements for dower reimbursement: *CDI* 2: 1, 5, 15, 21, 22, 29, 98–99, 102; *CPR 1247–1258*: 175. Suits between Agatha Ferrers and William and

NOTES   145

Joan de Valence: *CDI* 2: 184, 190, 194, 196, 211, 220, 221, 242, 244; KB 27/1 m. 24; KB 27/16 m. 11d; KB 27/21 m. 36d; KB 27/26 mm. 4d, 47d; KB 27/39 m. 16; KB 27/43 m. 13d.

27. CP 40/27 m. 60d; JUST 1/763 m. 49d; JUST 1/788 m. 71; KB 27/26 m. 26d; CP 25/1/283/15 no. 450.
28. *CFR 1272–1307*: 65. KB 26/206 m. 24d; KB 26/208A m. 37d.
29. KB 26/160 mm. 21, 34d.
30. KB 26/181 m. 11; *CDI* 2: 94, 133, 137; *ClR 1256–1259*: 331–32; *ClR 1264–1268*: 401–02. See also, Otway-Ruthven, "The Medieval County of Kildare," 189.
31. KB 27/31 m. 20; *CDI* 2: 247.
32. See Otway-Ruthven, *History of Medieval Ireland* (London: Ernest Benn, Ltd., 1968), 209.
33. *CDI* 2: 152–53, 162, 164, 172–73, 183–84, 191–92, 242; *CDI* 4: 227; *CClR 1272–1279*: 48–49; *CClR 1296–1302*: 165, 213; *Calendar of the Justiciary Rolls for Ireland, 23–31 Edward I, 1295–1303* (Dublin, 1905), 143, 282–83; *RP* 1: 171, 182–83; C 47/10/15 no. 10; KB 27/1 mm. 8d, 18; KB 27/3 m. 13d; KB 27/11 m. 7. For commentary on the travails of the Ferrers coheirs, see Otway-Ruthvin, "The Medieval County of Kildare," 195–96; Otway-Ruthvin, *A History of Medieval Ireland*, 218–19; and G. J. Hand, *English Law in Ireland*, 122. On the division of Leinster among the Marshal coheirs, see esp. Orpen, *Normans in Ireland* 3: chs. 25 and 26. Phillips, "Anglo-Norman Nobility," 99, makes particular reference to the Ferrers's partition.
34. *CPR 1266–1272*: 441.
35. Agnes's second son, William, had an illegitimate son, William de Vescy of Kildare, who survived him and, by royal license, succeeded to the Vescy lordship of Alnwick. The lordship ultimately devolved to the Percy family after William of Kildare's infant son died. There are several significant references to this complicated arrangement in the Year Books of Edward II.
36. Mentioned in a charter confirmation. *CChR* 1: 328.
37. It is interesting to note that Peter de Chauvent had been granted the marriage of Joan Ferrers Mohun when her husband, John de Mohun, died in 1256. Joan took matters into her own hands, however, and eloped with Robert Aguillon. This grant must have been compensation for the failure of the earlier grant. *CPR 1247–1258*: 495.
38. *CPR 1258–1266*: 36; *ClR 1259–1261*: 9, 15, 33, 36, 38, 88, 205, 212, 274, 484; *Excerpta é Rotuli Finium* 2: 365–66; KB 26/168 m. 10. Scott Waugh's statement that Ingram de Percy married one of Maud's daughters, in "Reluctant Knights and Jurors: Respites, Exemptions, and Public Obligations in the Reign of Henry III," *Speculum* 58 (1983): 979, is in error.
39. This family never seems to have adopted a true patronymic, as most of the surviving male progeny referred to themselves as fitzReginald, and then, eventually, as fitzJohn. This makes it almost impossible to find them in most extant records, although they appear in chancery records in connection to the Beauchamps of Somerset enough to demonstrate that the family survives at least until the mid-1300s.

40. Maud sued her daughter, Joan fitzPeter, for an advowson in the church of Shepton Malet, but the suit was probably motivated by a desire to straighten out a confusing tenurial situation than by outright hostility. CP 40/106 m. 135.
41. Sibyl and Guy de Rochechouard do not seem to have had any children. Both died before the other sisters and their husbands and, moreover, may have lived in France, so there are no records of their interactions with the rest of the family.
42. CP 25/1/284/21 no. 250; CP 25/1/285/24 no. 250; CCIR 1313–1318: 189.
43. CPR 1317–1321: 188.
44. CPR 1340–1343: 275.
45. CP 40/164 m. 33.
46. CPR 1307–1313: 147, 182; CP 25/1/285/25 no. 298. When Joan died, in 1314, Reginald received the lands due him. CCIR 1313–1318: 120.
47. *Register of William Wickwane, Lord Archbishop of York, A. D. 1279–85* (Surtees Society, 1907), 46.
48. Thomas Corbridge 1: 120.
49. Thomas Corbridge 1: 199.
50. John le Romeyn 1: 160.
51. E 13/37 m. 64.
52. E 159/68 m. 55.
53. E 159/73 m. 43d; CP 40/142 m. 1; CPR 1292–1301: 602.
54. E 159/63 m. 64.
55. Joan's son, William, received leave to attend university and to remain in the living of Bedhampton, granted to him by his mother while he was studying. *Registrum Johannis de Pontissara, Episcopi Wintoniensis, AD 1282–1304* (Canterbury and York Society 19, 1915), 1: 147.
56. James's last presentation from the family was to the living of Sheperton: E 159/68 m. 55.
57. As will be seen in chapter 5.
58. CCIR 1339–1341: 299–300.
59. CPR 1343–1348: 370.

Chapter 3 Like Mother, Like Daughter: The Parallel Careers of Margaret de Quency and Maud de Lacy

1. Relationships between mothers and sons are occasionally discussed.
2. The Common Law form of dowry is discussed in greater detail in chapter 2.
3. For example, the extortionate fines imposed by King John for widows to attain their dower or enter their inheritances.
4. Most notably Michael Altschul, who includes a substantial discussion of her in *A Baronial Family in Medieval England: The Clares, 1217–1314* (Baltimore: Johns Hopkins University Press, 1965).

5. According to GEC, the original grant is found in BL Cott. Charter 24, 6. Ranulph died in 1232, and the king then granted the third penny of the county to Hawise—signifying her accession to the earldom. GEC 7: 676.
6. There are no entries in the Curia Regis Rolls identifying any litigation concerning the grant of the earldom to Hawise de Quency; neither are there any extant chyrographs or deeds by which the other putative heirs released their rights to it.
7. According to GEC, Hawise encouraged the king to grant the earldom to John de Lacy about ten years after his marriage to Margaret (7: 678–79). This implies that Hawise gave the property to John alone, and may be the result of a misreading of the *CPR* entry (1232–47: 3) in which Hawise received permission to grant John the third penny of the county, the symbol of his position as earl. This grant could not have been a late *maritagium* of sorts, since such a large grant would never have been made in "retroactive" frankmarriage. The grant was clearly made to both John and Margaret and was restricted to her direct heirs because their son, Edmund, who died before his mother, never received the title or the issues of the title, as is mentioned by Dugdale, *Monasticon* 5: 535. Finally, Margaret, rather than Edmund, seems to have been liable for the debts of her uncle, Earl Ranulph, and she paid them until her death. E 159/25 m. 22d; E 159/33 mm. 14, 16, 17d; E 159/46 m. 20.
8. A Close Rolls entry (1242–47: 54) implies that there were more children, but since the entry appears two years after John's death, around the time of Margaret's remarriage, it may simply be in error or a calculated bit of creativity on the part of Henry III's chancery: the letter instructs Margaret that her daughters by John will be raised in the king's household.
9. His son, Henry de Lacy, achieved the title after the death of his grandmother.
10. Matthew Paris, who was notably critical of both the Lacys and the Clares (he calls John de Lacy one of the "infamous and mistrusted men" who were "exceedingly hateful to the English nobles"), insists that John de Lacy in effect "stole" Richard de Clare from under Henry's nose without the king's knowledge, a move that prompted both Richard, earl of Cornwall, and Gilbert le Marshal, earl of Pembroke, to rebel against the king. Not only is he completely mistaken, but he also claims that John himself married the sister of Simon de Montfort that same year, an impossibility since he was still married to Margaret. Matthew Paris 1: 68, 121.
11. She married, after the death of Earl Gilbert de Clare, Richard Plantagenet, earl of Cornwall and brother of Henry III.
12. Alice is described as "very young" at the time of her marriage, which suggests she was well below the canonical age of marriage. John de Vescy was younger than Edmund, and so he and his wife were likely to have been toddlers at the time of their marriage. Dugdale 5: 535.
13. Many historians—most recently Loveday Lewes Gee, in *Women, Art and Patronage from Henry III to Edward III: 1216–1377* (Woodbridge,

Suffolk: The Boydell Press, 2002)—assume that Edmund received the title earl of Lincoln at his father's death. This was not the case, as the earldom was his mother's inheritance and, although she released some of the lands relating to the title to him, he never achieved the title. Edmund is always referred to as Constable of Chester and lord of Pontefract in the sources for his career.

14. Most recent edition with translation: *Walter of Henley and other Treatises on Estate Management and Accounting*, trans. and ed. Dorothy Oschinsky (Oxford: Clarendon Press, 1971) introduction: 191–99; text: 387–416. Oschinsky does not mention who initiated the work, Grosseteste or Countess Margaret, but I infer from her introduction that the bishop wrote the treatise on his own initiative. He later adapted the work for use in his own household. General introduction, 5.
15. Introduction to the *Rules*, 198–99.
16. This reinforces the statement that Edmund had never attained the title, since Margaret seems to have had total control of the lands involved and Walter assumed the title.
17. Walter apparently died of dysentry or some other short-term illness while he was at Chepstow castle, the *caput* of the Striguil lordship.
18. Anselm had not been recognized officially as the earl of Pembroke at the time of his death.
19. According to GEC (and repeated without question by subsequent scholars) Margaret married, for the third time, one Richard de Wiltshire. This conclusion is based upon a single entry in the *CChR 1226–1257*: 393. Richard was most assuredly a tenant or a knight in Margaret's household, but not her husband. The king granted a fair in the manor of Chelbury, Lincolnshire, to Margaret and Richard jointly. Chelbury pertained to the earldom of Lincoln, and thus Margaret was probably acting as Richard's patron and warrantor in the royal gift. During the time of this supposed marriage Margaret litigated alone and dealt with the Crown and Chancery as a single person. Thus, there is no evidence of a marriage ever taking place between Margaret and Richard.
20. Alice had another son, John, who died sometime between 1258 and 1266.
21. This is discussed in greater detail in chapter 2. For discussions of the partition of Leinster and its subsequent divisions, see Goddard Henry Orpen, *Ireland Under the Normans*, 4 vols. (1920; reprt, Oxford: Clarendon Press, 1968) 3: ch. 26; A. J. Otway-Ruthven, "Knights' Fees in Kildare, Leix, and Offaly," *Journal of the Royal Society of Antiquaries of Ireland* 91 (1961): 163–81; Otway-Ruthvin, "The Medieval County of Kildare," *Irish Historical Studies* 11 (1959): 181–99; and W. F. Nugent, "Carlow in the Middle Ages," *Journal of the Royal Society of Antiquaries of Ireland* 85 (1955): 62–76. Margaret's assignment of Kildare can be found in *ClR 1247–1251*: 71, 156–57, 159, 294; *CPR 1247–1258*: 41; *CDI* 1: 440, 446–47, 459.
22. E 159/25 m. 8d; E 159/28 mm. 3, 3d, 7, 12d.
23. *CDI* 2: 113. A mark was two-thirds of a pound and was a common unit of measurement in the royal chancery, although not an actual unit of currency.

24. E 159/47 m. 21d.
25. Henry's sister, Margaret, was already married, to yet another Marshal connection, George de Cantelou. George's mother, Eve de Braose, inherited one-fourth of one-fifth of the Marshal estates of her mother, Eve la Marshal, and one-fourth of her father, William de Braose's, estates. The marriage was contracted in 1252, when George was two years old. He died s. p. in 1273; Margaret never remarried. GEC 1: 22–23.
26. For discussions of female control of wardships, see Waugh, *Lordship of England*; Walker, "Free Consent" and "Widow and Ward: The Feudal Law of Child Custody in Medieval England," in *Women in Medieval Society*, ed. Susan Mosher Stuard (Philadelphia: University of Pennsylvania Press), 159–72; Labarge, *Small Sound of the Trumpet*; and Mertes, *English Noble Household*, to name only a few.
27. The earldom of Northumberland and the dukedom of York were not established until the following century.
28. This was more or less customary. Their first daughter was named after Richard's mother, Isabel, so it was almost required that the second daughter be named after her maternal grandmother. The names of their third and fourth daughters, Rose and Eglantina, as well as the names of their second and thirds sons, Thomas and Bogo, are not connected to anyone within either family's lineage. Again, as was customary, their eldest son was named Gilbert after his paternal grandfather. It is perhaps significant that they did not name any of their sons after men in Maud's lineage.
29. Writs of admeasurement were brought by the heir against a dowager when he believed that she had received more than her "reasonable" third of his land. See Loengard, "*Rationabilis Dos.*" KB 26/177 mm. 2, 3, 13; *CPR 1266–1272*: 49. See a full discussion of this in Altschul, *A Baronial Family*, 96–101.
30. Including cousins such as John de Vescy and newly belted peers such as Richard de Ferrers, earl of Derby.
31. Agnes received lands that had been forfeited by rebels after the Battle of Evesham. See chapter 2.
32. The chyrograph was made in 1250. CP 25/1/175/35 no. 574.
33. According to "Bracton," the presence of a signed chyrograph was virtually the only way that a wife could not contest the granting away of her property against her will. *On the Laws and Customs of England*, ed. Samuel Thorne.
34. CP 40/9 m. 47; CP 40/15 mm. 6, 10d.
35. Margaret litigated three dower pleas against sub-feofees who vouched the heirs to warranty. All were introduced in the Cambridge Eyre of 1247: JUST 1/81 mm. 16d, 18, 18d.
36. Detinue in 1259 and 1265 (KB 26/162 m. 32, KB 26/165 m. 13d, KB 26/210 m. 9); Quare Impedit in 1258 (KB 26/162 m. 23); Novel Disseisin in 1248 (JUST 1/909A m. 5); Concord in 1261 (JUST 1/82 m. 16d).
37. Two Trespass suits in 1258 (KB 26/160 mm. 22, 28d and KB 26/162 m. 23); Accounting/Debt in 1254 (KB 26/154 m. 24); Wardship in 1254 (KB

26/154 m. 24); Advowson in 1250 (KB 26/143 m. 21); Wardship in 1247 (JUST 1/81 m. 14) and a few debt pleas in the Court of Exchequer of Pleas—mostly involving the problems over Eleanor de Montfort's Marshal dower—were the only suits litigated against Margaret in twenty years.
38. These suits are too numerous to list. The dower suits were all against sub-feofees, introduced shortly after Richard's death. The remainder of the pleas introduced by Maud encompasses the usual range of suits—trespass, detinue, debt, etc.—over the next twenty-five years. The suits brought against her also span the litigation spectrum, from dower, detinue, and warranty to trespass, right, debt, and *quare impedit*.
39. Edmund and Alice de Lacy also had a son, John, but he died in childhood. Henry, their younger son, became their heir. Margaret was appointed by King Henry III to negotiate the marriage settlement between Henry and Margaret. See Waugh, *Lordship of England*, 57–58. It is also likely that the discussion of the marriage between her granddaughter, Margaret de Lacy, and George de Cantelou had included her input as well.
40. Altschul, *A Baronial Family*, 36.
41. The fourth daughter, Eglantina, died in infancy.
42. Henry's marriage to Margaret Longespee brought the earldom of Salisbury into the Lacy family. His second marriage, to Joan Martin, whose mother, Eleanor, was part of the extended Marshal family by both lineage and marriage, reinforced the connections to that power bloc, which were also forged by the marriage of Henry's sister to George Cantelou, another Marshal heir. Eleanor was the daughter of Reginald fitzPeter and Joan de Vivonia, one of the daughters and coheirs of Maud de Ferrers, and also the widow of John de Mohun, her mother's first cousin.
43. Altschul, *A Baronial Family*, 177–80. Bogo was treasurer of York and chancellor of Llandaff, two positions that demonstrate his interests in the Church to be economic rather than spiritual.
44. Advowson: KB 26/195 [m. 1, 2, 3, or 4], KB 26/188 m. 25d, JUST 1/1050 m. 91; Debt: JUST 1/368 m. 26; Quitclaim: CP 40/31 m. 63d. This account from the plea rolls differs slightly from Michael Altschul's description, taken from the registers of the archbishops of York. *A Baronial Family*, 183–85. See, also, *Register of Archbishop of York Walter Giffard*, nos. 48, 49, 83, pp. 20, 27 and *Register of Archbishop of York John le Romeyn* 1: 47. This case suggests that Bogo was pursuing his own agenda to such a degree that filial gratitude was beyond his abilities.
45. Detinue in 1275–76 (CP 40/11 m. 3d, /15 m. 16), 1278–83 (see n. 46), 1282–84 (CP 40/44 m. 33, /55 m. 99d); withholding of charter in 1279 (CP 40/31 m. 112); homage and service 1276–78 (CP 40/17 m. 5, /24 m. 67, /27 m. 58); debt in arrears in 1285–86 (CP 40/59 m. 73, /64 mm. 92d, 116d); *recordare* in 1277 (CP 40/19 m. 25d).
46. CP 40/19 m. 25d.
47. CP 40/23 m. 13.
48. CP 40/28 m. 42d, /38 m. 35, /44 m. 62d.
49. KB 27/66 m. 3, KB 27/67 m. 2d.

NOTES   151

50. BL, Harleian Manuscript 4835: Cartulary of Clare Priory, folios 2v, 3r, 4r, 5v, 6r. See also Dugdale, *Monasticon* 6.3: 1599–1600 and Altschul, *A Baronial Family*, 36 37. This and Maud's other acts of ecclesiastical patronage have also been discussed by Gee, *Women, Art, and Patronage*, 13, 31, 66, 128–29, 136, 166.
51. *Papal Registers: Letters* 1: 448.
52. *Papal Registers: Letters* 1: 478; Dugdale 6.1 1: 333. See also the papal inhibition to the abbess of Leigh from selling the church plate: *Papal Registers: Letters* 1: 485.
53. BL, Harleian Manuscript 3660: Cartulary of Canonsleigh Priory, folios 103, 122v, 127r.
54. Harley 3660 folios 121r, 135v–136r, 156.
55. *Register of Archbishop of York Walter Gray, 1215–1255*, 209.
56. Dugdale, *Monasticon* 2: 61. Maud also laid his sword and spurs on the tomb at the dedication ceremony.
57. Thomas did well for himself, gaining a lordship of his own in Ireland.

Chapter 4 Heroism and Duty: Maud Mortimer of Wigmore's Contributions to the Royalist Cause

A portion of this chapter was included in Linda E. Mitchell, "Noble Widowhood in the Thirteenth Century: Three Generations of Mortimer Widows, 1246–1334," in *Upon My Husband's Death: Widows in the Literature & Histories of Medieval Europe*, ed. Louise Mirrer (Ann Arbor: University of Michigan Press, 1992), 169–91.

1. A march is the territory demarcating a border—usually volatile—between two politically independent regions. England was bounded on the West by the March of Wales and on the North by the March of Scotland.
2. The names of these commotes changed frequently in the twelfth and thirteenth centuries to reflect the development away from autonomous Welsh kingdoms and principalities to combinations of marcher baronies, Welsh principalities, and hybrid regions that shared characteristics of both. By the fourteenth century, the border regions had become truly balkanized into contiguous baronies and English-style counties.
3. Davies, *Lordship and Society in the March of Wales, 1282–1400* (Oxford: Clarendon Press, 1978), 25.
4. An exception, of sorts, was land held in socage tenure, which retained some local legal relationships. Most nobles did not hold land in socage; it was more typical of the free peasantry. Disputes regarding socage land did, however, appear in the central courts. It was not totally free from Common Law control.
5. Reginald ultimately retained Abergavenny but granted Bramber to John de Braose, lord of Gower, whose father, William, had been Reginald's older brother. He was the noted rebel during the reign of King John whose wife and eldest son had been starved to death by the king.

6. Eve married William le Cantelou, Eleanor married Humphrey de Bohun (another Marshal heir), and Isabel married David, son of Llewelyn ab Iorwerth—an arrangement that was in the works at the time of Isabel's father's death (indeed, was the apparent reason for William's presence at Llewelyn's court in the first place). All shared in the Marshal inheritance from their mother, but only the three older sisters inherited the Braose estates.
7. This negotiation is in itself somewhat unusual because none of the other girls were as yet married. Although no sources identify the dates of the birth of the girls, it is possible that they were very young—infants to toddlers—in 1230 and that this negotiation was designed to solidify a political alliance between Llewelyn and William Braose at a time of considerable tension between the marcher baronage and the prince of North Wales.
8. *Calendar of Ancient Correspondence Concerning Wales*, ed. J. Goronwy Edwards (Cardiff: University Press Board, 1935), 51–52. Also appears in Shirley, *Letters of Henry III's Reign* 1: 369. A number of chronicles comment on the incident, among them the *Brut y Tywysogyon*, which states matter-of-factly, "That year William Breos [sic] the Younger was hanged by Llewelyn ab Iorweth, after he had been caught in the prince's chamber with king John's daughter, the prince's wife." Ed. Thomas Jones (Cardiff: University of Wales Press, 1952), 229. Roger Turvey, more recently, claims that William was still a hostage in Llewelyn's court when this incident occurred, but sources document the incident differently. Roger Turvey, *The Welsh Princes, 1063–1283* (London: Longman, 2002), 61.
9. *Ancient Correspondence Concerning Wales*, 51–52; Shirley, *Letters of Henry III's Reign* 1: 368.
10. In 1242, Eve was cited by the Exchequer because she had failed to pay the entire fine she had made in order to marry her daughter, Eleanor, to Humphrey de Bohun, earl of Hereford and Essex. *Excerpta e Rotula Finium* 1: 367. There are no records identifying the negotiations of the marriages of Maud and Eve, but the men they married were connected significantly to Eve's natal family, as will be seen later, thus suggesting that she had had a hand in those arrangements as well.
11. *CPR 1232–1247*: 46, 52.
12. Eve's third brother, Gilbert, had died in 1242.
13. The tortuous nature of the relations between the Braose family and Llewelyn are amply demonstrated by this marriage alliance, since Joan was the woman with whom Reginald's son William committed adultery and the step-mother of David ap Llewelyn who married Maud de Braose's youngest sister, Isabel.
14. Roger was about fifty years old at his death in 1282, according to GEC. All three children contributed to the family's alliances along the Welsh Marches. Hugh, who founded the lordship of Chelmarsh in Shropshire, married Agatha de Ferrers, one of the seven coheirs of Sibyl la Marshal, daughter of Earl William le Marshal, while Joan married Peter Corbet, lord of Caus in Shropshire.

15. Davies, e.g., neglects to mention that Mortimer's success stemmed primarily from his wife's inheritance and is completely silent about Maud's nineteen-year widowhood, during which her son was unable to solidify his position in her lands. *Lordship and Society*, 25.
16. Eleanor was married to William le Marshal the younger, and retained the title but virtually no property from the Pembroke estates, since there was a question whether the marriage had ever been consummated. Henry III negotiated an annuity of £400 a year for her, which was to be divided among all the heirs to the earldom, but made the typically shortsighted move to agree to pay her the annuity himself, relying on the heirs to repay him. They soon amassed thousands of pounds of debts to the Crown, which apparently were never entirely paid.
17. The number of books about the Barons' War and the rebellion of Earl Simon are too numerous to list here, and historical opinions vary widely as to Simon's agenda in the rebellion. A good recent biography is that of J. R. Maddicott, *Simon de Montfort* (Cambridge: Cambridge University Press, 1994).
18. Possibly because all of the children of Roger and Maud would have been too young to be embroiled in the conflict. Certainly, the actions of their sons, Edmund and Roger, after they had attained their majority demonstrate that they would not have been averse to siding against their parents had they been old enough to do so.
19. *Documents of the Baronial Movement*, ed. Treharne and Sanders, no. 37 B, 267; *Annales Cambriae*, 101–02; Matthew Paris 3: 340, 351–53.
20. The chronicle descriptions of this range from the terse to the gruesome. A selection: Matthew Paris 3: 356; Nicholas Trivet, *Annales* (London, 1845), 266; *Opus Chronicorum* in *Chronica Monasterii S Albani*, ed. Henry Thomas Riley (Rolls Series, 1866), 18–19; *Annales Londoniensis* in *Chronicles of the Reigns of Edward I and Edward II* (Rolls Series, 1882), 1: 69.
21. Several chronicles mention the death of Earl Simon, but few describe the desecration of his corpse. See *Opus Chronicorum* in *Chronica Monasterii S Albani*, ed. Henry Thomas Riley (London, 1866), 18–19; and *Annales Londoniensis* in *Chronicles of the Reigns of Edward I and Edward II*, ed. William Stubbs (London, 1882), I: 69. Michael Prestwich, *Edward I*, 51, mentions the incident, but he does not even bother to give "Roger Mortimer's wife" a name, nor does he cite his source. Maddicot cites *De Antiquis legibus liber Chronica Maiorum et Vicecomitum Londoniarum*, ed. T. Stapelton (Camden Society, 1846), 75–76. See Maddicot, *Simon de Montfort*, 344.
22. BL, Harley 1240, f. 8, no. 1; f. 35, no. 1.
23. All of these issues will be discussed in context and greater depth later.
24. *Documents of Baronial Reform and Rebellion*, 51.
25. *Calendar of Ancient Correspondence Concerning Wales*, 49. Maud's daughter, Isabel, was married to John fitzAlan, lord of Oswestry and Clun, so this might also indicate a close relationship between them that kept Maud well informed of activities in the region.
26. *Calendar of Ancient Correspondence Concerning Wales*, 84.

27. *Welsh Rolls*, 280–81.
28. *Welsh Rolls*, 308, 311–16.
29. *Welsh Rolls*, 350–51; CP 40/106 mm. 71, 89. There is a question in the Welsh Rolls whether the list of landholders sent to Wales was for 1292 or 1294. As the entries in the Common Pleas roll for Michaelmas 1294 are the only indications that Maud was ever respited for pleas, I believe that the summons to Wales probably occurred in 1294 rather than 1292. *Novel disseisin* was one of the "petty" assizes created by Henry II. If a tenant was forcibly evicted from his property without having lost a court case to a plaintiff, then he purchased a writ of *novel disseisin*. Novel disseisin is probably the most common civil case in the courts of medieval England. *Darrein presentment* was another "petty" assize that sought to determine who had last presented a cleric to a particular ecclesiastical living.
30. *CClR 1296–1302*: 132.
31. E. J. L. Cole, "The Castles of Maelienydd," *The Radnorshire Society Transactions*, Sixth Annual Report 16 (Dec. 1946): 6.
32. *CPR 1281–1292*: 8, 115. SC 8/312 no. E-26. In 1297 she paid £50 for farm of the manor of Aure.
33. Quittances in 1287 and 1292, *CClR 1279–1288*: 471; and *1288–1296*: 262, 271; respites E 159/57 m. 1d; E 159/58 m. 1d; E 159/61 m. 18.
34. *CPR 1281–1292*: 130; *1292–1301*: 501.
35. Harley 1240 f. 117r and 62v. William died without progeny in 1297 and his lands returned to his mother. *CClR 1296–1302*: 73.
36. For example, CP 40/50 mm. 23d, 26; CP 40/51 m. 46d; CP 40/52 m. 40; CP 40/53 mm. 26, 26d, 30, 65d; CP 40/57 mm. 24d, 38d. This is just a small selection. Maud's grandsons from her daughter Margaret's marriage to John de Vere and her nephews, from Joan Mortimer's marriage to Peter Corbet, were also involved because Roger and Maud had alienated lands to those collateral branches as well as to their own sons.
37. JUST 1/302 m. 38d and JUST 1/740 m. 46.
38. Maud pursued few suits (aside from dower) in her widowhood: two of accounting, two for debt, and one of *novel disseisin*. This would suggest that Maud experienced little trouble from her tenants, even in the volatile Marches. On the other hand, Maud was sued six times for right and once for entry, as well as twice each for dower and detinue and three times for *novel disseisin*. Her success in such suits against her, however, was unusually high. In the three cases in which Maud vouched her son, Edmund, to warranty, they won once and Maud received equivalent lands in the other two (CP 40/53 m. 52d [1284] to CP 40/139 m. 112 [1301]; CP 40/64 m. 76 [1286] to CP 40/101 mm. 169d, 170, 170d [1293]; CP 40/55 m. 4 [1284] to CP 40/83 mm. 166–166d [1290]). The last case, in which Maud was sued along with her Braose coheirs, disappeared without a decision (CP 40/76 m. 11 [1289] to CP 40/86 m. 93 [1290]). She even achieved unusual success in the other pleas brought against her. Maud won all three *novel disseisin* cases. The remaining cases do not contain decisions. This brief description of Maud's litigation suggests that she retained firm control over her tenants as well as her family.

39. *CClR 1279–1288*: 451; E 159/60 m. 2d.
40. Although Roger of Chirk's allegiance tended to waver between the royalist and the baronial sides.

Chapter 5 Welshness, Englishness, and the Problem of Dowagers and Heiresses in Wales: The Lestrange Family's Marital Adventures in Powys

1. The classic essay on the development of these legal texts is that by J. Goronwy Edwards, "Hywel Dda and the Welsh Lawbooks," in *Celtic Law Papers* (Aberystwyth, 1971), 137–60.
2. For more complete accounts of the differences between Welsh and English law, as well as comparisons between Welsh law and other Celtic legal systems, see R. R. Davies, "The Status of Women and the Practice of Marriage in Late-Medieval Wales," in *The Welsh Law of Women*, ed. Dafydd Jenkins and Morfydd E. Owen (Cardiff: University of Wales Press, 1980), 93–114; D. A. Binchy, *Studies in Early Irish Law* (Dublin: Royal Irish Academy, 1936); G. J. Hand, *English Law in Ireland, 1290–1324* (Cambridge: Cambridge University Press, 1967).
3. A note about Welsh naming systems and spelling: Welsh names have no lineage-based patronymic. Instead, like Germanic naming systems (the use of the term "fitz"), men include their biological father's name as their patronymic, connected by the preposition "of" (ap or ab)—i.e., "son of" (e.g. Llewelyn ab Iorwerth, Rhys ap Tewdr, etc.). Some men and women also adopted or were given nicknames or cognomens by which they became known. For example, Llewelyn ab Iorwerth was called Llewelyn Fawr (the Great) by some and, occasionally, Llewelyn Gwynedd—the cognomen most typically associated with his grandfather, Owain. Women's cognomens tended to be related to personal appearance (Gwladus Ddu—"Dark-eyed" Gladys) or personality (Hawise de la Pole was called "Gadarn"—"The Hardy"—by the Welsh: see later). Although a Welsh-language board exists today, the spelling of Welsh names is still not entirely standardized, and medieval Welsh names are particularly difficult. Latinized forms—David for Dafydd, Griffin for Gruffud, Gladys for Gwladus, etc.—appear in the Latin and French sources and those are used by some historians instead of the Welsh spelling. Unfortunately, Welsh historians who use the traditional forms do not always agree on the spelling of these names, either. To alleviate all confusion, I follow the orthographical convention used by R. R. Davies.
4. The earldom had been held by the Montgomery family, who were the most powerful in the region during the reign of King Stephen, but whose failure to support Henry II's mother, Empress Maud, led to their downfall when Henry attained the throne. Robert de Montgomery's tomb still rests in the Abbey of SS Peter and Paul in Shrewsbury. In fact, the county that presently describes the medieval lordship of Upper Powys is called Montgomeryshire, after the earls of Shrewsbury, but the name of the county

town is Welshpool, after the adopted name of Gwenwynwyn's son, Gruffud, who changed the family's name to the more French "de la Pole."
5. A. J. Roderick, "Marriage and Politics in Wales, 1066–1282," *Welsh History Review* 4.1 (1968): 15.
6. Not only did Llewelyn marry Joan, illegitimate daughter of King John, but he also arranged marriages for all of his children—both male and female— with members of the Anglo-Norman marcher baronage. In addition, the Corbets and Pantulfs were often associated in the twelfth and thirteenth centuries. See Janet Miesel, *Barons of the Welsh Frontier*. Caus is just north of Powys.
7. Madoc, according to Bridgeman, had a daughter, Efa, to whom passed land that was apparently held of Gruffud as a sub-feofee. G. T. O. Bridgeman, "The Princes of Upper Powys," *Montgomeryshire Collections* 1 (1868): 21.
8. Yes, another marcher baronage.
9. *Brut y Tywysogyon*, 180–83.
10. *Brut y Tywysogyon*, 189.
11. *Brut y Tywysogyon*, 195.
12. *Brut y Tywysogyon*, 207.
13. Morris Charles Jones, *The Feudal Barons of Powys* (London: J. Russell Smith, 1868), 3.
14. *CChR* 1: 266.
15. Richard Morgan, "The Barony of Powys, 1275–1360," *The Welsh History Review* 10 (June 1980): 5. This will be discussed in greater detail later.
16. The castle now known as Powis Castle went through a variety of names over the years: Trallwng, Pool, Castel Coch, Powis. D. J. Cathcart King, "Castles and the Administrative Divisions of Wales: A Study of Names," *The Welsh History Review* 10.1 (1980): 93–96. The burning of the village is mentioned in the *Annales Cambriae*, ed. John Williams ab Ithel (Rolls Series, 1860), 92.
17. A source mentioned by Bridgeman actually suggests this: a deed requiring witnesses to attest the date of a grant proved the date by mentioning that it was the year that "Llewelyn, son of Griffin [was] with Griffin son of Wenhunwen, with no small army to destroy the March, and particularly Roger de Mortimer." The witnesses should know: one of them was destined to be Gruffud's eldest son's father-in-law. Bridgeman, 31.
18. Bridgeman, 31–37.
19. Although I am sympathetic to the attitude of many historians of medieval Wales with respect to the issues of Welsh identity, culture, and nationhood being obviated by the English conquests I feel their condemnation of Gruffud ap Gwenwynwyn for being a "turncoat" is antithetical to historical analysis. In terms of survival, Gruffud clearly made the right choices for his family, and he clearly tried to encourage, by his example, other Welsh princes to use his hybrid model of land tenure as a means of survival. For an unpolemical analysis of this situation, see R. R. Davies, *Conquest,*

Coexistence, and Change: Wales, 1063–1415 (Oxford and Cardiff: Oxford University and University of Wales Press, 1987), 233–36.
20. Jones, *Feudal Barons of Powys*, 7. The author goes on to dispute whether Owain in fact "had the power to surrender the title of prince...to the prejudice and deprivation of his male collaterals...without their express consent" in a clear bid to claim an ongoing Welsh title to the lordship.
21. Gruffud and Hawise also had a daughter, Margaret, who married Fulk fitzWarin of Whittington, but she does not enter into this inheritance because gavelkind tenure disinherited her. She may have received a *maritagium* from English estates held by the family. Bridgeman, 46.
22. Gruffud seems not to have used the name, preferring the traditional Welsh system of Gruffud ap Gwenwynwyn (which appears in Latin and French records as "Griffin son of Wenowen"). As a result, historians seem to have assumed that Owain, Gruffud's son, was responsible for the change of name. If that were the case, then only his immediate family—Owain, his children, and his wife—would have used the Normanized patronymic. That is not the case: all of Gruffud's legitimate sons and his widow, Hawise, used the designation "de la Pole." This suggests strongly that the name was in place before Gruffud's death, and before the lordship changed officially from a Welsh principality to a marcher lordship. The designation "de la Pole" may also have significance with respect to the welter of family members engaged in intra-family warfare in the fourteenth century, which I will discuss in greater detail later.
23. Bridgeman includes what he claims to be the original charters, collected in the Welsh Rolls of Edward I: Bridgeman, 125–28. The last version of the charters was enrolled by Edward III in 1343: *CPR 1340–1343*: 496–97.
24. The difficulties of identifying Welsh lands using Anglo-Norman records written in Latin and translated into modern English are extraordinary. However, G. T. O. Bridgeman, "The Princes of Upper Powys," *Montgomeryshire Collections* 1 (1868): 5–89 provides invaluable assistance, despite the usual orthographical eccentricities (Bridgeman spells the name Gruffud four different ways, e.g., depending on the source he uses).
25. The Pantulfs were another important alliance, but one that was more tangential to the family fortunes.
26. Gruffud's maternal grandmother was also a Tregoz.
27. There were several cadet branches of the Lestranges of Knockyn, most importantly the Lestranges of Blackmere, which was also involved in the political effects of these alliances.
28. This might be in error: Margaret's *maritagium* would have been a more likely cause of conflict with her brother.
29. Miesel, *Barons of the Welsh Frontier*, 20–22.
30. The marriage of close cousins was more typical among Welsh families than among Anglo-Norman, but they would still have had to be granted dispensation for first cousins to marry, as Owain and Joan did.
31. It is impossible to identify Sibyl's parentage. She and Llewelyn engaged in extensive litigation over her Pauncefot dower, which continued after

Llewelyn's death. She may also have remarried again, to Gilbert de Bohun. CP 40/134 m. 140d.
32. The Audleys were growing in importance in the March at this time and the Giffards were very important barons of the region near Powys, as lords of Brimpsfield. Ela remarried twice after Gruffud's death: James de Perrers and Peter Corbet. GEC 10: 641–42.
33. *CFR 1272–1307*: 351.
34. *CFR 1272–1307*: 335, 351, 358, 534; *CClR 1288–1296*: 336, 340, 341, 379; *CPR 1292–1301*: 140.
35. Owain agreed to allow Lewis to grant Sibyl a "nominated" dower—the manor of Gorgennon and the lands of Mechain Uchcoed—at the church door. It turned out to be greater than a third of his estate, so Sibyl's share underwent a revaluation. *CIPM, Edward I* 3: 138–39. Also, *CClR 1288–1296*: 424.
36. Sibyl may well have opted out of the picture entirely, more intent on wresting her dower from the heir of her first husband.
37. *CPR 1292–1301*: 163.
38. Demonstrated by the flurry of commissions sent to investigate.
39. *CPR 1292–1301*: 458, 464, 470–71, 473.
40. Joan had three children with Roger during their thirty-five years of marriage: Roger, Robert, and Eleanor. All three children acted as her executors at her death in 1348.
41. Hilda Johnstone, ed., *Letters of Edward Prince of Wales 1304–1305* (Cambridge: Cambridge University Press for the Roxeburghe Club, 1931), 154.
42. *RP* 1: 274.
43. Bridgeman, 55. It is likely that Joan had placed Gruffud in Edward's household during the years of her guardianship, although it is not clear whether Edward's decision was a general response to the ongoing crisis in Powys or referred specifically to Joan and Roger's petition.
44. Bridgeman, 48.
45. William de la Pole was dead by December 1311, when Gwladus his widow was acquitted of half of the farm she had been charged for an assarting project. The steward on the estate would not allow cultivation on the land to occur because it would have disrupted the herds of deer that abounded there. William and Gwladus had a son, Gruffud, who was declared of age in 1319; he held his inheritance as a sub-feofee of Gruffud ap Gruffud ap Gwenwynwyn, according to the Close Roll—which is probably in error, since William's original grant designated him as a sub-feofee of Owain. The association of William's heir with his younger brother in this way could have been another attempt to legitimize Gruffud's argument that Powys should be held in gavelkind with himself as the principle heir. Ironically, the Welsh nationalist historians of the nineteenth century, such as Morris Charles Jones, refer to Gruffud ap William as the "true" heir to Powys. *CClR 1318–1323*: 86.

46. Evidence of this mother–daughter alliance comes from the association of their husbands and the Trumwyne and Cherleton children in activities related to the family feud.
47. The Ordinances were provisions brought by the baronial party led by Henry de Lacy, earl of Lincoln, and his son-in-law, Thomas, earl of Lancaster, against King Edward II in an attempt to remove royal favorites such as Piers Gaveston and Henry and Isabella Beaumont from positions of power. For a few years immediately following Earl Henry's death in 1311, Thomas of Lancaster was effectively the ruler of England. This will be discussed in greater detail in chapters 7 and 8.
48. *Annales Londoniensis* 1: 224–25.
49. *CPR 1307–1313*: 546–47 describes one such complaint.
50. *CPR 1307–1313*: 547.
51. *CClR 1307–1313*: 424.
52. *CClR 1307–1313*: 417. This claim is just as deliberately mendacious as William's claim that he held his estates from Gruffud, his brother. It also formed the basis of Joan and Roger's attempt to gain control of La Pole from Joan's mother-in-law, Hawise Lestrange de la Pole.
53. *CClR 1307–1313*: 459. Also mentioned in Jones, *Feudal Barony of Powys*, 11.
54. According to Jones, 11.
55. *CClR 1307–1313*: 555.
56. *CClR 1307–1313*: 555–56.
57. Roger and the queen had formed an invading army against Edward II.
58. *Cartulary of Haughmond Abbey*, ed. Una Rees (Shropshire Archaeological Society, 1985), 100–01.
59. *The Chartulary of the Priory of St Pancras of Lewes*, ed. L. Salzman (Sussex Record Society, 1934), 13.
60. *CPR 1313–1317*: 21–25, 26, 66, 142–43.
61. *CClR 1307–1313*: 569; *CClR 1313–1318*: 29, 30. See also, Bridgeman, 67. Gruffud was supposed to receive Dender as his share of the patrimony after Hawise's death.
62. *CClR 1313–1318*: 29.
63. It may be recalled that Hawise Gadarn's brother, Gruffud, had married Ela daughter of Nicholas de Audeley.
64. *CPR 1313–1317*: 150–51. This commission was reissued in 1315. *CPR 1313–1317*: 315–16.
65. *CClR 1313–1318*: 272, 345, 351, 352; *CClR 1318–1323*: 18, 427; *CPR 1313–1317*: 444, 472, 548.
66. *CPR 1317–1321*: 327. John himself was appointed as justiciar of Ireland; he and his brother, Bishop Thomas, went to Ireland together in the 1330s. John, however, was removed as justiciar and replaced by Thomas. *CPR 1334–1338*: 478; *CPR 1338–1340*: 80.
67. *CPR 1321–1324*: 157–58, 307, 340; *CClR 1318–1323*: 665; *Calendar of Ancient Petitions Relating to Wales*, 387–90.

68. *CPR 1321–1324*: 157–58. I have not changed the spelling of the entry, as it outlines not only the variation of spelling of names, but also the problems inherent in trying to translate Welsh into Latin and thence into English. "Owen ap Griffud ap Gwen" may have been an illegitimate son of Gruffud ap Gwenwynwyn, if his name is accurate.
69. *Petitions Relating to Wales*, 387–89.
70. An exemplification made at the request of John de Cherleton in 1336, of a charter that was "accidentally lost" confirms a charter made in 1283 granting Mechain Iscoed in fee to Roger de Sprenghose. The property was in John de Cherleton's hands because of the forfeit of Gruffud Vaghan. *CPR 1334–1338*: 307.
71. *CPR 1321–1324*: 451–52.
72. *CClR 1327–1330*: 202–03; *CPR 1327–1330*: 97, 269, 270, 273–74, 331–32.
73. *CPR 1327–1330*: 76.
74. *CPR 1327–1330*: 561–62; *CClR 1327–1330*: 500.
75. Bridgeman suggests that Gruffud Vaghan might not have had any surviving male children, but that he might have had two daughters, who may have married Sir Roger Chamber and Hugh Montgomery. This might have been a reason for Gruffud to change his mind about the usefulness of Common Law tenure over gavelkind. Bridgeman, 75.
76. *CPR 1330–1334*: 142; *CClR 1330–1333*: 379–80, 435.
77. *CPR 1330–1334*: 267.
78. *Bridgeman*, 59–60.
79. Cecily married Thomas Rotherik and received the lordship of Dynas as her *maritagium*. *CPR 1340–1343*: 225; *CClR 1339–1341*: 206, 256.
80. *CPR 1340–1343*: 496–97; *CPR 1343–1345*: 37. There was a brief return to past strategies around this time, when Maud, Gruffud's wife, was imprisoned in La Pole castle, but the king reprimanded John de Cherleton and he released her. *CPR 1343–1345*: 175.
81. *CClR 1349–1354*: 576. John de Cherleton held the barony of Powys Wenwynwyn by right of curtesy after Hawise's death.
82. Despite her Welsh cognomen, Hawise Gadarn was actually the most "English" of the three women.

Chapter 6 Murderous Maud? The Case Against Maud Mortimer of Richard's Castle

A version of this chapter was read at the Mid-Eastern Region Congress on British Studies of the North American Congress on British Studies, New York City, April 1997. I am grateful to Barbara Harris, who commented on this paper.

1. Gaol Delivery Roll 39 m. 22, as quoted in Hilda Johnstone, ed., *Letters of Edward Prince of Wales 1304–1305* (Cambridge: Cambridge University Press for the Roxburghe Club, 1931), xxxviii.
2. English justices were allowed to utilize "pressing," the suspending of a millstone on a pulley and the lowering of it onto the chest of the accused, in

order to extract a confession, but this was not considered the equivalent of the kinds of torture typically mandated by both Canon Law and the Inquisition and by Roman Civil Law (such as the use of strappado), which were more or less obligatory in the interrogation of both the accused and of recalcitrant witnesses.
3. Robert C. Palmer, *The Whilton Dispute, 1264–1380: A Social-Legal Study of Dispute Settlement in Medieval England* (Princeton: Princeton University Press, 1984), 169. In fact, Palmer's characterization of the circumstances surrounding Hugh's death are so dismissive that they merit quoting in full:

> A poet did mention Hugh for his part in the siege of Caerlaverock in 1300: "Hugh Mortimer, who well knew how to make himself beloved." Whether the poet was being ironic or Hugh simply never used his talent with his wife, Matilda (*sic*), is not known, but she killed him by poison on 5 August 1304. Queen Margaret seems to have thought that action not entirely reprehensible and interceded to obtain a pardon for her. It is thus likely that the personalities involved would only have exacerbated the difficult legal situation.
>
> Hugh Mortimer was poisoned at the age of 31, leaving his wife and two daughters, Joan and Margaret.... [T]he girls were not long burdened by the provision of dower to Hugh's widow: Matilda died in 1308.

That Palmer never mentions the additional charges against Maud demonstrates his lack of interest in one of the figures who contributed to the complexities surrounding the ownership of the manor of Whilton.
4. Johnstone, *Letters of Edward Prince of Wales*, introduction, xxxviii–xl.
5. *CPR 1301–1307*: 334, 378, 402.
6. GEC 9: 265. See, also, John Carmi Parsons, *The Court and Household of Eleanor of Castile in 1290* (Toronto: Pontifical Institute of Medieval Studies, 1977), 16. This William le Marshal is no relation to the earls of Pembroke.
7. Among them, John de Vescy's marriage to Isabella de Beaumont, as is discussed in chapters 2 and 7. See, also, Parsons.
8. *CPR 1301–1307*: 142–48. Apparently, Hugh did indeed exercise this privilege. See Palmer, *Whilton Dispute*, 147–48.
9. Despite Palmer's less than generous characterization of it.
10. *CIPM* 4: 142–44; 5: 22–25.
11. *CPR 1292–1301*: 304.
12. CP 40/122 m. 22d. See also, CP 25/1/285/24 no. 238 and *Devon Feet of Fines* (Devon and Cornwall Record Society, 1939) 2: 104–05.
13. There are connections among various Kyngesmedes and *other* parties in the Whilton dispute, however. See later.
14. See Historical Manuscripts Commission, *Report on the Manuscripts of Wells Cathedral* (London, 1885), 94–95; and *Calendar of the Manuscripts of the Dean and Chapter of Wells* (London, 1907) 1: 211–14.
15. *CPR 1301–1307*: 41, 53, 62.

16. *CFR* 1: 497; *CIPM* 4: 142–44.
17. *CPR 1301–1307*: 261, 265.
18. *CClR 1302–1307*: 180–81, 221.
19. SC 8/320 doc. E. 450.
20. *CPR 1301–1307*: 334; *CClR 1302–1307*: 328, 337.
21. *CIPM* 5: 25.
22. Johnstone, *Letters*, 34.
23. *CPR 1301–1307*: 379, 402.
24. Johnstone, *Letters*, 34.
25. Johnstone, *Letters*, 50–51.
26. *CClR 1302–1307*: 319.
27. *CPR 1301–1307*: 343–44.
28. *CClR 1302–1307*: 319.
29. Johnstone, *Letters*, 58.
30. Johnstone, *Letters*, 75–76.
31. *CPR 1301–1307*: 402.
32. Johnstone, *Letters*, 92, 105–06. Also quoted in introduction, xxxix.
33. *CPR 1301–1307*: 378.
34. Johnstone, *Letters*, 123. "Et creez a nostre dite Cosine de ceo que elle vous disra de bouche depar nous."
35. *CPR 1301–1307*: 486.
36. Palmer, *The Whilton Dispute*, 226–27. Alice was the daughter of Hugh's half-sister, Felicia de Whelton de Montgomery.
37. *CPR 1301–1307*: 343–44. This Roger Mortimer was probably Roger Mortimer of Chirk, uncle of Roger Mortimer of Wigmore, who did several terms as justiciar of Wales; William Mortimer was probably related to Hugh of Richard's Castle through his East Anglian kin.
38. CP 40/153 m. 459d. They defaulted.
39. CP 40/158 m. 116d. Maud claimed, through her attorney, that she owed only £10 and she apparently did pay that amount, because Richard the Mercer returned to court in 1307 to claim the remaining sum.
40. CP 40/159 m. 67.
41. *CPR 1301–1307*, 410.
42. *CPR 1301–1307*, 440.
43. CP 40/162 mm. 23, 274d.
44. CP 40/160 m. 202.
45. Which contradicts entirely Robert Palmer's offhand dismissal of these events.

Chapter 7 Isabella de Vescy and the Lords Ordainer: Marital Politics and the Crown, 1272–1327

1. Two recent biographies of these queens highlight these issues. Margaret Howell, *Eleanor of Provence: Queenship in Thirteenth-Century England* (Oxford: Blackwell Publishers, 1998) and John Carmi Parsons, *Eleanor of Castile: Queen*

and Society in Thirteenth-Century England (New York: St. Martin's Press, 1995). There is also ample evidence from chronicle sources to suggest that neither queen was particularly well liked by their contemporaries.

2. Both Isabella and her brother, Henry, took their mother's family name as their own. Henry inherited the lordship of Beaumont.

3. William was the child of Isabella of Angoulême, the widow of King John, and Hugh le Brun de Lusignan. He and his other siblings arrived in England as teenagers and Henry III welcomed them with open arms. He showered them with gifts and benefits and married them to the sons and daughters of the most prominent barons. William was particularly well rewarded, marrying Joan de Munchesney, one of the coheirs (through her mother Joan) of the Marshal earldom of Pembroke. He was exiled during the Barons' War, although he returned soon after, and seems to have made his peace with the other barons after that because William became one of the "grand old men" of Edward I's reign.

4. John's first wife was also a royal connection: he married Agnes of Saluzzo, cousin of Eleanor of Provence and sister of Alice, wife of Edmund de Lacy. She died before the marriage produced any children, in 1265, around the time John was wounded at the battle of Evesham. John survived the wound and became a close friend of Edward and Eleanor. There was talk of a betrothal to Mary de Lusignan (yet another royal cousin) but nothing came of it. GEC 12.2: 278–80.

5. Thomas was the earl of Lancaster and Leicester in his own right and earl of Lincoln and Salisbury by right of his wife, Alice de Lacy, daughter of Henry de Lacy, earl of Lincoln, and Margaret Longespee, *suo jure* countess of Salisbury.

6. Michael Prestwich wrote a short article on Isabella's wardship of Bamburgh Castle and scattered mentions of her appear in works concerning the rebellion of Thomas of Lancaster, but most of these references support the Ordainer position that she was a foreigner who should never have acquired the power she amassed. See Prestwich, "Isabella de Vescy and the Custody of Bamburgh Castle," *Bulletin of the Institute of Historical Research* 44 (1971): 148–52; and Michael Prestwich, *Edward I* (Berkeley: University of California Press, 1988), 550.

7. This was discussed in more detail in chapter 2.

8. Another marriage arranged by Eleanor had been that of Maud la Mareschal and Hugh de Mortimer of Richard's Castle—see chapter 6.

9. Parsons, *Eleanor of Castile*, 34.

10. Several estates that John had held in chief were regranted to the couple in jointure and John received a grant of land directly from Queen Eleanor, which was regranted to Isabella during her widowhood. *CChR 1257–1300*: 246; and *CPR 1281–1292*: 474.

11. John's grandfather, Eustace de Vescy, had married Margaret, illegitimate daughter of William the Lion, king of Scotland. Sanders, *English Baronies*, 103.

12. According to the Register of Archbishop Le Romeyn of York, Isabella presented James to the living of Brompton in 1286, although this date is

suspect since both Agnes, who had the living of Brompton, and John were still alive at that date. *Register of John Le Romeyn*, 1: 160. See, also, chapter 2 for a discussion of the Ferrers patronage of James.

13. Her litigation began in the Michaelmas term of 1289 and continued only for about six months, being completed by the end of the Hilary term of 1290. CP 40/80 mm. 68, 160; CP 40/81 mm. 20d, 34d.
14. *CPR 1281–1292*: 409, 410, 476; *CPR 1292–1301*: 3.
15. Otway-Ruthven describes William de Vescy as one "whose activities produced a greater surviving volume of complaint than those of any other chief governor of the middle ages." A. J. Otway-Ruthven, *A History of Medieval Ireland* (London: Ernest Benn, 1968), 209.
16. William's son, John, who had been married in 1290 to another of Queen Eleanor's cousins, Clemencia, died in 1295 without any heirs of his body. William managed to negotiate to have his illegitimate son, William de Vescy of Kildare, gifted with the lordship of Alnwick, but he had no direct dealings with the legitimate kin. He died at Bannockburn in 1314, leaving no heir.
17. *CPR 1292–1301*: 185.
18. *CPR 1292–1301*: 228, 302. Two daughters of Edward I and Eleanor of Castile.
19. *CClR 1296–1302*: 10; *CClR 1302–1307*: 311.
20. *CClR 1296–1302*: 46.
21. *CPR 1292–1301*: 513, 577; *CClR 1296–1302*: 508; *CPR 1301–1307*: 124.
22. *CChR 1300–1326*: 49, 50, 58.
23. Prestwich, "Isabella de Vescy and the Custody of Bamburgh Castle," 149. Prestwich mentions the entries in the memoranda rolls (E 159/78 m. 7d and E 368/75 m. 4). The Fine Roll entry was made in 1305: *CFR 1272–1307*: 528.
24. Prestwich, "Isabella de Vescy," 148–52.
25. Although William's Irish estates had devolved to his illegitimate son, the English lordship of Alnwick would eventually devolve to the Percy family and form the center of the earldom of Northumberland.
26. She would eventually appoint clerics to livings in Clemencia's gift as her representative. *Register of Archbishop of York Greenfield* part 3, 1306–1315, ed. William Brown and A. Hamilton Thompson (Surtees Society, 1936), 179–80; and part 5 (1940), 269.
27. *CClR 1302–1307*: 299.
28. His grandson apparently sued in the court of the Exchequer of Pleas for repayment of a large sum that John de Warenne had allegedly spent on repairs to the castle, but it is unclear whether those repairs had been made early or late in his tenure. *CPR 1307–1313*: 270.
29. *CPR 1301–1307*: 511.
30. *CPR 1307–1313*: 26; *CClR 1307–1313*: 6.
31. *CPR 1307–1313*: 20.
32. *CClR 1307–1313*: 31.

33. *CPR 1307–1313*: 236. See also, *The Household Book of Queen Isabella of England for the Fifth Regnal Year of Edward II, 8th July 1311 to 7th July 1312*, ed. F. D. Blackley and G. Hermanson (Edmonton: University of Alberta Press, 1971), xiii–xiv.
34. *RP* 1: 284; also BL, Harley Charters 43.D.18; *Annales Londoniensis*, in *Chronicles of the Reigns of Edward I and Edward II*, ed William Stubbs, Rolls Series (London, 1882) 1: 201; *Gesta Edwardi de Caernarvon auctore canonico Bridlingtoniensis*, in *Chronicles of the Reigns of Edward I and Edward II*, 2: 41.
35. *CFR 1307–1319*: 121.
36. *Household Book of Queen Isabella*, xxiv, 133.
37. *CPR 1307–1313*: 427.
38. *CFR 1307–1319*: 131–33.
39. *CPR 1307–1313*: 552, 580; *CPR 1313–1317*: 85.
40. *CPR 1313–1317*: 29.
41. *CPR 1313–1317*: 83, 88.
42. CP 25/1/270/92 no. 3; CP 25/1/181/10 nos. 49, 50; CP 25/1/189/15 no. 36; CP 25/1/10/46 no. 23; CP 25/1/136/89 no. 9. See, also *CPR 1317–1321*: 354–55, 444.
43. This was the transfer of Boulton Percy to Isabella for her life at a rent of a rose per year. CP 25/1/270/92 no. 3.
44. *Feet of Fines for the County of York, from 1327 to 1347: 1–20 Edward III*, ed. W. Paley Baildon (Leeds: Yorkshire Archaeological Society, Record Series, 1910) 42: 58–59.
45. More on this in chapter 8.
46. *CPR 1321–1324*: 204.
47. *CFR 1319–1327*: 444.
48. GEC 2: 60.
49. *CClR 1327–1330*: 29; *CPR 1327–1330*: 134. The grant was free of any rent or payment.
50. GEC 1: 307–08.
51. Fryde, *The Tyranny and Fall of Edward II, 1321–1326* (Cambridge: Cambridge University Press, 1979), 220–25. I have found no evidence of this in the Close or Patent Rolls.
52. *CPR 1330–1334*: 182.
53. *CPR 1324–1327*: 316. She also ratified a donation to the Gilbertine house of Bolington, which had been made by Philip de Kyme a few years before her own mortmain grant. B. L. Harley Charters 45.I.38.
54. *Papal Registers 1305–1342*: 347.
55. *CPR 1330–1334*: 288, 312, 397.

Chapter 8 Martyr to the Cause: The Tragic Career of Alice de Lacy

Versions of this chapter were presented at Alfred University's Bergren Forum, October 1999, and at the Midwest Medieval History conference, Cincinnati, Ohio, October 1999.

1. The cursory comments of modern-day historians about Alice will be addressed in greater detail later.
2. Margaret's and Alice's activities are discussed in greater detail in chapter 3.
3. And also Derby, although the title was not used.
4. Edmund drowned in a well at Denbigh Castle and John died when he tripped and fell over the edge of a parapet at Pontefract. GEC 7: 686n.
5. There is a remarkable similarity between this arrangement and that which transferred the earldom of Lincoln from the hands of Ranulph, earl of Chester, to the Lacy family in the first place. Ranulph granted the earldom to his sister, Hawise de Quency, who then granted it to her daughter, Margaret, and her husband, John de Lacy, in theory disinheriting the right heirs of Ranulph de Blundeville. It also resembles Gilbert de Clare's arrangement with the king at the time of his marriage to Joan of Acre, which will be discussed later. Some of the deeds certifying the property transfer are found in DL 42/5 mm. 103d–104, 104d–104; DL 42/11 ff. 9–9d, 11; DL 10/195.
6. Henry's aunt, Maud de Lacy, married Richard de Clare. She was the great-grandmother of Eleanor, Elizabeth, and Margaret de Clare, who divided the earldoms of Gloucester and Hertford after their brother's death at Bannockburn in 1214. All three sisters were in similarly precarious positions as that of Alice during the reign of Edward II.
7. Such as that of John de Trokelowe, who claims that the greatest nobleman in England, Thomas of Lancaster, was unanimously acclaimed as the savior of the people. Trokelowe's Annales in *Chronica Monsaterii S Albani*, ed. Henry Thomas Riley (Rolls Series, 1866), 69–70.
8. Prestwich states: "A more effective leader than Lancaster would have been able to deal with the incompetent Edward II long before 1322..." *The Three Edward*, 93.
9. A note appended to BM Add. Mss. 5844, f. 96 (a letter from Henry de Lacy to Edward I concerning the priory of Spalding), e.g., describes Henry as "a very conscientious good man, and true patron of the convent." James F. Baldwin, in 1927, stated "Needless to say the reputation of the earl as an able administrator, a man of thrift and liberality, is abundantly confirmed." Baldwin, "The Household Administration of Henry Lacy and Thomas of Lancaster," *The English Historical Review* 42.166 (1927): 182. More recent evaluations of Henry's career have not altered this consensus.
10. According to Capgrave's Chronicle, Henry advised his son-in-law to lead the resistance against Edward II. "And whan this Herry schuld dye, he cleped Thomas to him, and commaund him to stand with the rite of the reme, and that he schuld be governed be the councel of Gy erl of Warwik." Quoted in GEC 7: 686n.
11. *CClR 1307–1313*: 314–15, 350, 370, 390, 434.
12. October 1313: Amnesty for Thomas's adherents, although the king did try to interfere in their lands despite the amnesty. *CPR 1313–1317*: 21–26, 142–43. October 1314: King grants a market and two fairs to Thomas and Alice at Burton Stather, Lincolnshire. *CChR* 3: 242. April 1315: John de la

Chaumbre of Coleham grants a small property to Thomas and Alice. DL 25/1880.
13. Baldwin, "Household Administration," 180–200. The author, interestingly, implies in the text that Alice was extravagant, too, but he then appends his edited version of Thomas's account roll, which belies his statement. In fact, Alice and her stepmother spent about the same amount (which, in the case of Joan, is described as "entirely reasonable"), which suggests that Alice was very frugal, indeed, if one takes into account the inflation that occurred between 1295 and 1314.
14. Such as the *Annales Paulini*, ed. William Stubbs (Rolls Series, 1882), 280.
15. Anno sequente, consecratus fuit dictus Lodowicus apud Westmonasterium in episcopum Dunelmensen a cardinalibus; et Johannes comes de Warenne Thomae comiti Lancastriae sponsam suam abripuit, non tamen causa adulterii sed in despectu comitis antedicti. *Chronica monasterii de Melsa, auctore Thoma de Burton, abbate*, ed. Edward A. Bond (Rolls Series, 1867), 2: 334–35.
16. Item eodem anno uxor Thomae Lancastriae, videlicet filia Henrici de Lascy comitis Lincolniae, recessit de comitiva et potestate domini sui supradicti, et comes de Warenna eam in suam custodiam tunc recepit. *Gesta of Edward of Caernarvon by the Canon of Bridlington*, in *Chronicles of Edward I and Edward II* 2: 54.
17. I am grateful for Douglas Biggs's reminding me of this context.
18. Thomas Walsingham, *Historia Anglicana*, ed. Henry Thomas Riley (Rolls Series, 1863) 1: 148–49.
19. *Vita Edwardi Secundi auctore Malmesberiensi* in *Chronicles of the Reigns of Edward I and Edward II* 2: 228–29.
20. May McKisack, *The Fourteenth Century, 1307–1399* (Oxford: Oxford University Press, 1959), 51 and note.
21. *Flores Historiarum*, ed. Henry Richards Luard (Rolls Series, 1890) 3: 179.
22. *Flores Historiarum*, 3: 149.
23. *Flores Historiarum*, 3: 17–18.
24. *Flores Historiarum*, 3: 149.
25. The description in the *Flores Historiarum* of a lame knight might well have derived from Walsingham's account. McKisack's identification of the knight as Ebulo Lestrange is a complete fabrication: Alice's future husband was, in 1216, an adherent of Thomas of Lancaster fighting the good fight in Wales.
26. *CPR 1313–1317*: 401, 434, 481, 528–29.
27. References to this are found in the letters of Archbishop William Greenfield, extracted and edited by Jennifer Ward, in *Women of the English Nobility and Gentry, 1066–1500* (Manchester: Manchester University Press, 1995), 66–67 and note 54.
28. *CClR 1313–1318*: 554, 575.
29. As John had no legitimate heirs, this settlement did not unduly disenfranchise him.
30. *CPR 1317–1321*: 263–64, 319.
31. *CPR 1321–1324*: 79, 81. The inclusion of Robert de Ferrers was Edward's revenge for the dispute over the earldom of Derby that had been going on

since the 1270s. Thomas's father, Edmund Crouchback, had received guardianship of the earldom after Evesham, earl of Derby, Robert de Ferrers (this Robert's grandfather) having supported Simon de Montfort. A massive indemnity of £50,000 was awarded to Edmund, who demanded it in one lump sum. When Robert could not pay, Edmund retained control of the earldom. Nearly forty years later, John de Ferrers, Earl Robert's son, sued Thomas of Lancaster in Court Christian for usury, claiming that the profits from the wardship had already paid the indemnity several times over. John lost on a technicality. See Mark Bateson and Jeffrey Denton, "Usury and Comital Disinheritance: The Case of Ferrers versus Lancaster, St. Paul's London 1301," *Journal of Ecclesiastical History* 43.1 (1992): 60–96.

32. *CPR 1321–1324*: 84, 141, 178; *CClR 1318–1323*: 564, 571, 574–77, 578–79, 589, 596, 605.
33. *CPR 1321–1324*: 175, 324.
34. Lincoln, Lincolnshire Archives, 3 ANC 2/2/1.
35. *CPR 1321–1324*: 194. See also DL 41/105. Most of the deeds occur later, but the original release was at this time.
36. Hugh had also acquired a stake in the dispersal of the Clare earldoms of Hertford and Gloucester by marrying Eleanor, one of the sisters and coheirs of Gilbert de Clare, who had died in 1314 at the battle of Bannockburn.
37. *CPR 1321–1324*: 179–80, 181, 183, 196, 197, and DL 25/170.
38. *CPR 1321–1324*: 215.
39. Although she would never entirely regain Pontefract (she got certain parts of the property but probably not the castle itself), Alice did eventually succeed in regaining her favorite castle, Bolingbroke (more on this later).
40. *CClR 1318–1323*: 674–75.
41. Hugh received Gretham, which Alice's stepmother, Joan, had held in dower. DL 41/105.
42. *CClR 1323–1327*: 28. This is also mentioned in Barker, "Household Administration."
43. *CPR 1321–1324*: 349–50. There is a certain irony here, as Alice had been stripped of control of the honor of Clifford.
44. *CPR 1321–1324*: 355.
45. First mentions: *CClR 1323–1327*: 103, 114, 124, 231. In all fairness to Edward II, the sheriffs of the succeeding reign were equally recalcitrant.
46. *CPR 1324–1327*: 63–64, 103; CP 25/1/286/32 nos. 245, 247, 248, 249, 250. See, also, Wiltshire Archaeological and Natural History Society, Records Branch, *Wiltshire Fines* (1939) 1: 132–33; and Devon and Cornwall Record Society, *Devon Feet of Fines* (1939) 2: 237–38.
47. *CClR 1323–1327*: 269–70.
48. *CPR 1324–1327*: 220.
49. BL, Harley 1240, f. 27; DL 36/1/200.
50. Since the estates in question had originally been inherited by Alice, her permission and "voucher to warranty" would have been necessary; Ebulo would have acted in her stead as her husband.

51. DL 25/3347; CP 25/1/194/11 no. 44; and *CPR 1330–1334*: 74.
52. Since Alice was *suo jure* countess of Lincoln, Edward II would not have been able to take the control of Lincoln Castle and its court out of her hands without declaring her a traitor and her lands forfeit. If he had done so, however, the constableship and control of the bailey would have gone immediately to Henry de Lancaster, the brother of Thomas, who would have been a much more powerful adversary in the region. Thus, it behooved Edward II to allow Alice to retain the privilege.
53. Original grant, DL 36/2/199; orders upon Talbot's death, *CClR 1327–1330*: 28, 169; orders to pay arrears, *CClR 1323–1327*: 142–43, 167, 626. Problems continued into the next years: *CClR 1327–1330*: 255, 283–84, 434, 562; *CClR 1330–1333*: 255 and on.
54. *CPR 1327–1330*: 338. Writ *de intendendo* to tenants in 1331: *CPR 1330–1334*: 113.
55. They exchanged the manor of Buckeby for £50 of land and tenements in Colston Basset for their lives. DL 25/2273 and CP 25/1/176/72 no. 9.
56. *CPR 1330–1334*: 36.
57. This suggests that Alice and Ebulo were in on the plot as well. *CChR* 4: 199. The entry was vacated because of technical errors.
58. *CChR* 4: 199, 357.
59. *CClR 1330–1333*: 178.
60. *CClR 1330–1333*: 325–26. His release appears also in a memorandum, *CPR 1330–1334*: 246.
61. *CPR 1330–1334*: 293, 299, 348, 441; *CClR 1330–1333*: 569, 610, 617; *CClR 1333–1337*: 21.
62. DL 25/74. The lease was for a year but it was apparently extended indefinitely.
63. CP 25/1/272/106 no. 13.
64. DL 10/274, DL 10/287; *CClR 1330–1333*: 273; *CPR 1334–1338*: 10, 34, 112, 121.
65. DL 10/272. This is in response to a letter patent of July 28, 1314, which coincides with Ebulo's association with Thomas of Lancaster and the other Ordainers. See earlier.
66. Custody of the lands and marriage of Roger de Cubbeldik, *CPR 1334–1338*: 57, 82. Pardon for amercement, *CPR 1330–1334*: 420. Commissions of oyer and terminer upon their request, *CPR 1334 1338*: 34, 65.
67. *CClR 1333–1337*: 492.
68. *CClR 1333–1337*: 444–45, 450–52, 460.
69. *Papal Letters* 2: 544. More on this later.
70. *CPR 1330–1334*: 31; *CClR 1330–1333*: 104.
71. Prestwich, *The Three Edwards*, 157. As usual, he fails to cite his source for this episode; I have been unable to locate it.
72. Prestwich, *The Three Edwards*, 157.
73. *CClR 1333–1337*: 561–62, 564.
74. *CClR 1337–1339*: 18–20, 25.

75. *CPR 1334–1338*: 450.
76. *CPR 1334–1338*: 463.
77. *CClR 1339–1341*: 107, 109; *CPR 1338–1340*: 534–38; *CPR 1340–1343*: 184–85.
78. *CClR 1337–1339*: 392–93; *CPR 1338–1340*: 529; *CPR 1340–1343*: 390.
79. *CClR 1337–1339*: 301; *CClR 1339–1341*: 140; *CClR 1341–1343*: 2, 429, 608; *CClR 1343–1346*: 499.
80. A number of complaints by Alice that her tenants had harvested beached whales before she could claim them were investigated in 1340. Robberies committed against her were also swiftly adjudicated that same year. *CPR 1338–1340*: 422, 483–84, 487. Arrests of men involved in Alice's complaints were also processed and concluded. *CPR 1340–1343*: 60; *CPR 1343–1348*: 353.
81. *CPR 1348–1350*: 60.
82. See, e.g., the grants and transfers outlined in the deeds, CP 25/1/286/37 no. 111 (printed in *Wiltshire Fines*, 29) and DL 36/1/188; CP 25/1/138/104 no. 38; DL 36/1/219, DL 36/3/187, and DL 36/3/189.
83. DL 36/2/48 and DL 7/1 part 1, f. 3, no. 7A [8]. The latter is undated, but is most likely to date from this period.
84. *CPR 1340–1343*: 278–79; *CClR 1341–1343*: 217.
85. Alice was not that usual a name at the time; the frequency of its use in that part of England, at that particular time, suggests a desire to both please and to be associated with the most important ladies of the Lacy family.
86. DL 25/2365. The language is unusual: *du commencement du mounde*.
87. *CPR 1343–1345*: 196–97, 249, 343.
88. K. B. McFarlane, *The Nobility of Later Medieval England* (Oxford: Clarendon Press, 1973), 248–67.

Chapter 9   The Rise and Decline of the Medieval English Noble Widow?

1. Discussion of this can be found in Eileen Spring, "The Heiress-at-Law: English Real Property Law from a New Point of View," *Law and History Review* 8 (1990): 273–96; and Spring, *Law, Land, and Family: Aristocratic Inheritance in England, 1300 to 1800* (Chapel Hill: University of North Carolina Press, 1993); and Joel T. Rosenthal, *Patriarchy and Families of Privilege in Fifteenth-Century England* (Philadelphia: University of Pennsylvania Press, 1992).
2. Despite the negation of the principle of the perpetual entail. See Spring. The *De Donis* statute is discussed extensively in C. M. A. McCauliff, "The Medieval Origin of the Doctrine of Estates in Land: Substantive Property, Family Considerations, and the Interests of Women," *Tulane Law Review* 66 (1992): 919–1013.
3. With the exception of statutes limiting price gouging during the Great Famine.

4. *A Baronial Household of the Thirteenth Century* (NY: Barnes and Noble, 1965).
5. Matthew Paris V: 721, 726, 730.
6. Cynthia J. Neville, "Widows of War: Edward I and the Women on Scotland During the War of Independence," in Sue Sheridan Walker, ed., *Wife and Widow in Medieval England* (Ann Arbor: University of Michigan Press, 1993), 109–40.
7. Matthew Paris, e.g., considered Isabella Marshal, the mother of Earl Richard de Clare, to have the courage and "heart" of a man. Matthew Paris, III: 246–47.
8. Suzanne J. Kessler and Wendy McKenna, *Gender: An Ethnomethodological Approach* (Chicago: University of Chicago Press, 1978).

BIBLIOGRAPHY

Manuscript Sources

Lincoln, Lincolnshire Records Office. ANC/.
London, British Library. ADD. MSS. 5844.
———. Cotton Charters.
———. Cartulary of Lewes Priory. Cotton Vesp. F. xv.
———. Cartulary of the Mortimer Family (Liber Niger). Harley 1240.
———. Cartulary of Canonsleigh Priory. Harley 3660.
———. Cartulary of Clare Priory. Harley 4835.
———. Harley Charters. 43.A.–45.I.
London, Public Record Office. Ancient Petitions. SC 8/.
———. Chancery Miscellanea. C 47/.
———. Charter Rolls. C 53/44.
———. Duchy of Lancaster Ancient Deeds. DL 25/.
———. Duchy of Lancaster Cartae Miscellania. DL 36/.
———. Duchy of Lancaster Coucher Books. DL 34/.
———. Duchy of Lancaster Deeds. DL 27/.
———. Duchy of Lancaster Miscellanea. DL/7; DL 41/; DL 42/; PRO 3/.
———. Duchy of Lancaster Royal Charters. DL 10/
———. Final Concords *Pedes Finium*. CP 25/1.
———. Rolls of the Court of Common Pleas. CP 40/.
———. Rolls of the Court of Exchequer of Pleas. E 13/.
———. Rolls of the Justices Itinerant. JUST 1/.
———. Rolls of the King's Bench, Henry III. KB 26/.
———. Rolls of the King's Bench. KB 27/.
———. Rolls of the King's Remembrancer. E 159/.

Published Primary Sources

The Administration of Ireland, 1172–1377. Ed. H. G. Richardson and G. O. Sayles. Dublin: Irish Manuscripts Commission, 1963.
Annales Cambriae. Ed. John Williams ab Ithel. Rolls Series, 1860.
Annales Paulini. Ed. William Stubbs. Rolls Series, 1882.
Bracton on the Laws and Customs of England. 4 vols. Ed. George E. Woodbine. Trans. Samuel E. Thorne. Cambridge, MA: The Belknap Press, 1968–77.

Brut y Tywysogyon. Ed. Thomas Jones. Cardiff: University of Wales Press, 1952.
Calendar of Ancient Correspondence Concerning Wales. Ed. J. Goronwy Edwards. Cardiff, 1935.
Calendar of Ancient Petitions Relating to Wales. Ed. William Rees. Cardiff, 1975.
Calendar of Charter Rolls. 6 vols. London, 1903–27.
Calendar of Close Rolls. Edward I–Edward III. 23 vols. London, 1900–13.
Calendar of Documents Relating to Ireland. Ed. H. S. Sweetman and Gustavius Frederick Handcock. 5 vols. London, 1875–86.
Calendar of Fine Rolls. Edward I–Edward II. 3 vols. London, 1911–12.
Calendar of Inquisitions Post Mortem. Henry III–Edward III. 14 vols. London, 1904–54.
Calendar of Liberate Rolls. Henry III, 1216–72. 6 vols. London, 1916–75.
Calendar of Papal Registers: Papal Letters. 2 vols. London, 1893–95.
Calendar of Patent Rolls. Henry III–Edward III. 31 vols. London, 1891–1916.
Calendar of the Justiciary Rolls or Proceedings in the Court of the Justiciar of Ireland. 2 vols. Dublin, 1905–14.
Calendar of the Register of John de Drokensford, Bishop of Bath and Wells (AD 1309–1329). Ed. Rev. Bishop Hobhouse. Somerset Record Society 1, 1887.
Calendar of Various Chancery Rolls, A.D. 1277–1326: Welsh Rolls. Hereford, 1912.
Cartae et Alia Munimenta quae ad Dominium de Glamorgancia Pertinent. Ed. G. T. Clark. vol. 3: 1271–1331. Cardiff, 1910.
Cartulary of Haughmond Abbey. Ed. Una Rees. Shropshire Archaeological Society, 1985.
The Chartulary of the Priory of St Pancras of Lewes. Ed. L. Salzman. Sussex Record Society, 1934.
Chronica monasterii de Melsa, auctore Thoma de Burton, abbate. Ed. Edward A. Bond. Rolls Series, 1867.
Chronica Monsaterii S Albani. Ed. Henry Thomas Riley. Rolls Series, 1866.
Chronicles of the Reigns of Edward I and Edward II. 2 vols. Ed. William Stubbs. Rolls Series, 1882.
Civil Pleas of the Wiltshire Eyre, 1249. Ed. M. T. Clanchy. Wiltshire Record Society, 1971.
Close Rolls. Henry III. 14 vols. London, 1902–38.
Devon Feet of Fines. Devon and Cornwall Record Society, 1939.
Excerpta è Rotulis Finium in Turri Londonensi Asservatis, Henrico Tertio Rege, A.D. 1216–1272. 2 vols. London: Record Commission, 1835–36.
Feet of Fines for the County of York, from 1327 to 1347: 1–20 Edward III. Ed. W. Paley Baildon. Leeds: Yorkshire Archaeological Society, Record Series, 42 (1910).
Flores Historiarum. Ed. Henry Richards Luard. Rolls Series, 1890.
Historical Manuscripts Commission. *Report on the Manuscripts of Wells Cathedral*. London, 1885.
Historical Manuscripts Commission. *Calendar of the Manuscripts of the Dean and Chapter of Wells*. London, 1907.
The Household Book of Queen Isabella of England for the Fifth Regnal Year of Edward II 8th July 1311 to 7th July 1312. Ed. and trans. F. D. Blackley and G. Hermanson. Edmonton: University of Alberta Press, 1971.

BIBLIOGRAPHY 175

Letters of Edward Prince of Wales, 1304–1305. Ed. Hilda Johnstone. Cambridge: University Press for the Roxburghe Club, 1931.
Liber Feodorum. The Book of Fees commonly called Testa de Nevill. 2 vols. London, 1920–23.
List of Welsh Entries in the Memoranda Rolls, 1282–1343. Ed. Natalie Fryde. Cardiff, 1974.
Monasticon Anglicanum. Ed. Sir William Dugdale. New ed., ed. John Caley, Henry Ellis, and Rev. Bulkeley Bandinel. 6 vols. London, 1817–30.
Paris, Matthew. *English History.* 3 vols. Trans. J. A. Giles. London: Henry G. Bohn, 1852. Reprint, AMS Press.
Paris, Matthew. *Chronica majora.* 7 vols. Ed. Henry R. Luard. Rolls Series. London, 1872–83.
Register of Archbishop of York Walter Giffard, 1266–1279. Surtees Society, 1904.
Register of Archbishop of York Walter Gray, 1215–1255. Surtees Society, 1872.
Register of John le Romeyn, Lord Archbishop of York, 1286–96. 2 parts. Surtees Society, 1913–17.
Register of Thomas Corbridge, Lord Archbishop of York, 1300–14. Part 1. Surtees Society, 1925.
Register of William Greenfield, Lord Archbishop of York, 1306–15. 5 parts. Surtees Society, 1931–40.
Register of William Wickwane, Lord Archbishop of York, 1279–85. Surtees Society, 1907.
Registrum Johannis de Pontissara Episcopi Wyntoniensis, A.D. *1282–1304.* Vol. 1. Canterbury and York Society 19, 1915.
Roll and Writ File of the Berkshire Eyre of 1248. Ed. M. T. Clanchy. Selden Society 90, 1973.
Rotuli Parliamentorum; ut et Petitiones, et Placita in Parliamento. Vol. 1. London: Record Commission, 1783.
Rotuli Ricardi Gravesend, Diocesis Lincolniensis, A.D. *1258–79.* Canterbury and York Society 31, 1925.
Royal and Other Historical Letters Illustrative of the Reign of Henry III. 2 vols. Ed. Walter Waddington Shirley. Rolls Series 27, 1862–66.
Thomas of Walsingham. *Historia Anglicana.* Ed. Henry Thomas Riley. Rolls Series, 1863.
Trivet, Nicholas. *Annales.* London, 1845.
Walter of Henley and Other Treatises on Estate Management and Accounting. Ed. and trans. Dorothy Oschinsky. Oxford: Clarendon Press, 1971.
The Welsh Assize Roll, 1277–1284. Ed. James Conway Davies. Cardiff, 1940.
Wiltshire Fines. Wiltshire Archaeological and Natural History Society, Records Branch (1939).

Secondary Works

Altschul, Michael. *A Baronial Family in Medieval England: The Clares, 1217–1314.* Baltimore: The Johns Hopkins University Press, 1965.
Archer, Rowena E. "'How ladies...who live on their manors ought to manage their households and estates': Women as Landholders and Administrators in the

Later Middle Ages." In *Women in Medieval English Society*, ed. P. J. P. Goldberg. Stroud: Sutton Publishing, Ltd., 1992.

Archer, Rowena E. "Rich Old Ladies: The Problem of Late Medieval Dowagers." In *Property and Politics: Essays in Later Medieval English History*, ed. Tony Pollard, 15–35. Gloucester: Alan Sutton, 1984.

Baldwin, James F. "The Household Administration of Henry Lacy and Thomas of Lancaster." *The English Historical Review* 42.166 (1927): 180–200.

Bateson, Mark and Jeffrey Denton. "Usury and Comital Disinheritance: The Case of Ferrers versus Lancaster, St Paul's London 1301." *Journal of Ecclesiastical History* 43.1 (1992): 60–96.

Binchy, D. A. "Family Membership of Women" and "The Legal Capacity of Women in Regard to Contracts." In *Studies in Early Irish Law*, 180–86 and 207–34. Royal Irish Academy, 1936.

Bridgeman, Hon. and Rev. G. T. O. "The Princes of Upper Powys." *Collections Historical and Archaeological Relating to Montgomeryshire* 1 (1868): 1–103.

Carlson, Cindy L. and Angela Jane Weisl, eds. *Constructions of Widowhood and Virginity in the Middle Ages*. NY: St. Martin's Press, 1999.

Carpenter, Jennifer and Sally-Beth MacLean, eds. *Power of the Weak: Studies on Medieval Women*. Urbana: University of Illinois Press, 1995.

Cockayne, G. E. *The Complete Peerage of England, Scotland, Ireland, Great Britain, and the United Kingdom*, 2nd ed. 13 vols. London: St. Martin's Press, 1910–40.

Coss, Peter. *The Lady in Medieval England, 1000–1500*. Mechanicsburgh, PA: Stackpole Books, 1998.

———. *Lordship, Knighthood and Locality: A Study in English Society c. 1180–c. 1280*. Cambridge: Cambridge University Press, 1991.

Crouch, David. *The Image of Aristocracy in Britain, 1000–1300*. London: Routledge, 1992.

Davies, R. R. *Conquest, Coexistence, and Change: Wales, 1063–1415*. Oxford: Clarendon Press/University of Wales Press, 1987.

———. "Law and National Identity in Thirteenth-Century Wales." In *Welsh Society and Nationhood*, ed. R. R. Davies, Ralph A. Griffiths, Ieuan Gwynedd Jones, and Kenneth O. Morgan, 51–69. Cardiff: University of Wales Press, 1984.

———. "The Status of Women and the Practice of Marriage in Late-Medieval Wales." In *The Welsh Law of Women*, ed. Dafydd Jenkins and Morfydd E. Owen. Cardiff: University of Wales Press, 1980.

———. "Kings, Lords, and Liberties in the March of Wales, 1066–1272." *Transactions of the Royal Historical Society*, 5th ser., 29 (1979): 41–61.

———. *Lordship and Society in the March of Wales, 1282–1400*. Oxford: Clarendon Press, 1978.

Dillon, Myles. "The Relation of Mother and Son, of Father and Daughter, and the Law of Inheritance with Regard to Women." In *Studies in Early Irish Law*, 129–79. Royal Irish Academy, 1936.

Edwards, J. G. "The Normans and the Welsh March." *Proceedings of the British Academy* 42 (1956).

Fryde, Natalie. *The Tyranny and Fall of Edward II, 1321–1326*. Cambridge: Cambridge University Press, 1979.

Given-Wilson, Chris. *The English Nobility in the Late Middle Ages: The Fourteenth-Century Political Community*. London: Routledge and Kegan Paul, 1987.

Harding, Alan. *England in the Thirteenth Century*. Cambridge: Cambridge University Press, 1993.

Holmes, George A. *Estates of the Higher Nobility in Fourteenth-Century England*. Cambridge: Cambridge University Press, 1957.

Holt, J. C. "Feudal Society and the Family in Early Medieval England: IV. The Heiress and the Alien." *Transactions of the Royal Historical Society*, 5th ser., 35 (1985): 1–28.

———. "Feudal Society and the Family in Early Medieval England: III. Patronage and Politics." *Transactions of the Royal Historical Society*, 5th ser., 34 (1984): 1–25.

Jones, Morris Charles. *The Feudal Barons of Powys*. London: J. Russell Smith, 1868.

Kaeuper, Richard W. "Law and Order in Fourteenth-Century England: The Evidence of Special Commissions of Oyer and Terminer." *Speculum* 54 (1979): 734–84.

Kessler, Suzanne J. and McKenna, Wendy. *Gender: An Ethnomethodological Approach*. Chicago: University of Chicago Press, 1978.

Knowles, C. H. "The Resettlement of England after the Barons' War." *Transactions of the Royal Historical Society*, 5th ser., 32 (1982): 25–41.

Labarge, Margaret Wade. *A Baronial Household of the Thirteenth Century*. New York: Barnes and Noble, 1965.

Loengard, Janet Senderowitz. "*Rationabilis Dos*: Magna Carta and the Widow's 'Fair Share' in the Earlier Thirteenth Century." In *Wife and Widow in Medieval England*, ed. Sue Sheridan Walker, 59–80. Ann Arbor: University of Michigan Press, 1993.

———. "Legal History and the Medieval Englishwoman: A Fragmented View." *Law and History Review* 4, no.1 (Spring 1986): 161–78.

———. " 'Of the Gift of her Husband': English Dower and Its Consequences in the Year 1200." In *Women of the Medieval World: Essays in Honor of John H. Mundy*, ed. Julius Kirshner and Suzanne F. Wemple, 215–55. Oxford: Basil Blackwell, Ltd., 1985.

McFarlane, K. B. *The Nobility of Later Medieval England*. Oxford: Clarendon Press, 1973.

Mason, Emma. "*Maritagium* and the Changing Law." *Bulletin of the Institute of Historical Research* 49 (1976): 286–89.

Maynes, Mary Jo, Ann Waltner, Birgitte Soland, and Ulrike Strasser. "Toward a Comparative History of Gender, Kinship, and Power." In *Gender, Kinship, Power: A Comparative and Interdisciplinary History*, ed. Maynes et al., 1–23. NY: Routledge, 1996.

Meisel, Janet. *Barons of the Welsh Frontier: The Corbet, Pantulf, and FitzWarin Families, 1066–1272*. Lincoln: University of Nebraska Press, 1980.

Mertes, Kate. *The English Noble Household, 1250–1600: Good Governance and Politic Rule*. Oxford: Basil Blackwell, Ltd., 1988.

Mitchell, Linda E., ed. *Women in Medieval Western European Culture*. NY: Garland Publishing, 1999.

———. "The Lady is a Lord: Noble Widows and Land in Thirteenth-Century Britain." *Historical Reflections/Réflexions Historique* 18 (1992): 71–97.

Mitchell, Linda E. "Noble Widowhood in the Thirteenth Century: Three Generations of Mortimer Widows, 1246–1334." In *Upon My Husband's Death: Widows in the Literature & Histories of Medieval Europe*, ed. Louise Mirrer, 169–91. Ann Arbor: University of Michigan Press, 1992.

Morgan, Richard. "The Barony of Powys, 1275–1360." *Welsh History Review* 10, no. 1 (June 1980): 1–42.

Orpen, Goddard Henry. *Ireland Under the Normans*. 4 vols. 1920. Reprint, Oxford: Clarendon Press, 1968.

Otway-Ruthven, A. J. "The Medieval County of Kildare." *Irish Historical Studies* 11 (1959): 181–99.

———. *A History of Medieval Ireland*. London: Ernest Benn, Ltd., 1968.

Palmer, Robert C. *The Whilton Dispute, 1264–1380: A Social-Legal Study of Dispute Settlement in Medieval England*. Princeton: Princeton University Press, 1984.

Parsons, John Carmi. *Eleanor of Castile: Queen and Society in Thirteenth-Century England*. NY: St. Martin's Press, 1995.

———. *The Court and Household of Eleanor of Castile in 1290*. Toronto: Pontifical Institute of Medieval Studies, 1977.

Pierce, T. Jones. *Medieval Welsh Society: Selected Essays*. Ed. J. Beverley Smith. Cardiff: University of Wales Press, 1972.

Prestwich, Michael. *Edward I*. Berkeley and Los Angeles: University of California Press, 1988.

———. *The Three Edwards: War and State in England, 1272–1377*. London: Weidenfeld and Nicolson, 1980.

———. "Isabella de Vescy and the Custody of Bamburgh Castle." *Bulletin of the Institute of Historical Research* 44 (November 1971): 148–52.

Rees, William. *South Wales and the March, 1284–1415*. Oxford: Oxford University Press, 1924.

Rigby, S. H. *English Society in the Later Middle Ages: Class, Status and Gender*. New York: St. Martin's Press, 1995.

Roberts, Glyn. "Wales and England: Antipathy and Sympathy, 1282–1485." *Welsh History Review* 1.4 (1963): 375–96.

Roderick, A. J. "Marriage and Politics in Wales, 1066–1282." *Welsh History Review* 4 (1968): 1–20.

Rosenthal, Joel T. *Patriarchy and Families of Privilege in Fifteenth-Century England*. Philadelphia: University of Pennsylvania Press, 1991.

———. "Aristocratic Marriage and the English Peerage, 1350–1500: Social Institution and Personal Bond." *Journal of Medieval History* 10 (1984): 181–94.

Sanders, Ivor J. *English Baronies*. Oxford: Clarendon Press, 1960.

Sheehan, Michael M. "The Influence of Canon Law on the Property Rights of Married Women in England." *Medieval Studies* 25 (1963): 109–24.

Simpson, Grant G. "The *Familia* of Roger de Quincy, Earl of Winchester and Constable of Scotland." In *Essays on the Nobility of Medieval Scotland*, ed. K. J. Stringer, 102–29. Edinburgh: John Donald Publishers Ltd., 1985.

Somerville, Robert. *History of the Duchy of Lancaster*. London: The Chancellor and Council of the Duchy of Lancaster, 1953.

Spring, Eileen. *Law, Land, and Family: Aristocratic Inheritance in England, 1300 to 1800.* Chapel Hill: University of North Carolina Press, 1993.

———. "The Heiress-at-Law: English Real Property Law from a New Point of View." *Law and History Review* 8 (Fall 1990): 273–96.

Stacey, Robin Chapman. *The Road to Judgement: From Custom to Court in Medieval Ireland and Wales.* Philadelphia: University of Pennsylvania Press, 1994.

Stephenson, David. "The Politics of Powys Wenwynwyn in the Thirteenth Century." *Cambridge Medieval Celtic Studies* 7 (1984): 39–61.

Stuard, Susan Mosher. "The Chase After Theory: Considering Medieval Women." *Gender and History* 4 (Summer 1992): 135–46.

Suppe, Frederick. "Anglo-Welsh Cross-cultural Marriages in Wales and the Marches, 1050–1330." Unpublished paper.

Swabey, ffiona. *Medieval Gentlewoman: Life in a Gentry Household in the Later Middle Ages.* NY: Routledge, 1999.

Underhill, Frances A. *For Her Good Estate: The Life of Elizabeth de Burgh.* NY: St. Martin's Press, 1999.

Walker, David. *Medieval Wales.* Cambridge: Cambridge University Press, 1990.

Walker, Sue Sheridan. "Litigation as Personal Quest: Suing for Dower in the Royal Courts, circa 1272–1350." In *Wife and Widow in Medieval England*, ed. Sue Sheridan Walker, 81–108. Ann Arbor: University of Michigan Press, 1993.

———. "Wrongdoing and Compensation: The Pleas of Wardship in Thirteenth- and Fourteenth-century England." *The Journal of Legal History* 9 (1988): 267–307.

———. "Free Consent and the Marriage of Feudal Wards in Medieval England." *Journal of Medieval History* 8 (1982): 123–34.

———. "Feudal Constraint and Free Consent in the Making of Marriages in Medieval England: Widows in the King's Gift." *Historical Papers* (1979) (Saskatoon): 97–110.

———. "Widow and Ward: The Feudal Law of Child Custody in Medieval England." In *Women in Medieval Society*, ed. Susan Mosher Stuard, 159–72. Philadelphia: University of Pennsylvania Press, 1976.

Ward, Jennifer C. *English Noblewomen in the Later Middle Ages.* London: Longman, 1992.

Waugh, Scott L. *The Lordship of England: Royal Wardships and Marriages in English Society and Politics, 1217–1327.* Princeton: Princeton University Press, 1988.

———. "Marriage, Class, and Royal Lordship in England under Henry III." *Viator* 16 (1985): 182–207.

———. "Reluctant Knights and Jurors: Respites, Exemptions, and Public Obligations in the Reign of Henry III." *Speculum* 58 (1983): 937–86.

Woolgar, C. M. *The Great Household in Late Medieval England.* New Haven: Yale University Press, 1999.

INDEX

Beaumont
    Agnes de, 96; Henry de, son of Agnes, 94, 96, 99–100, 102–3, 104; Isabella de, wife of John de Vescy, 25, 93–104, 108, 130

Bigod, Roger, earl of Norfolk, 50

Blundeville, Ranulph de, earl of Chester, 15, 30–1

Bohun, John de, lord of Midhurst, son of Franco de Bohun and Sibyl de Ferrers, 15, 20, 27

Braose, lords of Abergavenny, Gower, and Bramber, 45, Table 4.1, 46, 48, 54
    Reginald de, 45, 48; William de, son of, 46–7; Eve la Marshal, wife of, 45, Table 4.1, 46–7; Eleanor de, daughter of William and Eve la Marshal, wife of Humphrey de Bohun 19, Table 4.1, 46; Eve II de, daughter of William and Eve la Marshal, wife of William de Cantelou, Table 4.1, 46; Isabel de, daughter of William and Eve la Marshal, wife of Dafydd ap Llewelyn, Table 4.1, 46; Maud de, daughter of William and Eve la Marshal, wife of Roger de Mortimer of Wigmore, 17, 43–55, Table 4.1

Cherleton, *see* Pole, de la

children
    and parents, 30, 35, 38–9, 42, 67–9
    and marital arrangements, 23–4, 37–8, 66–7

Clare, earls of Hertford and Gloucester, 37
    Gilbert I de, 20; Richard de, son of, 31–2, 33, 34, 36; Maud de Lacy, wife of, *see under* Lacy; Bogo de, son of Richard and Maud de Lacy, 37; Gilbert II de, son of Richard and Maud de Lacy, 37, 50, 52, 54, 99, 123

commissions
    of Oyer and Terminer, 68, 70, 122
    special, 86

Corbet, lords of Caus
    Robert, 59; Margaret, daughter of Robert and Emma Pantulf, wife of Gwenwynwyn ab Owain Cyfeilog, 59, Table 5.1, 62, 65

Corbet, lords of Morton Corbet
    Robert and Catherine Lestrange his wife, Table 5.1, 65; Joan, daughter of Robert and Catherine Lestrange, wife of Owain de la Pole and Roger de Trumwyne, 65–77, Table 5.1
    Thomas, 65

crime
    homicide, 79–81, 84; as a form of "self-help," 91–2
    legal procedure in criminal cases, 86–7
    abduction and rape, 108–11, 112–3, 115, 120

curtesy, 9

INDEX

Despencer
   Hugh, earl of Winchester, and Hugh his son, 74, 101, 114, 115, 116, 117; Hugh III, son of Hugh II and Eleanor de Clare, 118
dower, 7, 8–9, 16, 17, 18, 19, 20, 24, 25, 27, 30, 33–4, 35, 36, 37, 42, 47, 48, 53, 54, 58, 62, 63, 64, 65, 67–8, 73, 76, 84, 89, 90, 95, 108, 123, 126, 130

ethnomethodology, 3–4
   and gender issues, 133–6

family, 12
   natal, 17, 22–3, 24, 25, 27–8, 98–9, 101; co-heirs, 19–21, 25
   marital, 48, 95, 99, 106
Ferrers, earls of Derby
   William de, 12–14, Table 2.1; Sibyl la Marshal wife of, 12–14, 15, Table 2.1; Agatha de, daughter of William and Sibyl la Marshal, wife of Hugh de Mortimer, 11–28, Table 2.1, Table 4.1, 46; Agnes de, daughter of William and Sibyl la Marshal, wife of William de Vescy, 11–28, Table 2.1, 36, 133; Eleanor de, daughter of William and Sibyl la Marshal, wife of William de Vaux, Roger de Quency, and Roger de Leyburn, 11–28, Table 2.1; Isabel de, daughter of William and Sibyl la Marshal, wife of Gilbert Basset and Reginald de Mohun, 11–28, Table 2.1; Joan de, daughter of William and Sibyl la Marshal, wife of John de Mohun and Robert Aguillon, 11–28, Table 2.1; Maud de, daughter of William and Sibyl la Marshal, wife of Simon de Kyme, William "le Forz" de Vivonia, and Emery de Rochechouard, 11–28, Table 2.1, 133; Sibyl de, daughter of William and Sibyl la Marshal, wife of Franco de Bohun of Midhurst, 15, 16, 20, Table 2.1; Robert de, son of William, 13, 114

Gruffud ap Gwenwynwyn, see Pole, de la
Gwenwynwyn ab Owain Cyfeilog, see Pole, de la

Kings of England
   John (r. 1199–1216), 6, 124, 127, 131
   Henry III (r. 1216–1272), 6, 13, 17, 18, 24, 31, 34, 36, 47, 49–50, 51, 53, 60, 62, 93, 105, 114, 127–8, 129, 130, 131, 132, 133, 137; Eleanor of Provence, wife of, 32, 93, 95
   Edward I (r. 1272–1307), 6, 21, 38, 44, 49, 50, 51, 52, 53–4, 62, 63, 68, 79, 80, 93, 94, 95, 96, 97, 98, 99, 105, 106, 107, 108, 123–4, 126, 128, 129–30, 131, 135; Eleanor of Castile, wife of, 38, 93, 94–5, 96; Margaret of France, wife of, 86
   Edward II (r. 1307–1327), 55, 64, 68, 70, 71, 73, 74, 80, 84–6, 93, 94, 97, 98, 99, 100, 101–2, 105, 108, 109, 110–1, 113, 114, 115, 116, 117, 124, 128, 130, 131, 132, 133, 137; Isabella of France, wife of, 54, 55, 74, 93, 100, 101–2, 118
   Edward III (r. 1327–1377), 73, 74, 75–6, 102, 103, 105, 117, 118, 119, 120, 121, 124, 128–9, 130, 131, 132

Lacy, constables of Chester and earls of Lincoln, 14, 15, 95
   John de, 30–2; Margaret de Quency, wife of, see under Quency;

INDEX

Edmund de, son of John and
Margaret de Quency, 32; Alice
of Saluzzo, wife of, 32; Henry
de, son of Edmund and Alice of
Saluzzo, 99; Margaret
Longespee, wife of, 37, 99, 105,
106, 122; Alice de, daughter of
Henry and Margaret
Longespee, wife of Thomas of
Lancaster, Ebulo Lestrange, and
Hugh de Frenes, 99, 101,
105–24, 130, 131, 132–3; Maud
de, daughter of John and
Margaret de Quency, wife of
Richard de Clare, 26, 29–42
land
  inheritance of, 13–5, 26–7, 30–1;
division of inheritance, 17
  acquisition of and exchange of,
116–7, 119
  jointure, 83
law
  status of women in, 6–7, 123–4, 125,
126–7, 136
  inheritance, 7 12, 13–4, 58
  Welsh, 58
  royal manipulation of, 81
Lestrange
  family connections in Powys, 57–77,
Table 5.1
  Ebulo, husband of Alice de Lacy,
115, 116–20, 121, 123, 124
  Fulk, 70, 71, 72
  John, 60, 62; Hawise, daughter of
John and Lucy Tregoz, Table
5.1, 62, 64–9, 77
  Roger, 52, 116, 119, 121, 122, 123
litigation, 7, 39
  over inheritance, 20–1, 36, 75–6,
87–8
  over dower and/or jointure, 18, 19,
33–4, 36, 65, 88–9
  over debt, 88
  over advowson rights, 88
Llewelyn ab Iorwerth, 43, 44, 46–7, 48,
49, 58, 59, 60, 62

Llewelyn ap Gruffud, Prince of North
Wales, 50, 51, 52, 55, 59
Longespee, earls of Salisbury
  William; Ela, wife of, 30, 41, 42,
106; Margaret, daughter of
William and Ela of Salisbury,
wife of Henry de Lacy, 37, 99,
105, 106, 122

maritagium, 7–8, 9, 15, 36, 40, 64, 107,
126, 131
marriage, 48, 55
  arrangements and alliances, 13, 14–6,
31–2, 37–8, 46–7, 65, 66, 82,
93–4, 94–5, 106–8, 123
  and remarriage, 33, 68, 116
  legal disabilities of wives in, 9
  strife in, 108, 113
Marshal, earls of Pembroke and lords
of Leinster
  heirs of, 13, 14, 15, 16, 17, 19, 22,
23, 33–4, 35, 47, 48, 49, 50, 133
  widows in family, 17
  William le, 12, 19, 23, 31, 45; Isabella
de Clare, wife of, 12, 32, 45;
Eve daughter of William and
Isabella de Clare, wife of
William de Braose, 45, Table
4.1, 46–7; Isabel daughter of
William and Isabella de Clare,
wife of Richard earl of
Cornwall, 32; Sibyl daughter of
William and Isabella de Clare,
wife of William de Ferrers,
12–4, 15, Table 2.1; Richard
son of William and Isabella de
Clare, 15, 47; Walter, son of
William and Isabella de Clare,
33; Margaret de Quency, wife
of, *see under* Quency; William
II, son of William and Isabella
de Clare; Eleanor sister of King
Henry III, wife of, 17, 18, 34
Mohun, lords of Dunster
  Reginald, 20, Table 2.1; Isabel de
Ferrers, wife of, *see under*

Mohun, lords of Dunster—*continued*
  Ferrers; John, son of Reginald
    and first wife, 20, Table 2.1;
    Joan de Ferrers, wife of, *see
    under* Ferrers; James, son of
    John and Joan de Ferrers, 25–7,
    95; John II, son of John and
    Joan de Ferrers, 27
Mortimer, lords of Wigmore and earls
  of March, 49
  Hugh, lord of Chelmarsh, 17, Table
    2.1; Agatha de Ferrers, wife of,
    see under Ferrers; Hugh II son
    of Hugh and Agatha de Ferrers,
    25; Hugh III son of Hugh II,
    25, 27
  Roger, lord of Wigmore, 17, 48, 50,
    51, 54–5; Maud de Braose,
    wife of, *see under* Braose;
    Roger, lord of Chirk, son of
    Roger and Maud de Braose,
    69, 70, 71, 72, 73
  Roger II, lord of Wigmore and earl
    of March, 74, 75, 101, 102, 116,
    117, 118, 128; Margaret de
    Fiennes, wife of, 131
Mortimer, Hugh de, lord of Richard's
  Castle, 79, 82–4, 87–8, 90, 91–2
  Maud la Marshal, wife of, 79–92,
    130
motherhood
  relationships between mothers and
    daughters, 30, 35; between
    mothers and sons, 38–9, 42,
    67–9; between grandmothers
    and grandchildren, 34–5

patronage
  by women; of monasteries, 39–41,
    114–5, 116, 120, 123; of clerics
    and dependents, 25–6, 95, 122;
    of art and artists, 41–2
  by royal family of women, 85, 96–7,
    99, 100, 119
Pole, de la, 57–77, Table 5.1

Gwenwynwyn ab Owain Cyfeilog,
  57, Table 5.1, 59–61
Gruffud ap Gwenwynwyn, Table 5.1,
  60–3, 65–6; Hawise Lestrange,
  wife of Gruffud ap
  Gwenwynwyn, Table 5.1, 62,
  64–9, 77, 133; Owain, son of
  Gruffud and Hawise Lestrange,
  62–3, 66–7; Joan Corbet, wife of
  Owain and Roger de
  Trumwyne, 65–77, Table 5.1;
  Hawise "Gadarn" daughter of
  Owain and Joan Corbet, wife of
  John de Cherleton, Table 5.1, 66,
  69–76; Cherleton family derived
  from Hawise Gadarn and John
  de Cherleton, 66, 69–76;
  Trumwyne family derived from
  Joan Corbet and Roger de
  Trumwyne, 68–9, 71–3, 76
politics, 127–9
  women and, 51–3, 96–8, 100,
    101–4, 129–32
  rebellion and, 47, 49–50, 99–100; led
    by Simon de Montfort, 49–50;
    led by Thomas of Lancaster,
    72–3, 74, 99–100, 101, 114; in
    Wales, 60, 62
  deposition of King Edward II, 100

Queens, *see under* Kings of England
Quency
  Robert de, 30; Hawise, sister of
    Ranulph de Blundeville, earl of
    Chester, wife of, 30–1;
    Margaret de, daughter of
    Robert and Hawise of Chester,
    17, 18, 20, 29–42, 132–3
  Roger de, earl of Winchester, 13,
    Table 2.1

Thomas, earl of Lancaster and Leicester,
  husband of Alice de Lacy, 64, 69,
  70, 71, 72–3, 74, 93, 95, 97, 99–101,
  102, 104, 106–14, 115, 116, 123

Trumwyne, *see* Pole, de la

Vescy, lords of Alnwick
    William, 14; Agnes de Ferrers, wife of, *see under* Ferrers; John, son of William and Agnes de Ferrers, Table 2.1, 32, 93–5; Isabella Beaumont, wife of, 25, 93–104, 108, 130; William II, son of William and Agnes de Ferrers, Table 2.1, 19, 21

Vivonia
    Hugh de, 23; William "le Forz" son of Hugh and Mabel Malet, Table 2.1, 23; Maud de Ferrers, wife of, *see under* Ferrers; Cecily, Joan, Mabel, and Sibyl, daughters of William and Maud de Ferrers, and their heirs, 24, 25, 26

war
    private warfare, 64, 65, 67–75, 114, 121
    in Wales during reign of King Edward I, 52–3
wardship, 102, 106
Warenne, John de, earl of Surrey, 97, 98, 108, 109–13, 114, 115–6
Welsh Marches and marcher lordships, 45, 57–8
    conflicts between marcher barons and the Welsh, 46–7, 64, 65, 67–75
    tenurial arrangements and changes within, 59, 62–4
widowhood
    and law, 7, 9, 16, 44–5, 58
    and social relationships, 32–3
    see also individual women by name